Nurturing the One, Supporting the Many

■

Detail from *The One and the Many*, 1978 Center for Family Life in Sunset Park brochure

Nurturing the One, Supporting the Many

THE CENTER FOR FAMILY LIFE IN SUNSET PARK, BROOKLYN

Peg McCartt Hess
Brenda G. McGowan
Michael Botsko

Columbia University Press New York

Columbia University Press
Publishers Since 1893
New York   Chichester, West Sussex

Library of Congress Cataloging-in-Publication Data

Hess, Peg McCartt.
Nurturing the one, supporting the many : the Center for Family Life in Sunset Park, Brooklyn / Peg McCartt Hess, Brenda G. McGowan, Michael Botsko.
p. cm.
Extends into 1999 a study funded 1993–1997 by the Annie E. Casey Foundation, providing detailed information beyond that in previous publications on the Center.
Includes bibliographical references and index.
ISBN 0-231-11594-6 (alk. paper)
ISBN 0-231-11595-4 (alk. paper)
1. Center for Family Life (New York, N.Y.)
2. Community development—New York (State)—New York.
3. Family services—New York (State)—New York.
4. Children—Services for—New York (State)—New York.
5. Family social work—New York (State)—New York.
I. Title: Center for Family Life in Sunset Park, Brooklyn.
II. McGowan, Grenda G. III. Botsko, Michael. IV. Title.

HN49.C6 H47 2002
306.85'09747'1—dc21   2002073988

Columbia University Press books are printed on permanent and durable acid-free paper.

Printed in the United States of America

c 10 9 8 7 6 5 4 3 2 1
p 10 9 8 7 6 5 4 3 2 1

TO THE MEMORY OF

the late Dr. Carol H. Meyer and
the late Sr. Geraldine Tobia, RGS

CONTENTS

■

FOREWORD

SUSAN P. KEMP

■

> The one thing to be dreaded in the Settlement is that it lose its flexibility, its power of quick adaptation, its readiness to change its methods as its environment may demand. It must be open to conviction and have a deep and abiding sense of tolerance. It must be hospitable and ready for experiment. Its residents . . . must be content to live quietly side by side with their neighbors, until they grow into a sense of relationship and mutual interests. . . . They are bound to see the needs of their neighborhood as a whole . . . to devote themselves to the arousing of the social energies which too largely lie dormant in every neighborhood given over to industrialism.
>
> Jane Addams, 1910

Jane Addams wrote these words about her beloved Hull House. Yet she could just as well have been describing the Center for Family Life, which to many contemporary observers stands as an equally remarkable example of the power and possibility of neighborhood-based services.

Admiration for the Center for Family Life and its work extends from the highest echelons of America's prestigious national foundations to people from every walk of life in Sunset Park, Brooklyn, the diverse, urban community in which the center is located. In her influential volumes on services to low-income families and communities, Lisbeth Schorr (1988, 1997) showcased the center as a bellwether program in the arena of holistic, neighborhood-based services. The Annie E. Casey Foundation, which funded the research that forms the basis for this book, has honored the center as a national exemplar in family- and community-centered social services and has played a major role in disseminating information about the center and its work to a national and international audience. The center's neighborhood foster care program serves as a model for New York City's community-based foster care services. And, as this richly detailed case study makes abundantly clear, local children and families love and respect the center and its staff.

It is fitting, therefore, that this deeply informative book is a testament to the Center for Family Life and its many accomplishments. Among the proliferation of social programs that address the complex needs of low-income children, families, and communities, the center stands out for the excellence of its practice, the clarity of its vision, the sense that it grows out of and is one with its community. To underline the value and importance of this work is an essential contribution: only through careful and detailed examination of the center's practice can we begin to learn how it might be possible to carry the lessons learned here to other cities, other neighborhoods, and other families.

There is more to this volume, however, than an extended analysis of the center and its programs, important as this may be on its own terms. Indeed, the opportunity to reflect at length on the center's contributions provides insights into issues both larger and more fundamental than the program itself. From that perspective this book, like the work of the center, is an important contribution to national discourse on the philosophy and structure of services for vulnerable children and families. Many dimensions of the center's practice are noteworthy. In the larger scheme of things, however, the ways in which the center and its work bridge a series of disabling polarities in contemporary child and family services are particularly salient.

Take, for example, the center's efforts to support and sustain local families. Its mission and programs offer an important corrective to the unhelpful dichotomies that frame current debates over the balance in child and family welfare between preserving families and saving children. Advocates for children—Elizabeth Bartholet (1999) is a prominent example—worry that efforts to promote community partnerships in child welfare will erode the already tenuous grip this society has on structures to ensure children's safety. At the other pole community advocates are perhaps overly confident in the ability of depleted communities to support very troubled families and children. In both constructions ties to family and community are set against the "welfare of the child," creating the impression that these values can indeed be separated. Buffeted by high-profile child abuse cases, and lacking secure footings in a potentially more useful middle ground, public and political opinion swing from one pole to the other, with troubling consequences for child and family policies and services.

The multifaceted, carefully calibrated services of the Center for Family Life offer a possible alternative—a "third space" with the potential to move the public conversation on the best interests of children and their families beyond such long-standing and deeply unprofitable polarities. In its core philosophy, as well as in its practices, the Center for Family Life frames the needs of children, families, and communities as inherently and inextricably connected. Thus framed, questions about the dimensions of child and family welfare shift, more usefully, to an integrative focus on the well-being of "children in families in communities" (to borrow Salvador Minuchin's felicitous phrase).

The center's holistic, systems-oriented, and inclusive approach is clearly evident in the details of its programs, which run the gamut from therapeutic and counseling services to services focused on housing, employment, and community development. The center's approach to service delivery disrupts conventional categories, leaving room for vibrant, boundary-crossing solutions to local needs. The late Carol Meyer, professor of social work at Columbia University, cherished the center for its ability to bridge the chasm that so often exists between community-centered and clinical services. Although the center closely resembles the Progressive-era settlement houses, its community-centered programs feature the best of contemporary clinical insights and practices. At the same time, its clinical practice is deeply contextualized, responding to the needs of residents as these are expressed through the particular economic, racial, political, and demographic realities of the Sunset Park community. This approach revitalizes clinical practice at the same time as it enhances community services.

In yet another boundary-spanning move, the center's work balances a clear professional vision with an equally clear commitment to the central value of community participation and leadership. Unlike some influential approaches to community building, this community-centered program is forthrightly organized around professional social work values and a deeply held belief in the value of professional services, including clinical services. At the same time, the center sets aside many of the artifacts that social work has acquired on its historical journey from neighborliness to professionalism, including its investments in forms of professional practice that separate service provision from the everyday lives and sociocultural contexts of those in need. To borrow a vision and language from Bertha Capen Reynolds (1934), this is truly "social work at the cross-roads of life where ordinary traffic passes by (p. 13)."

The center's integrative and transformative practices gain integrity and power from its sustained investment in its particular neighborhood. In a funding and services environment that for many reasons (from fiscal constraints to commitments to timely permanency for children) is increasingly oriented to time-limited interventions, the center's long-term presence in

Sunset Park and open door approach to service provision suggests another model—one that responds to the ebb and flow of patterns of local and family need and that (in its refusal of categorical funding, for example) has deliberately resisted many pressures to define needs and their solutions in other than local terms. For the families in this community the center is thus a resilient and present article of faith and hope in a constantly changing environment.

There is much to admire in the work of the center and much in this book that should be brought to the table as we try to shape policies and services to better serve multiply vulnerable families and communities. But can a program like the center, which is so closely tied to the vision and energies of the remarkable women who founded it, be replicated elsewhere? Peg Hess, Brenda McGowan, and Michael Botsko conclude that there is much here that will travel well to other places and other communities. I agree with them. This is not a model that can be replicated whole cloth, nor does this book provide a protocol that if followed will produce the same results as we see mapped out in this volume. Nonetheless, the center's vision, and the accounts of its practices detailed here provide an accessible, authentic, and generative template for services in which, as Sister Mary Paul Janchill says, "family work [is] the task of the community itself."

Obviously, this program and its particular approach to community-centered social work practice resonates strongly with me. So does this book. It offers, I think, an increasingly rare commodity: a detailed, carefully observed, and thoughtfully weighed reflection on the multiple dimensions of good social work practice with vulnerable families through the lens of a particularly fine exemplar. Few programs have the heft and longevity to be worth such analysis. Equally (and sadly), few scholars of social work practice have the sense of the whole of the profession's work that so deeply informs this book. Peg Hess, Brenda McGowan, and their junior colleague, Michael Botsko, are just the right authors for such a book. It would accomplish far less than it does if it were not for their distinguished ability to make visible for us the possibilities this program suggests not only for children, families, and their communities, but for social work itself. They have written a book that offers a way forward for a profession that in many ways has lost its sense of self. I look forward to teaching from it, to recommending it to my colleagues in the field, and to turning to it when I need ro remind myself why good practice framed by social work values and commitments is so vitally important.

ACKNOWLEDGMENTS

We have been engaged in studying and writing about the work of the Center for Family Life in Sunset Park, Brooklyn, since 1993. During that period we have been provided resources, access, and support, all of which we are pleased to be able to gratefully acknowledge here.

As described in the introduction to this volume, the Center for Family Life was selected by the Annie E. Casey Foundation as a grantee for its Evaluation Grants Program in 1993. The center was identified through a competitive process in which leaders in the field of children's services nominated well-established programs nationwide that were preventive, collaborative, comprehensive, flexible, and family focused. We were fortunate to be selected as the center's evaluation team by its codirectors, Sister Mary Paul Janchill and the late Sister Geraldine Tobia, in consultation with Ms. Cindy Guy, senior research associate with the Annie E. Casey Foundation. As an evaluation team, we relished the opportunity to engage in a collaborative research effort with the center's administrators, practitioners, and clients and to focus on processes as well as products, words and feelings as well as statistics. We are grateful to the Annie E. Casey Foundation for providing the funding required to conduct this exciting research. We hope that, as the foundation intended, the results will encourage program funders, administrators, and practitioners to experiment with the innovative service concepts and program initiatives that contribute to the center's success.

We are especially indebted to Sisters Mary Paul and Geraldine for providing us the opportunity to study and write about this outstanding community institution. Both were very committed to the aims of this research and consistently enthusiastic about its potential benefits. They provided us with volumes of information, candidly answered our questions, and facilitated our access to the many staff members, program participants, and community constituents we interviewed, observed, and/or surveyed.

We also want to acknowledge the close cooperation we received from the center's program supervisors and staff. They were always willing to expose their work and to reflect upon their practice experiences. Staff members devoted extensive time to completing our research instruments, participated in in-depth interviews, and gave us thoughtful feedback as we developed reports. Special thanks are due to the three members of the staff, Edie Crockenberg, Mary Lou Duggan, and Jenny Robles, who graciously accepted the extra clerical burdens this research placed on their already overcrowded days. We are also grateful to Robert Hagen for his assistance with MIS data.

We are also very grateful to the center's clients and program participants who openly shared their stories with us and reflected about the meaning of the center to their families. Their perspectives helped us understand the ways in which the center's mission, philosophy, interrelated programs, and competent and committed staff members interact to create a family-focused, community-rooted resource that is "like home" to many Sunset Park residents. We are indebted to the children, youth, and parents who participated in focus groups, telephone surveys, and in-depth interviews and who allowed us to observe them as they participated in center activities.

Although we are solely responsible for the data and conclusions presented in this volume, we received invaluable assistance from others. Dr. Barbara Simon conducted a substudy of the connections between the Center for Family Life and the neighborhood of Sunset Park (1995). Several Columbia University School of Social Work (CUSSW) Ph.D. students assisted with data collection, entry, and/or analysis, including Don Allen, Kathy Kapila, Abbie Karic, Michael Powell, Julia Stewart, and particularly Yvonne Johnson, Murray Nossel, and Ernst VanBergeijk. Ernst completed his research practicum at the center, and Yvonne conducted an historical study of Sunset Park (1997). Murray videotaped research interviews and developed a pilot video that served as the basis for the Annie E. Casey Foundation's decision to support the production of a documentary about families served by the center with Roger Weisberg (*A Brooklyn Family Tale*, 2001). Sarah Crawford worked with youth served by the center to develop a community youth survey, and Kristen Hess assisted with data entry and analysis. Landra Haber transcribed many hours of interviews, and Sheryl Sodohoue produced tables and figures.

Sylvia Brewster, Julie Stein Brockway, Leora Cohen, Paige Sayle, and Stephannie Thomas generously provided photographs for the book.

Reporting in book form the massive amount of data generated through this multiyear study has required the assistance of many colleagues. Our efforts in this undertaking have been greatly facilitated by John Michel, our editor at Columbia University Press. In addition to advising us at each step with his ever present good humor, John enlisted three exceptionally helpful anonymous reviewers to review manuscript drafts. We are indebted to them for their assistance in shaping the organization and clarity of the final product. Several other colleagues gave very useful suggestions about the manuscript, including Sister Mary Paul, Julie Stein Brockway, and John Kixmiller at the center, Murray Nossel, journalist Michael Shapiro, whose discussion of "The Inevitability of Mother" in *Solomon's Sword* (1999) conveys his grasp of the center's philosophy and mission, Gary Mallon, a respected colleague in the child welfare field, and Denise Burnette, an expert in research methodology. Jeremy, Kristen, and Howard Hess, Dorothy McGowan, and Elaine Walsh read and made helpful comments on various versions of the manuscript.

We also gratefully acknowledge the patience of our partners: Howard, Elaine, and Joanne. Other professional commitments complicated the timely completion of this book; as a consequence, our partners, families, and friends have been living with it for a long time!

Finally, we are grateful for the professional vision and enthusiasm of two colleagues, the late Sister Geraldine Tobia, cofounder and codirector of the center, and the late Dr. Carol H. Meyer, Ruth Harris Norman Professor of Family and Child Welfare at Columbia University School of Social Work. Carol was a valued mentor and teacher of the center's codirectors as well as of the book's authors. She well understood and repeatedly taught others the strengths of the center's service model and the principles that guide it. In dedicating this book to their memory, we acknowledge their profound impact upon us and upon the field's appreciation of family-focused, community-based services as an essential and effective response to the needs of families and children.

Nurturing the One, Supporting the Many

■

INTRODUCTION: THE CENTER FOR FAMILY LIFE AND ITS PROGRAMS

■

This book tells the story of the first twenty-two years in the life of an outstanding community institution: the Center for Family Life. The center was established in 1978 with the mission of helping the families and children of Sunset Park, Brooklyn, a community of many immigrants struggling with poverty and unemployment. It is also the story of the two professional women—Sister Mary Paul Janchill and the late Sister Geraldine Tobia—who served as midwives at the center's birth and tenaciously guided and protected the center while nurturing both those who receive its services and those who provide them.

We present a narrative about development—the development of one organization and its innovative programs, of the thousands of families who have participated in its programs and activities, of the community to which it belongs, and of the staff who place their compassion, energy, and expertise at the service of the organization, the families, and the community. We have used a narrative approach because we believe it best allows us to convey the complex, multidimensional aspects of this unique organization's development over time.

It is an account placed in the context of over two decades of change—changes in the Sunset Park community, in professional social work practice approaches, in theoretical frameworks, and in social policy. Although some of these changes have shaped the center's programs, others have been resisted by the center's leadership and staff. Still others have been inspired by activities at the center.

Although the story of the Center for Family Life is interesting in its own right, it is also instructive to community-based programs in other urban areas that are attempting to assist families and children with a complex set of challenges. Within the child welfare system public and voluntary agencies throughout the country are attempting to respond more effectively to the needs of families in particular communities. The center's unique combination of community-rootedness and clinical sophistication offers the field a programmatic model for preserving and supporting families over time. There are two reasons we believe it is especially important to tell the story of the Center of Family Life now. First, in the past generation the child welfare field moved from what had traditionally been a focus on child saving to the adoption of what Schuerman (1997) has described as the three principles governing child welfare policy in the U.S. today: 1. reasonable efforts to prevent foster placement, 2. permanency planning for children in foster care, and 3. placement in the least detrimental alternative. This policy shift reflects increasing community and professional recognition of the negative consequences of overreliance on parent-child separation and foster care placement as the primary means of helping children whose parents are unable to provide adequate care. The evolution in public policy also represents increasing recognition of the potential for growth and change in high-risk families who receive services designed to enhance parental functioning and child well-being while children remain in their own families and communities.

Unfortunately, this family-centered orientation to the provision of services has come under increasing criticism in recent years (Murphy 1993; MacDonald 1994, 1999; Weisman 1994) in the context of the resurgence of conservative political forces eager to dismantle federal entitlement and service programs for low-income families. This has resulted not only in the adoption of the Personal Responsibility and Work Opportunities Act of 1996 (P.L. 104–193), commonly known as the "welfare reform" bill, but also the passage of the Adoption and Safe Families Act of 1997 (P.L. 105–189). The latter bill, which makes the safety of children the priority in all child welfare decision making, essentially reverses the pro-family stance implied in the Adoption Assistance and Child Welfare Act of 1980 and the Omnibus Budget Reconciliation Act of 1993. This reversal was justified on the basis of a nationwide rise in child maltreatment reports, broadly publicized research findings regarding the limited success of the "Homebuilders" model of family preservation services, and a dramatic increase in kinship foster care placements (McGowan and Walsh 2000).

What was ignored in the rush to "do something" about the continuing problems in the child welfare system and to prevent the occasional child fatalities that may result from poorly informed decision making by untrained and unskilled workers were the positive results that can be achieved with high-risk families and children when they are given the types of services and supports necessary to enable them to achieve their full potential. Our hope is that this book will provide policy makers, program administrators, and practitioners some of the evidence and conviction required to halt this effort to turn back the clock and "rescue" children from the family and community life in which they are most likely to thrive. Universally accessible, comprehensive, community-centered family-focused services provided by competent practitioners can make a real difference for low-income families and children.

The second important reason for telling the story of the Center of Family Life now is that there exists a strong sense of demoralization among child welfare practitioners, precipitated in large measure by the extensive public criticism of this service system. It is becoming increasingly difficult to recruit highly skilled young social workers to this field of practice (Alwon and Reitz 2000). What is missing from many of the debates about the family and child service system is informed discussion of the practice interventions that actually help families confronted with multiple problems and of the ways in which practitioners in this difficult field can retain a sense of optimism about their work and about the opportunities they can create for children at risk.

Social work educators frequently refer to the pioneering work of early professional leaders such as Jane Addams, but little attention is given to the successes of the leading practitioners today. Our hope is that this book will demonstrate that current practitioners are still able to have a significant impact on the lives of the families and children they serve and that there are role models available for front-line child welfare workers struggling with the complexities of the problems they confront on a daily basis.

This book is designed primarily to provide an in-depth "thick description" (Geertz 1973, 1983) of a single successful service program. It is not a report of a large-scale experimental study, as is more commonly produced in an academic setting. But we think these are equally valuable ways of knowing (Hartman 1994b) and believe our efforts to elucidate the subjugated knowledge (Foucault 1980; Hartman 1994a) of the practitioners and clients at the Center for Family Life may provide more meaningful guidance to policy makers, program administrators, child welfare practitioners, and social work students than would a report focused on our statistical findings.

THE STUDY UPON WHICH THIS BOOK IS BASED

Among those interested in the Center for Family Life's community-centered family-focused model has been the Annie E. Casey Foundation. The foundation's selection of the center as a grantee for its Evaluation Grants Program provided the opportunity for our study. The Center for Family Life, technically a satellite program of St. Christopher-Ottilie Services for Children and Families, a large voluntary agency based in Sea Cliff, Long Island, was one of several Evaluation Grants Program grantees. The grantees were selected nationally through a competitive process in which leading researchers, policy makers, and practitioners in the field of children's services nominated well-established programs with strong reputations that shared the defining characteristics of the foundation's own service initiatives, i.e., they are preventive, collaborative, comprehensive, flexible, and family-focused. The overall objective of this Evaluation Grants Program was to produce studies that could make significant contributions to the field of children's services, the agenda of the foundation, and the programs themselves. Weiss and Horsch (1998) report that the Evaluation Grants program

> differed from traditional foundation-funded evaluation in three fundamental ways. First, it established a partnership that involved shared power between an organization and an external evaluator. Organization staff selected the evaluator and participated actively in the evaluation. Second, the Grant Program emphasized both process and outcome studies. Third, in the evaluation process, it fostered broad participation of organization staff beyond the director level. In establishing this program, the Foundation sought to enable organization staff to learn more about their programs, to contribute to understanding in the broader field of family support, and to determine whether this new approach could be a model for future Foundation funding for evaluation. (pp. 2–4, 15)

Funded from 1993 to mid-1997, the study was extended informally into 1999 to collect follow-up data. In accord with the mandates of the foundation, the research focused on the center's mission and philosophy, historic and community context, program operations, service processes, and service results. Thus this research has generated detailed information that goes far beyond the articles and monographs about the center's programs that have been published previously.

The authors were selected as the research team by the center. One of the authors (McGowan) had studied the center's development in the context of prior research and had published several related reports (McGowan 1994, 1988; McGowan with Kahn and Kamerman 1990). Although the other members of the research team, Hess and Botsko, had previously conducted research in other child welfare agencies, they had not known the center's administrators and staff before conducting the study. We all relished the opportunity provided by the Annie E Casey Foundation's Evaluation Grants Program to engage in a collaborative research effort with the center's administrators, practitioners, and clients and to focus on processes as well as products, words and feelings as well as statistics.

We conceptualized the overall study design as a case study (Orum, Feagin, and Sjoberg 1991; Stake 1994, 1995; Yin 1994) of the Center for Family Life in the context of the Sunset Park community. Within this design we incorporated interrelated multiphased substudies of specific center programs. We were committed to designing an illuminative evaluation (Gordon 1991) that would capture the complexity, dynamism, and spirit of this organization. To this end we collected detailed information from multiple perspectives, including those of program staff (professional and volunteer) and administrators, family members participating in a broad range of center programs and activities, and community leaders. To explore the interrelationships of the center's various services and the interventive processes and outcomes of each program component, we conducted multiphased substudies of each service. We recognized that identifying and describing the "content and manner of the service being delivered" is a critical stage in the development and evaluation of a program (Cheetham 1992:276).

Multiple data sources and methods of collection included in-depth semi-structured interviews with center administrators and staff, families participating in center programs, and community leaders, review of center documents, records, and correspondence, the center's management information system regarding services to 4,630 families during a twenty-four-month period, and standardized case data collected on a prospective sample of 189 families served in the center's preventive program using the Family Assessment Form (McCroskey, Nishimoto, and Subramanian 1991; McCroskey and Meezan 1997), and several other instruments. Additional sources of data included participant observation in multiple programs, a telephone survey of

139 families participating in community school programs, focus groups of participants in a community school program as well as staff in the employment program, logs completed by staff in multiple programs, and other standardized instruments completed by program participants and staff. Collection of data from multiple sources, through multiple methods, and by multiple investigators permitted extensive triangulation (Denzin 1978). Greater detail concerning the study design and methodology is provided in appendix A.

As we began to disseminate the findings from our study of the Center for Family Life, it became clear that written words could not fully capture either the center's dynamic services and programs or the impact of these on the families and children of Sunset Park. Murray Nossel, a research assistant on our study, was inspired by his conversations with staff at the center and had videotaped a number of his interviews with the center's cofounders, staff, and program participants. We asked Murray to develop a brief edited video that could serve as a stimulus for discussion with the study's funder about a documentary on the center that would complement this book. Subsequent to our discussions with the Annie E. Casey Foundation about this option, Roger Weisberg agreed to join Murray as a codirector and coproducer for a series of documentaries. Broadcast by PBS Channel 13 on New York City's WNET and in cities, this series further elaborates the story of the center by providing an in-depth look at the people who use and provide its services. Seven Sunset Park families, all facing significant difficulties in their lives, were followed over a two-year period. The documentary series examines the holistic fashion in which the center approaches its work with these families through its many programs, portraying the intimate personal relationships among the community residents and the center staff and the complexity of the center's work.

WHAT IS THE CENTER FOR FAMILY LIFE?

The Center for Family Life is a community center that provides Sunset Park families comprehensive support services and activities at multiple neighborhood sites as well as sophisticated clinical social work services. The neighborhood map (figure 1) depicts the location of center services. The center is accessible to community residents from 8:00 A.M. to 11:00 P.M. daily, and the codirector and live-in staff member, Sister Mary Paul, is available for emergency services by telephone from 11:00 P.M. through 8:00 A.M. Funded through New York City and state government agencies, foundation grants,

Center for Family Life in Sunset Park
Employment Services
Counseling
Job Search
Job Placement
Follow-Up
Family Support Center
(Main Office)
Individual, Group and Family Counseling
Psychological and Psychiatric Evaluations
Family Camping
Family and Community Centered Activities
Immigration Issues
"Life Lines" Community Arts Project at Middle School 136
Afterschool Arts Program
In-school Interdisciplinary Arts Program
Traveling Theater and Dance Troupes
Summer Arts Day Camp
Family Special Events
Emergency Service Center
Advocacy Clinic
Thrift Shop
Emergency Food
P.S. 1 Community School
School-Age Child Care
Afterschool Recreation and Arts
Youth Leadership Program
Teen Evening Center
Parent/Teen Sewing Project
Parent Advisory Council
Summer Day Camp
Beacon School at P.S. 314
School-Age Child Care
Afterschool Recreation and Arts
Youth Leadership Program
Evening Center Programs
Year-Round Youth Employment Program
Outdoor Neighborhood Center
Family Night
Parent/Teen Advisory Council
Summer Day Camp
Coordinator of Beacon Programs
GOWANUS BAY
GREENWOO
CEMETER
SUNSET PARK

FIGURE 1

Map of Sunset Park, Brooklyn, and location of center programs

and gifts from corporations and individuals, all center services are free to family members. The center is a satellite program of St. Christopher-Ottilie Services for Children and Families, a large voluntary agency based in Long Island.

Since its establishment, the center's home has been Sunset Park, a community with a growing population and with incoming immigrants, both documented and undocumented, from Central America, South America, China, Hong Kong, and Arab countries in the Middle East. Children and families of the neighborhood are confronted daily by poverty and unemployment, maternal and child health concerns, drug-related difficulties, youth gang activity, a housing shortage, and oversubscribed schools. Almost 30 percent of the community's children and youth are participating in one or more center services over the course of a year.

The Center for Family Life provides extensive community school programs that incorporate after-school child care, summer camp, creative and performing arts programs, recreation, youth development and parent education; employment programs for adults and youth; comprehensive emergency services to meet families' needs for food, clothing, and financial assistance; individual, family, and group counseling, known as the "preventive program"; and neighborhood foster care. The center's staff members are also engaged in community development efforts.

Families may use one or more center services concurrently or sequentially over the course of the children's development. To illustrate, within one week a family could meet with a preventive program social worker for family treatment. Several individual family members might also meet with the worker for individual counseling and/or participation in a group. Children could attend daily one of the center's after-school child care programs; teens could participate daily in the center's youth development program; parents could participate in a center parent education group, the employment program, and/or the English as a Second Language program; the family could receive food and clothing from the center's food pantry and thrift shop. In addition, the family's preventive program social worker might refer family members to other community resources.

But the center provides much more than formal services to the Sunset Park community. Its staff join the community's children, youth, parents, and grandparents in their lives and in their daily life tasks. Community residents who participate in the center's programs have described staff members as "like family," "like big brothers and big sisters to me," and "friends."

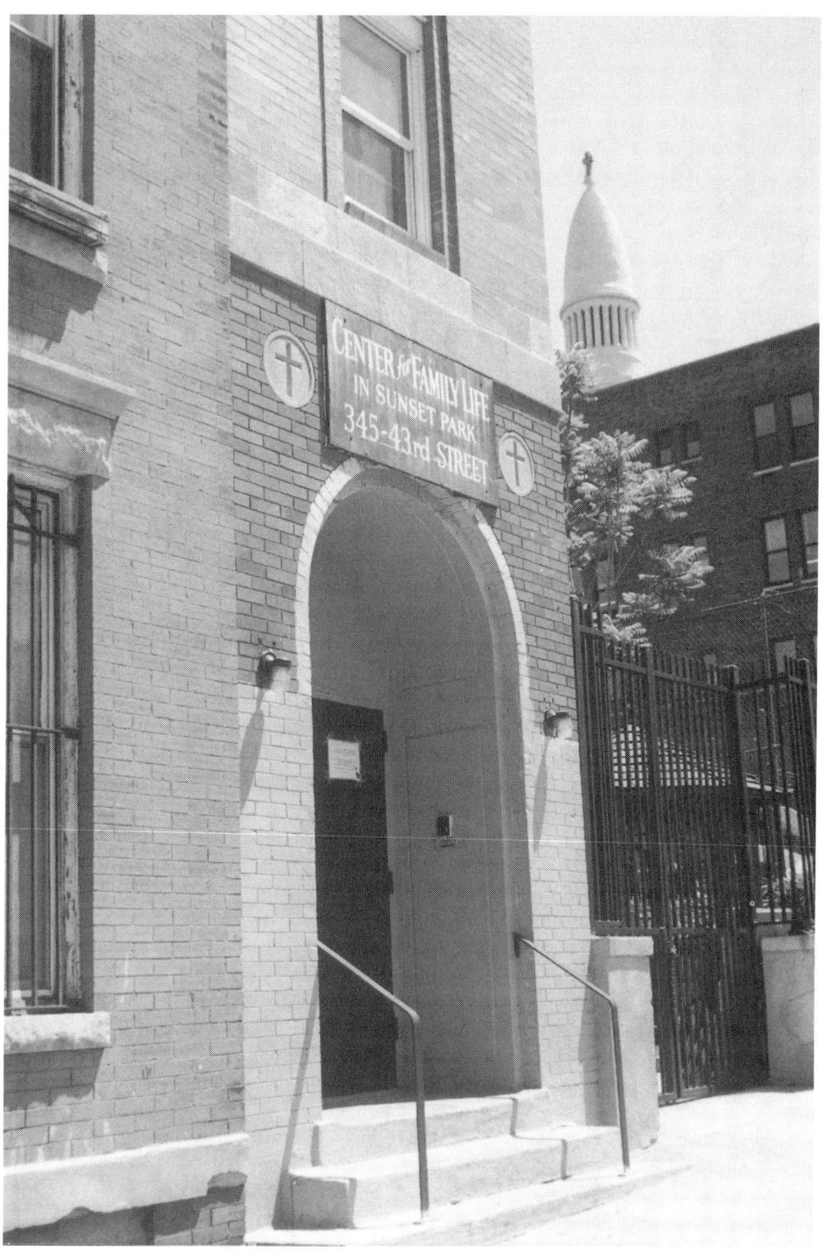

FIGURE 2

Main office of the Center for Family Life on 43d Street in Brooklyn

FIGURE 3

Sibling group enjoying after-school recreation

In our study of the center and its programs, we found that, although each center program component has an identifiable purpose, role, and integrity, the "whole (the center itself) is greater than the sum of its parts" (Hess, McGowan, and Botsko 1997:3). There is a synergy created as family members interact with various program staff and with other Sunset Park children and families using center services. We believe that the Center for Family Life's mission, philosophy, and program model provide a prototype for delivering comprehensive, integrated, and individualized services to families with a broad continuum of needs and complex problems, often significantly reflective of the effects of poverty.

SUNSET PARK: THE CENTER'S HOME

Located within sight of Manhattan, Sunset Park, Brooklyn, is a neighborhood with a distinct set of sights, sounds, and activities, as described below by Yvonne Johnson, an assistant to the research team:

If you take the downtown N subway from Manhattan you will, some half hour later, arrive in Sunset Park, Brooklyn. On this particular April day I get off at the 45th Street/Fourth Avenue station. As I climb the stairs to the street I hear the noisy traffic and subsequently see busy Fourth Avenue. The monotony of the fast-moving vehicles on the thoroughfare is in contrast with the sidewalk with its small shops that I walk past: a laundromat, a deli, a fast-food store—all with their doors open on this unusually warm and sunny spring afternoon. There are toddlers running in and out of the stores and adults chatting in Spanish as they stroll by.

I turn west, down 43d Street and pass the Center for Family Life, a social service family agency. Typically the center is my destination. Instead I walk on till I reach the Gowanus Expressway at the end of the block. This monstrous, thunderous motorway is on stilts, making Third Avenue dark beneath. There are a few pedestrians in view, but they are quickly out of sight. Within a few minutes hundreds of motor vehicles pass overhead on the expressway, and in its shadows I see that Third Avenue has its own share of voluminous traffic, but, on foot, one feels alone and vulnerable in this space.

I retrace my steps, glad to leave the Gowanus Expressway and pass the occupied brownstones again. It's after five o'clock. Elderly couples are sitting in their small front yards, and younger adults sit on the stoops of their large two- or three-family homes. Children are riding bikes, and a couple of teens are sweeping their paved front yard. I am struck by the activity—the stoops are being used more than they are in Greenwich Village. Unlike other neighborhoods where people's lives appear to be centered inside the house, rather than on the neighborhood or the community, private and public spaces are being used for social interaction. It seems that there is a feeling of community.

I reach Fifth Avenue, where there is a rising green mound: Sunset Park. Mounting the steps, I look down on Fifth Avenue and see a little beyond. I continue up the hill where there are families picnicking, having their early evening meal in the sunshine, and couples dating. At the summit, the second highest in Brooklyn, a magnificent view is revealed. To the north is Manhattan—the World Trade Center appearing nearby—and ahead, to the west, is the New York Bay, with angular shapes by the water, no doubt the unused piers . . . Atop Sunset Park the confusing contrasts experienced below recede and the neighborhood becomes an orderly part of this great city of New York. (Johnson 1997:3–4)

A Growing and Diverse Community

The only unchanging dimension of Sunset Park is its demographic changeability. It is one of the fastest growing communities in New York City, with incoming immigrants, both documented and undocumented. The 1990 United States Census indicated that Sunset Park, a geographic area of less than three square miles, was a neighborhood of 102,565 people, 4 percent more than in 1980 (Sheffer 1992:78). By the 2000 census the population had reached 120,063, an increase of 17.1 percent (City of New York Department of City Planning 2002). In 1997 28,075 children and youth under the age of eighteen lived in Sunset Park (Citizens' Committee for Children of New York 1999:156). Twenty-nine percent were under five years of age; 28.6 percent were five to nine years old; 24.5 percent were ten to fourteen years old; 18.3 percent were ages fifteen to eighteen.

Almost one-third (29 percent) of community residents are foreign born, and two-thirds (65.9 percent) of foreign-born residents are not naturalized U.S. citizens (City of New York, Department of City Planning 1993). Recent immigrants entering the community are primarily from China (28.9 percent), the Dominican Republic (20.3 percent), the former Soviet Union (6.8 percent), Poland (6.0 percent), Ecuador (4.8 percent), the Philippines (2.5

percent), India (2.3 percent), Guyana (2.2 percent), Bangladesh (1.8 percent), Trinidad and Tobago (1.8), and other countries (22.6 percent) (City of New York, Department of City Planning 1996). The City of New York Department of City Planning further reports that Sunset Park is one of the few New York City neighborhoods that absorbs immigrants from *all* the top forty countries of origin for immigrants to New York City (ibid.)

The neighborhood has been broken down into ten ethnic groups: Hispanic, Italian, Irish, Scandinavian, Polish, Chinese, Greek, other Asian, Middle Eastern, and other European (Winnick 1990:132). Specifically, 61 percent of the community's population is Hispanic, 16 percent white non-Hispanic, 18 percent of Asian, Pacific Islander, and American Indian descent, and 5 percent African American (Center for Family Life 2000:2–12). Interethnic rivalries and attendant political fractionization have troubled the community (Sheffer 1992).

In attempting to identify a New York City neighborhood similar to Sunset Park for comparative purposes, one of the research team members consulted with a statistician from the New York Department of City Planning Population Division. According to the statistician, there is no comparable neighborhood in the city. Sunset Park is "unique" in its blend of Hispanic and Asian residents. The current Hispanic community is highly diverse. It is composed of persons whose families have come from Puerto Rico, the Dominican Republic, El Salvador, Honduras, Ecuador, Mexico, Colombia, Cuba, and Peru. The countries of origin of most Asian and Asian American residents are China, Taiwan, Hong Kong, the Philippines, and India (Winnick 1990:144). Zhou reports that "today, most of Sunset Park's Chinese immigrants are Cantonese from the mainland and Hong Kong. . . . Immigrant Chinese now call Sunset Park 'Bat Dai Do,' a Cantonese translation of 'Eighth Avenue,' which means the road to good fortune and prosperity" (Zhou 2001:163).

Sunset Park's changing demography has impacted the center's program development and staffing patterns significantly. For example, as more Chinese residents have immigrated to Sunset Park, greater attention has been paid to the language, culture, and family dynamics of the different Chinese groups (China, Taiwan, Hong Kong) participating in programs. The changing nature of Sunset Park's Latino population has required that staff recognize the distinctions among national groups in its clinical and school-based interventions. In addition, recruitment of staff members who are bilingual, i.e., English/Spanish, English/Chinese, is a high priority.

The Families and Children of Sunset Park: Challenges

The specific nature of the services provided by the Center for Family Life over the past two decades has been significantly influenced by the needs of the community's families and children. The penetrating presence of poverty and unemployment has required continuing access to emergency services (i.e., food, clothing, financial assistance). The challenges facing immigrant parents in locating and retaining employment, including the need for job skills, English as a second language skills, and child care, prompted the creation of an employment program and shaped the services provided through the center's community school programs. Problems faced by the community's youth—gangs, drugs, and violence—reinforce the staff's strong commitment to providing educational, socialization, youth development, recreational, and employment programs for children and teens. The need for services to youth is underlined by an important finding from a survey of eighty-eight Sunset Park youth, conducted by students in an after-school ESL class at Dewey Junior High School, that 68 percent of the respondents were worried they might die before their twenty-fifth birthday (Crawford 1995).

Although Sunset Park is not as depressed as several other Brooklyn neighborhoods, it has continued to have serious problems that affect these children and their families. To illustrate, as reported by the Citizens' Committee for Children (1999), when Sunset Park is compared to seventeen other Brooklyn community districts with regard to the rate of adult unemployment, Sunset Park's rate of 8.0 percent is slightly lower than the Brooklyn mean of 9.2 percent. Sunset Park's percentage of households with incomes under $10,000 also compares favorably with other Brooklyn community districts, ranking fifth lowest. Yet when ranked according to the percentage of children born into poor families, Sunset Park fares less well, ranking third highest at 70.8 percent, much higher than the Brooklyn mean percentage of 54.2 percent and the New York City mean of 55.8 percent. The percentage of children receiving public assistance in 1998 was 27.9 percent, slightly higher than Brooklyn as a whole (mean = 26.2 percent). Births to teens (13.2 percent of Sunset Park births in 1996) and low-birth-weight infants (7.9 percent of infants born in 1996) are another cluster of problems confronting families. Child abuse and neglect reports for Sunset Park in 1996 totaled 676, or 25 reports per 1,000 children, and active cases in Sunset Park identified as receiving city funded placement prevention services for 1996 totaled 324. However, despite the high percentage of Sunset Park's children born into poverty (70.8 percent), the rate of placement in foster care is 9 per 1,000 children compared to 22 for Brooklyn as a whole and 25 for New York City. It is highly probable that this statistic reflects the center's presence in the lives of neighborhood children at risk for foster care placement.

Drug abuse and drug dealing also challenge Sunset Park's families. Heroin, crack, and cocaine are sold and used. In a recent survey of 266 Sunset Park residents, respondents identified drugs as the worst thing about raising a family in Sunset Park (Metis Associates 1999).

Overcrowded housing and schools are also serious community issues. In 1996 43.4 percent of Sunset Park's rental housing was rated fair to poor (Citizens' Committee for Children of New York 1999:162); almost a third (32 percent) of rental housing is overcrowded. Severely overcrowded schools are another problem confronting the community's children. Johnson reported that the rapid growth in the proportion of Hispanic children in Sunset Park, from 2 percent of the population in the 1950s to 70 percent twenty years later and to 85 percent in 1980 "has placed enormous pressure on teachers, both in terms of assisting students for whom English is a foreign language and of coping with teaching in environments that are operating beyond capacity" (1997:26).

Thus poverty and unemployment, maternal and child health concerns, drug-related difficulties, youth gang activity, housing shortage, and oversubscribed schools confront children and families of the neighborhood daily and test the skills and persistence of the center's staff members and volunteers.

The Families and Children of Sunset Park: Resources

Despite the community's depressed economic status, it has many resources. For example, Sunset Park has many small family-owned and operated businesses, most owned by immigrants (Winnick 1990:149–150). Such businesses include groceries, delicatessens, travel agencies, newspaper and stationery stores, laundries, butcher shops, fish stores, fruit and vegetable stores, restaurants, bars, clothing stores, and hardware dealers. In their ownership, staff, commodities, and store signs, street-level businesses reflect the immediate ethnic mixture of the surrounding few blocks. Thus, local retailers provide the vast majority of jobs and services in the community. The few larger employers in Sunset Park include the Lutheran Medical Center, garment factories, and the light manufacturers and goods assemblers of the industrial zone along the waterfront (ibid.:156–160).

Sunset Park's strengths also include the remarkable diversity of its population and cultures, the connectedness of residents to the neighborhood, and the demonstrated commitment of a significant number of its residents to making the neighborhood a good place to live, work, and raise children. In a 1999 neighborhood survey (Metis Associates), Sunset Park residents most frequently identified the social networks as the best thing about raising a family in Sunset Park (22.2 percent of respondents). Seventy percent of the respondents indicated they know most of the adults who live in or near their block, and 72 percent indicated they know most of the children who live in or near their block. Almost 20 percent indicated the best thing about the neighborhood was that services are nearby and good. Such services are strengthened by the thousands of hours of work provided each year voluntarily by parents, grandparents, teenagers, and neighbors at schools, churches, and organizations such as the Center for Family Life.

It is also a strength of Sunset Park's families and children that they are willing to use the neighborhood services available. To illustrate, data in the center's management information system indicate that 8,408 children—*almost 30 percent of the children in the community*—in 4,630 families used at least one center service in the twenty-four months of 1994 and 1995. During the twelve-month period of fiscal year 1999, 4,465 families were identified as using at least one center service (Center for Family Life 2000:2–20). We are certain that a greater number than identified actually accessed center services, with undercounts particularly likely in the recreation, youth development, emergency services, and advocacy programs.

In the neighborhood survey described above, Sunset Park residents were asked, "Have you ever heard of the Center for Family Life?" and, "If yes, how important is CFL to the neighborhood?" Over six in ten residents (63.2 percent) responded yes to the first question, and, of those, 88 percent indicated that the center is very important to the neighborhood.

Thus, despite the economic and social problems challenging Sunset Park's families and children, there are visible community strengths and resources. Not the least of these are residents' connections with each other and their connection to the community. The Center for Family Life is among these resources, and it is a more powerful resource because parents, grandparents, and youth volunteer their time and talents to expand and support

FIGURE 4, 5

Different views of the Sunset Park Community: (*top*) Fifth Avenue, one of the commercial strips in Sunset Park (*bottom*) Typical row houses on 43d Street between Fourth and Fifth Avenues

the center's programs. Thus families are connected with the center not only in their need for services but also as resources for other families in the community.

TWO DECADES OF PROGRAM DEVELOPMENT

For more than two decades the Center for Family Life and the community of Sunset Park have shaped each other's development through an ongoing iterative process. As a dynamic organization the Center for Family Life has sought input from its immediate and broader environments and actively gathered information about community residents' needs and interests. The directors and staff critically and collectively have weighed changes in the community against the center's mission and primary purposes, integrating what supports and enhances these purposes and setting aside or actively disregarding that which would undermine its work with Sunset Park's families and children. The center has thus enacted its deep commitment to the community that is its home.

Sister Geraldine and Sister Mary Paul, professional social workers and the center's founding codirectors, established the center with a "blueprint" based upon their earlier professional experiences. This blueprint included emergency services, counseling, and community school services, with family life education, socialization, and learning to be provided at the schools. Sister Geraldine spent six months in the community prior to the center's opening, determining the needs that were present. After the center opened, the staff members regularly identified the needs they heard from the community and the resources to be developed in response. Through this process, activities and services have been designed and implemented.

Sisters Mary Paul and Geraldine emphasized that the development of specific programs has often been due to the vision of center staff and community residents. Sister Mary Paul stressed that "we never could have written in 1978 what the center would be. You would not have found anything about performing arts, about dance. It just happened from the experiences of people." For example, staff members attracted to working at the center brought their talents in the arts and in dance, thereby shaping the development of the community school programs. Sisters Geraldine and Mary Paul credit Margie Santana, a VISTA volunteer, with the development and continuation of the Children's Corner at the neighborhood Income Maintenance Office, Ernie Santiago with pushing for more space for teen programming, Magda Santiago, a VISTA volunteer, with developing the storefront center and thrift shop, Frances Vargas with the development of the employment program, and Julie Stein Brockway with creating a full-fledged community arts program within a public school.

The First Five Years

When the center opened in November 1978 a number of core center services became operational. Over the first few months services were located at one site and provided by eight full-time staff, a part-time psychiatrist and part-time psychologist, and five full-time VISTA volunteers and four youth volunteers. Seven days a week center staff responded to the emergencies of Sunset Park families and children. Staff provided information about and referrals to community agencies and services, assessment and evaluation services, crisis-oriented counseling, individual, group, and family casework, and case consultation, direct intervention, and program planning with neighborhood schools. When staff observed that the reception room was filled with people who needed food, the emergency food pantry in the storefront center was created.

During the center's first year of operation its founders established the Community Advisory Board, which represented a cross-section of neighborhood residents as well as resource persons and professionals. Community development planning and outreach included ongoing needs assessment, liaison, and advocacy with neighborhood schools, community agencies, and service delivery systems. A number of recreational and socialization programs were established in 1979, including a weekly teen night and a monthly teen dance, a parents' night with a children's room program, numerous holiday outings for parents and children, summer day camp, and a drop-in center for children and adolescents who were mentally challenged. During its first sixteen months of operation the center "responded to 794 referrals for assistance" (691 families with 1,961 children and 103 single persons), and staff provided group services for "many hundreds" of Sunset Park children, adolescents, and parents (Center for Family Life 1980:6).

A working partnership with the community's schools was essential to the service model the directors wanted to develop at the center. The first community school project was initiated in the fall of 1979 at a large elementary school that had the lowest literacy and highest suspension rate in the district. Financed by a grant from the New York State Park and Recreation Commission and a matching grant from J. P. Morgan Charitable Trust, this project incorporated after-school child care, a learning and cultural environment program, which subsequently became the performing arts program, an evening center for teens, supervision and training of community youth interns, and establishment of a planning committee for the community school project.

During 1980 the emergency food pantry was expanded to include a thrift shop and advocacy service center where short-term crisis intervention and support were offered to neighborhood residents. A second community school project and the foster grandparents program were also initiated.

In response to community needs, several new programs were established in 1981 and 1982, including the employment services (job training and placement), the Life Lines community arts project–family life theater, and a basketball league. In the center's fifth year the third community school project was established. This project also incorporated a program for youth leadership training and a counselor-in-training (CIT) program for youth assisting with the after-school child care program. Registration for Fresh Air Fund Camp was also newly undertaken. Thus within a five-year period the center's extensive emergency services, individual, family, and group counseling, community school projects, and employment program were well established and stable. The second five years primarily brought additions to existing programs.

The Second Decade

In its tenth year (March 1988), the center admitted its first two children into neighborhood foster family care. This care was, and continues to be, provided under the auspices of the foster care license of the umbrella agency, St. Christopher-Ottilie. Since that time 146 children in 77 families have been served in this program. Facilitating frequent visiting and ongoing parent involvement with foster parents and the center's social workers, this pioneering program provides care in a Sunset Park family for neighborhood children who must, for their own safety, leave their families' homes temporarily. Placement in Sunset Park allows the children to experience less discontinuity in parent and sibling relationships, friendships, schooling, and recreational activities than would placement outside the community. It also enables the center's social workers and foster parents to work more closely with the child's parents and to model and encourage enhanced parenting skills.

In summer 1990 the Summer Youth Employment Project was established with funding by New York City's Department of Employment. Center staff coordinated the teens' work activity at nonprofit organizations in and near Sunset Park and offered training and supports for youth in preparing for future employment.

In 1991 a community school project was established at Middle School 136, including a family life education program, family learning center, and Life Lines community arts project and after-school program. In addition to program components incorporated in the center's other community school projects, an in-school school partners project was created. During the 1992–1993 academic year project youth was established at P.S. 314. This new program provided a mentor, a weekly family-life and sex-education class, and, when needed, a tutor to each counselor-in-training (CIT).

In its fifteenth year (1993) center staff undertook an important new initiative in collaboration with the Chinese-American Planning Council, Discipleship Educational Center, Lutheran Medical Center, Brooklyn College, and the New York City Board of Education. The center submitted a proposal and was selected to be the "lead agency" coordinating a Beacon School project at P.S. 314, which had been designated by the City of New York as one of its new Beacon Schools. Beacon Centers are open after-school and evenings, six days a week, and offer a range of social service, recreational, educational, and vocational activities designed to meet community needs. Needs are identified by the Community School Board and the Beacon School's own Community Advisory Council. As the lead agency, the center has worked closely with the Community Advisory Council to plan programming and to manage space in nonschool hours, making the space available to diverse community groups for meetings and activities.

Building on the additional services offered through the Beacon School, the center continued to expand its existing programs and add new programs, including a community carnival, parent workshops on immigration, and a family camping project. In 1997 Middle School 136 was awarded a four-year grant from the Center for Arts Education: NYC Annenberg Challenge for Arts Education with Life Lines as the lead arts group. Over time, Life Lines has been developed to include in-school learning projects integrating the arts, community services, and social group work, an after-school arts program and summer arts camp, traveling theater and dance troupes, and youth internship and mentoring and parent participation and leadership programs. In the following year five teaching artists in theater, dance, fine art, and vocals collaborated with two center social workers to provide extensive student instruction, interdisciplinary arts presentations, and leadership workshops.

In the Third Decade

In this third decade of service to the Sunset Park community, the center's paid and volunteer staff members continue to provide the rich array of programs and activities described above. Center programs are located at six sites, including the main office, and employ sixty-two full-time and seventy part-time staff. A large number of volunteers, including many parents and youth, help in the various component programs. Its budget (2000–2001) is $4,230,156, $2,708,020 of which comes from three New York City agencies: the Administration for Children's Services (formerly the Child Welfare Administration) for the preventive services program, the Department of Employment for the Summer Youth Employment Project (SYEP), and the Department of Youth and Community Development for the community

FIGURE 6

The Life Lines Traveling Theater Troupe in rehearsal

school programs. The balance comes from foundations, corporations, and individuals.

In just over two decades the Center for Family Life has grown from a small community-based program focusing initially on family counseling, information and referral services, and collaborative community service planning to a complex organization that integrates comprehensive family support services and activities at multiple neighborhood sites as well as sophisticated clinical and community development efforts. Since 1978 the center has served thousands of Sunset Park residents.

WHY FOCUS ON THE CENTER FOR FAMILY LIFE?

Almost since its inception the Center for Family Life has been recognized as a model program for delivering comprehensive, community-based, family-centered services (McGowan with Kahn, and Kamerman 1990; Rosenblatt 1985, 1995; Shapiro 1997, 1999; Sheffer 1992) and as a "successful program" for at-risk children and their families (Schorr with Schorr 1988; Schorr 1997). Its growing reputation has created widespread interest in its mission and philosophy, programs, processes, and results. A constant stream of social work practitioners and administrators, policy makers, academic researchers, representatives of public and private funding sources, and journalists have visited the center to observe its activities. In the national news and other publications they have reported the center's innovative, often pioneering programs, effective interventions in individuals' and families' lives, and contributions to development and change in the community it serves. These publications have reflected respect for the work undertaken by the center's directors and staff, documented aspects of the center's history and development, and contributed to awareness of its programs.

Early Recognition of the Center As an "Institution That Serves the Neighborhood"

Seven years after the Center for Family Life's doors opened to the community of Sunset Park, Brooklyn, its staff and programs and several families using its services were featured in a *Time* cover story titled "A Christmas Story in Sunset Park" (Rosenblatt 1985). Readers were introduced to the center as follows:

> What Sister Geraldine would have visitors understand is that it is not a matter of how much she gives to the people of Sunset Park but how much she gets back. The gift is their lives, she says: they trust us with their lives, and we offer them in return practical things like food and clothing, spiritual things like comfort and encouragement, hope, perhaps; sometimes we give them hope. But oh, what they give to us . . . They are wonderful people, wonderful. . . . Sure I love them. I'm supposed to love them as part of my vocation. But you can't love someone into life. They do it themselves. The process is slow but continuous. Sunset Park goes on and on. The work we do, it's not like your kind of work, not like most kinds of work, with beginnings, endings, and neat lines. (1985:18)

Using primarily the words of family members and of Sister Mary Paul and Sister Geraldine, the center's codirectors, Rosenblatt vividly portrayed the impoverished physical environments and interpersonal difficulties with which these families lived. The article also captured the broad range of center services in which these families participated, including individual, family, and group counseling, after-school programs, summer camp, the emergency food pantry and thrift shop, the employment program, literacy classes, and the theater workshop. The *Time* story also illustrated the philosophical commitments and theoretical orientation that underlie the center's programs and the staff's interactions with families, the extensive outreach and effort to engage clients in a shared sense of responsibility for change, the focus on all family members and on families as systems, the developmental and expressive emphasis, and the professional staff's "nonjudgmental quality of acceptance" (p. 22). Rosenblatt underlined the staff's expectation that change is slow but continuous: " 'I think that one must learn a different, less urgent sense of time here,' says Mary Paul, 'one that depends more on small moments than big ones' " (p. 29). Also stressed were the center's commitment and effective contributions to Sunset Park. Community leaders were found to "agree that the center is the social engine of the neighborhood. . . . The center is credited for the beginnings of [the neighborhood's] recovery" (p. 22).

Recognition of the Center As a "Successful Program"

In 1988, ten years after the Center for Family Life began providing services, it was referenced as a successful program in the widely acclaimed book

Within Our Reach (Schorr with Schorr 1988). This compelling book focused the country's attention upon highly successful social programs for children. Based upon their review of interventions that could prevent poor outcomes for children growing up at risk and of successful programs' commonalities (pp. 256–259), the authors concluded that

> the programs that work best for children and families in high-risk environments typically offer comprehensive and intensive services . . . are able to respond flexibly to a wide variety of needs . . . approach children not with bureaucratic or professional blinders, but open-eyed to their needs in a family and community context. Interventions that are successful with high-risk populations all seem to have staffs with the time and skill to establish relationships based on mutual respect and trust. (pp. xxii)

A New Approach to Foster Care That "Gives Promise"

In 1990 the Foundation for Child Development published a monograph reporting the center's "new model of providing foster care." In the foreword Jane Dustan noted that

> the Center for Family Life in Sunset Park, Brooklyn, the model described in this monograph, has been a leader in efforts to put into effect the kinds of reforms currently under discussion. . . . The core satellite model of the Center for Family Life offers a new approach to the provision of foster care that gives promise of reducing the length of stay in care and reuniting children with their families in a relatively short time. The program is embedded in the philosophy of the Center itself, offering a multiplicity of services to the children and families of the Sunset Park Community. (Lerner 1990:5–6)

The monograph's author, Steve Lerner, stated, "For the last year, Sister Mary Paul and her co-workers at the Center for Family Life have been demonstrating that it is possible to keep sibling groups together and to provide foster-care placements in the same community in which the children and their parents live" (p. 9). He noted that what distinguishes the center's foster care program from any other in New York City is that it "is a neighborhood-based program that will accept only foster children who come from the Sunset Park Community" (1988:10).

In the years since publication of this monograph several reform initiatives have drawn upon the center's neighborhood-based foster care model. For example, the Annie E. Casey Foundation's Family to Family Initiative identifies as a desired result of this initiative that "family foster care services should also become a neighborhood resource for children and families, investing in the capacity of communities from which the foster care population comes" (*Family to Family* 1998:7).

A "State-of-the-Art" Practice and Program Organization

As one component of a national social services study directed by Sheila B. Kamerman and Alfred J. Kahn, one of the current authors (McGowan) investigated family and child service programs that "are by professional and community reputation identified as 'strong' or 'promising'" (McGowan with Kahn and Kamerman 1990:12) to develop grounded hypotheses about directions for service program and delivery system reform. The Center for Family Life was among the ten sites selected.

McGowan, Kamerman, and Kahn emphasized, "What makes the [center's] model seem so promising is that, unlike most other publicly-funded family and child service programs, it places no diagnostic or categorical barriers on access to help and offers services designed to serve a broad spectrum of needs" (p. 124). They also stressed the center's flexibility "to adjust the level and range of services provided to families at risk as needs change over time, while insuring the availability of help before crises emerge" (ibid.).

"Professionalism and Practicality" Point the Way

Fourteen years after the center's establishment, the Surdna Foundation and the Foundation for Child Development published a monograph about the center's development, services, and infrastructure, the residents of Sunset Park, and those aspects of the center's approach most critical to its identity. Sheffer, the author, explicitly raised the question "Can the CFL model be replicated?" and concluded that

> an effort to produce an exact copy of the Center is probably infeasible as well as unwise. But it is almost certainly possible to create service agencies or modify the practices of existing agencies so that they resemble the Center in overall style and orientation. . . . The combination of pro-

fessionalism and practicality manifested over the last 14 years in the accomplishments and the leadership of the Center for Family Life in Sunset Park, Brooklyn, may point the way. (1992:67, 69)

Linking Family Service and Employment Needs

In 1994 the Foundation for Child Development published another monograph on the center (McGowan 1994) highlighting its innovative effort to pursue a "two-generation" strategy by training the job counselors in its Employment Services Program to assess and address the family service needs of parent participants with primary responsibility for child care.

An Effective Local Social Service Agency Devoted to Youth's Well-Being and Preserving Parent-Child Relationships

Two articles published in 1995 and 1997 each provided a different Sunset Park family's story and a compelling picture of the center's work with the respective families. Similarly to Rosenblatt's 1985 article, both also captured the philosophical and theoretical bases that undergird the center's programs.

An October 8, 1995 *New York Times Magazine* article about the society "that pretends to love children" described a sixteen-year-old Sunset Park youth, Henry (a pseudonym), and his observations about his life on the streets and at home. The author, again Roger Rosenblatt, described the Center for Family Life programs that Henry participated in, which were geared toward youth development, socialization, and recreation, and noted that Henry also worked with children in the center's summer camp.

Examining the state of children who, like Henry, are poor, exposed to violent and destructive behavior, neglected, and abused, Rosenblatt stressed:

> They are assaulted by everything, all at once. . . . Actually, the Henry of Sunset Park is a bit luckier than the tens of millions of American children, of all economic classes, races, and regions, whom the country pretends to love. At least this Henry has an effective local social service agency—the Center for Family Life to which he referred—that is devoted to his well-being." (p. 60, 61)

In 1997, in the context of New York City's plan to reform its child welfare services through decentralization, Michael Shapiro examined center services to another Sunset Park family coping with problems of severe mental illness, poverty, homelessness, substance abuse, and foster care. Published by *New York*, "Child Support" is "a story not only of a mother's struggle to stay in her child's life but the parallel struggle of the Center for Family Life to protect the child and still keep her relationship with her mother alive" (Shapiro 1997:44). In these two articles, as in earlier publications, readers were provided a sense of the extent and severity of the difficulties many Sunset Park families face as well as the persistence, compassion, and skill of the center's professional response to families' needs.

"A Template"

In a more recent publication, *Solomon's Sword*, Shapiro (1999) examined the experiences of "two families whose children the state took away" (p. xiii) and explored the dilemmas that characterize our nation's current public child welfare policies and service delivery system. Illustrating with the story told in his 1997 article described above, Shapiro describes the center's acceptance of what he calls the "inevitability of mother," i.e., the emotional bond between a child and his or her mother that affects the child's preferences and experiences regardless of the mother's competence as a parent. He also documents the extraordinary efforts made by center staff to prevent foster placement and the similarly tenacious efforts to maintain contact between mother and child when placement could no longer be avoided. Shapiro contrasts this acceptance with the public child welfare system's often adversarial approach to working with children's parents, an approach that sometimes appears to be based on the assumption that the emotional bond between children and their parents is nonexistent or can be easily set aside. He quoted Sister Mary Paul: " 'We don't have a choice about extricating that mother from that child's mind or reality' " (p. 252), and his conclusions reflected a similar point of view:

> Sometimes the state must take children from their parents, temporarily or permanently. But sometimes children will be better served by what might be called muddling through, taking on the sometimes interminable work of cobbling together a childhood, sometimes with several people who can assist in doing for those children what their parents cannot. . . . Those other adults, however, do not and cannot replace the parents. (p. 297)

In describing "the answers for failed children," Shapiro emphasized the importance of keeping children in care in their neighborhoods and "keeping the work of child welfare confined to the neighborhoods where people live" (pp. 289–290). He asserted that "Sisters Mary Paul and Geraldine established the Center for Family Life upon just such an idea. While the center is not necessarily a model of what all child welfare agencies could be, it is a template for the way agencies should be organized and money spent" (p. 291).

Rosenblatt, Schorr, Shapiro, and others writing about the Center for Family Life have emphasized that the center's programs illustrate what *can be done* for at-risk children and their families. Although largely anecdotal, the publications cited above have provided consistent images of both the extensive needs of many of the Sunset Park's families and children and the center's mission, philosophy, and skillful professional responses to these needs. Their conclusions were all confirmed in our research findings.

THE BOOK'S ORGANIZATION

In writing this book we describe the Center for Family Life and its programs and elaborate the lessons learned from our study of the center's first twenty-two years of service. We place the center's program model and the lessons learned in the context of what is known about effective programs for families. Thus we hope to contribute to the ongoing development of effective community-centered, family-focused programs. We also examine the implications of these lessons as they relate to professional education and practice, program design and implementation, social policy, and research. To achieve these multiple purposes, we have integrated our study findings with the voices of those who shared their own and the Center's stories with us.

In chapter 1 we describe the blueprint that Sisters Mary Paul and Geraldine used in establishing the Center for Family Life and the commitments, philosophies, and interests of the center's leadership and program staff. These commitments have shaped the center for over two decades and are evident in all program components.

Many of the developments at the Center for Family Life have been shaped by forces in the larger child welfare environment. And the programmatic developments at the center have anticipated and contributed to some of the shifts in family and child service policy and programming. In chapter 2 we examine the New York City, state, and federal policy context within which the center was established and has evolved.

In chapters 3–6 the goals, key characteristics, service delivery processes, and results of the center's core programs and services are identified in considerable detail. Programs highlighted include the center's family counseling program, known as the preventive program, the neighborhood foster care program, the community school programs, and the programs to support family and community development. These include the center's emergency services, employment program, and advocacy and community development initiatives. Drawing upon our in-depth interviews, we provide extensive illustrations of Sunset Park's residents' and the program staff members' experiences with the center over time.

Finally, in chapter 7 we identify the core components of the center's model, practice principles that inform the center's service design, and delivery and organizational principles that inform the center's leadership and management. We examine the ways in which these might be applicable in other settings and discuss the implications or lessons for professional practice, education, and research and for child welfare policy that can be derived from studying the center's experience.

There are multiple stories that could be told about the Center for Family Life, each from a somewhat different perspective. We have focused upon the perspectives of the two professional women who envisioned and established the center and provided leadership for its continuing development, those described to us by staff and volunteers who have enacted its mission daily, those shared with us by selected Sunset Park residents who have accessed its diverse programs and activities, and those recalled by others in the community who have collaborated with center staff over the past twenty-two years. Their stories, along with the study data we collected, have shaped our understanding of the center's mission, philosophy, programs, and outcomes.

Since the center opened its doors in 1978, it has developed its community-centered, family-focused programs in ways that have demonstrated a range of commitments, philosophies, and interests. These include its commitments to focus on the family, belong to the Sunset Park community, provide comprehensive, integrated, and holistic services that are both inclusive and nonstigmatizing, develop a range of working partnerships, integrate an intergenerational, developmental focus in program design, achieve continuity while maintaining a flexible learning stance organizationally, maintain professionalism and a theoretically grounded practice, and control focus and size while responding to emergent needs and opportunities. We explore these in chapter 1.

1

BUILDING A FAMILY-FOCUSED, COMMUNITY-CENTERED PROGRAM: COMMITMENTS, PHILOSOPHIES, AND INTERESTS

■

> From the deep springs of life there stirs the meaning of every human being; the irreducible dignity of every person as individual. In truth it has been said that "one person is of more value than a world." Paradoxically, personhood is nurtured and enhanced in a family, in a people, in a community. Individuality springs not in a fishbowl, but within the vitality and connectedness of community.
>
> The Center for Family Life in Sunset Park is devoted to the growth and development of the one—the individual child, adult, parent—and the development of the many that in diversity and richness of background come together for the fulfillment of human needs and aspirations, as a neighborhood.
>
> The Center for Family Life in Sunset Park—a place of welcome for neighbors who can become friends and partners, a place where each person can find a listening and understanding response to questions, problems or needs, and connectedness in this city and this setting of possibilities. The individual and the many in our caring!
>
> From *The One and the Many*, 1978 center brochure

Sisters Mary Paul and Geraldine, the center's founders and directors, began their work in Sunset Park as experienced social work practitioners. They brought with them priorities derived from years of professional work with families, individuals, groups, and communities. In recounting when the idea for a neighborhood family center first emerged, they described their work as

Portions of this chapter are adapted from Barbara Simon (1995), "'A Community of Interests:' An Account of the Connection Between the Center for Family Life and the Neighborhood of Sunset Park, Brooklyn, 1978–1995."

FIGURE 1.1

Sisters of the Good Shepherd (an order founded in France in 1641 as Sisters of the Refuge to shelter banished women) at the Euphrasian Residence, a program for young girls who were placed by the court system. Sister Mary Paul was director of social services for Euphrasian and several related programs, and Sister Geraldine was program director of Euphrasian. Sister Geraldine recalled that "it was out of a deep experience of working with children and teenagers that we were convinced that we were just working at the symptomatic end, postponing the essential tasks [of family work]. The kids were just symptom bearers. We were convinced that we had to work with families." She remembered the significant impact of the parting words of one child who had been living at Euphrasian as she was being discharged to her family:

> She was just crying. She said to me, to Mary Paul, and to the worker, "It's not that I don't want to go home. I'm not upset about that. I don't want to

leave here, because everything worked here for me—if only I could go home and somebody would still meet with my mom and me and help us to get along and if there would be a school where I got the attention I got here, I could do better in school."

And Mary Paul and I looked at each other, and we said, "Why not? What's to stop us?"

Their first attempt to implement a neighborhood center with a strong family focus was in 1972 in Park Slope, Brooklyn, a neighborhood where the Sisters of the Good Shepherd had a preexisting service program. Sister Mary Paul recalled the challenges inherent in that initial effort: "There was nothing out there like that—a family center. . . . The family support movement had not been identified anywhere in the United States. There was no such thing as preventive services funding, no funding for family work. We really had no base on which to rest. We started on a belief system." Sister Mary Paul noted that while they were in Park Slope "the model was defined—the clinical services, the community school relationship, emergency services. We had defined the need for foster care. . . . We made some mistakes. But when we came to Sunset Park, what was really clear was that we wanted to be serving families."

Thus Sister Mary Paul and Sister Geraldine approached the establishment of the Center for Family Life with a blueprint based upon their earlier professional experiences. That blueprint included counseling, emergency help, and community school services, with family life education, socialization, and learning to be provided at the schools. As the center staff identified community needs and developed resources, specific activities and services were designed and implemented. Thus the blueprint was adapted to meet the needs in Sunset Park.

Although the blueprint outlined the focus and structure of the center's services, it is the certainty and intensity of the commitments, philosophies, and interests of the organization's leadership and program staff that have shaped the Center for Family Life. The specific nature of these emerged from our in-depth interviews with the center's directors, program directors, staff, and participants, and community leaders, our direct observations of the center's activities, and our review of numerous documents. Over the past two decades these commitments, philosophies, and interests have been tested and refined as both the center and the community to which it belongs have evolved. The center is historically and currently characterized

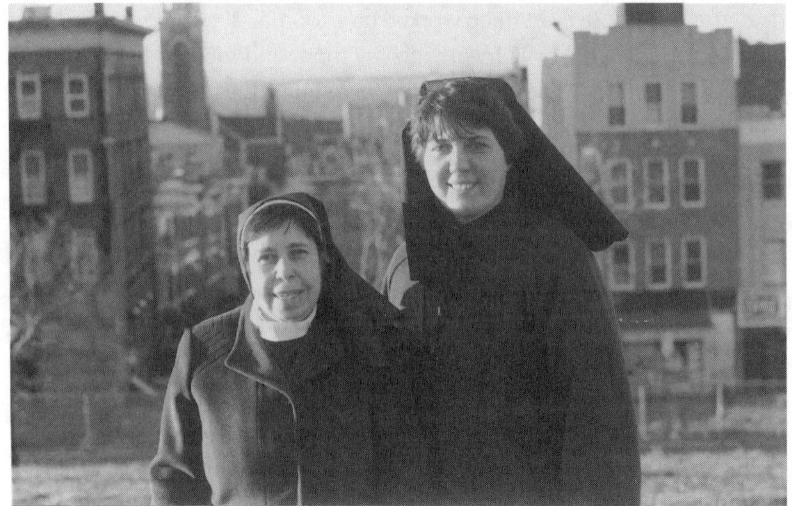

FIGURE 1.2

Sr. Mary Paul and Sr. Geraldine, cofounders of the center

by its commitments, which, as described in this chapter, are evident in all its program components.

THE FAMILY AS THE UNIT OF ATTENTION

From the beginning the keystone of the center's philosophy has been that the family is the unit of attention. Over the many years of the center's operations no shift is evident in the primary investment of the center's leadership and the larger center staff in Sunset Park's families. Sister Mary Paul has stated that

> you have to look for some level of commonality. Somewhere there has to be a possibility of a community of interests. And for me, in a multiracial, multiethnic community, I think family is the plane on which you find things to appreciate in each other. I don't really know what else there is if it's not that. The word family in Spanish, familia . . . it's in each culture here. It is really strong. In the Chinese culture and the Arab culture love of family is equally strong.

The center's staff members have always assisted at least two generations of family members at a time. For example, providing employment training and job placement services for adults in a family is deemed as critical as offering a range of programs, activities, and services for children and teens. Involving grandparents whenever they are available and able in the activities of younger family members is a priority. "What's good for the families of Sunset Park is good for the community of Sunset Park, since families anchor the community," agreed Dr. Jennifer Howse, chairperson of the center's Advisory Board.

Staff in the center's preventive services program, which provides individual, family, and group counseling as well as other family support services, articulated the importance of understanding family systems in the process of assessment, in identifying and supporting each family's strengths, and in engaging all family members in center activities. A preventive program staff member stressed that "the key is that we work with the family, with everybody. . . . In my own cases I'm more successful when I've been able to engage everybody—every single one of the persons that lives in that particular household. That makes a big, big change. For me, that's the key to the whole thing."

Early support for the development of the center's capacity to focus on families—both financially and from a policy standpoint—emanated from New York State. Funding from the New York City Special Services for Children, the New York State Department of Social Services, and foundation grants made it possible to start the center. The New York State Child Welfare Reform Act of 1979 placed an increased emphasis on keeping families intact through the expansion of decentralized, community-based, and integrated services, and the federal Adoption Assistance and Child Welfare Act of 1980, P.L. 96–272, reinforced the state's policy direction. With the passage of these two laws, the center was assured continued funding for community-based services for high-risk families and public support for the staff's efforts to keep families together (McGowan with Kahn and Kamerman 1990:29).

After the center was well established, its ability to serve families with school-aged children was further enhanced by the New York City Department of Youth and Community Development Beacon School grant program, initiated in 1993. Through this initiative the center has coordinated efforts with other community agencies to create year-round activities for children, teens, and their parents seven days and evenings at one school and to study ways to enrich other school sites.

BELONGING TO THE COMMUNITY

> We wanted to be in the community, part of the community, and working with families around family issues. . . . We brought with us the idea that the neighborhood was the base for family services. We were convinced that family work had to be the task of the community itself. Sister Mary Paul

In the Community

Why did the community of Sunset Park become the home of the center? In recalling their decisions regarding the establishment of the Center for Family Life, Sister Geraldine and Sister Mary Paul both stressed the importance of rooting their work in a community, agreeing to locate the center in one that was experiencing very serious problems but was not too thoroughly debilitated. As the center's founders, they considered several Brooklyn communities for the center's home. They concluded that Sunset Park fit their criteria: a very troubled and underserved community, but a community in which they believed "a momentum is building for a many-faceted approach to the social and economic recovery of this neighborhood and the development of its people" (Center for Family Life 1979:5). They saw the newly founded center as "very privileged to be contributing to this effort" (ibid.).

Sister Mary Paul reported that during the period of their assessment and planning, which began in 1978, they were urged to locate in Sunset Park by the New York City Special Services for Children commissioner, the District 15 superintendent of schools, Community Board 7's district manager, many from the 72d Police Precinct, and social service agencies. All identified Sunset Park as a very troubled community, particularly gang-ridden at that time, and distinctly underserved other than by Lutheran Medical Center. The director of community relations at the Lutheran Medical Center, Kathryn Wylde, felt that at the time of the center's establishment, "a new organization, with a multiservice approach, was badly needed for families who would not respond to the traditional services of mental health clinics, but who needed recreational programs for their children and help in addressing very serious gang problems" (Sheffer 1992:18).

Another factor in locating the Center in Sunset Park was the consensus among those with whom the founders consulted that it would be productive to locate it within the geography of the major systems (schools, police, social service agencies, etc.) that served nearby Park Slope, a nearby community where the two sisters' credibility was already strong, based upon their work there from 1972 to 1977.

A long-time supporter of the center, Barbara Blum, who was the commissioner of the New York State Department of Social Services in 1978, recalled that she would have preferred "to see a model like this tested in a somewhat more devastated neighborhood [than Sunset Park]." She noted, however, that "the sisters were very practical. You have to have, they felt, some other things that are viable [in a neighborhood] in order to make this model effective." Blum observed that the neighborhood's attraction for immigrant groups may contribute to a "positive force" not present in other neighborhoods: "The neighborhood is constantly being infused with people searching for opportunity and that may very well create some positive force that one doesn't find in these more devastated neighborhoods where people are quite walled in and not able to be motivated so well."

A comment from state senator Christopher Mega, cited in the *New York Times*, was included in the center's first progress report: " 'Sunset Park hasn't reached the point of complete disaster like the South Bronx or Bushwick. . . . There is noticeable deterioration here *that can be turned around*' " (emphasis added) (Center for Family Life 1979:5). His comment, noted as "widely shared in the community" (ibid.), lent external credibility to the directors' choice of neighborhood for the center's home.

Belonging to the Community

Sisters Geraldine and Mary Paul were concerned not only about locating the center in a community but also that the center's services would belong to that community. To be present with and accountable to Sunset Park families day to day, year in and year out, has been a chief goal of the center founders. Sister Mary Paul stated, "We're here, and we're available. It's just like years ago in the settlement house. The settlement house and its staff belonged to the community . . . joining people in their life space on a daily basis, joining them in their daily life tasks."

Thus making the center's staff and programs accessible to the neighborhood has been a high staff priority since it opened. Describing this priority, a Center for Family Life preventive program social worker elaborated:

This is community-based social work, broadly. We limit ourselves geographically [to Sunset Park], but within that geographic area I see the families, businesses, schools, the hospital, enclosed in that area as all being interconnected. I'm connected to guidance counselors and teachers and assistant principals at the school, people at the hospital, my neighborhood foster care families. So when I see a family beginning to deteriorate, falling apart, I can almost visualize pulling in nets or supports to keep them going, and it's all by their friends and neighbors. I believe very much in that. It makes sense to me. . . . We draw on the community resources, not just the social workers of the program, but drawing energy from all the supports that are in the community, to keep the family growing and alive and feeling good about itself. All the resources are right here in the community. Very rarely do they [clients] have to go outside of that.

Belonging to the Sunset Park community inevitably means being responsive to the political, economic, and social changes that affect the community. For example, the changing demography of Sunset Park has significantly influenced the center's program development and its staffing patterns. To illustrate, as more Chinese residents have joined center activities, greater attention has been paid to the language, culture, and family dynamics of the respective Asian groups participating in programs. The changing nature of Sunset Park's Latina/o population has required center staff to recognize the distinctions between national groups in its clinical and school-based interventions. Political divisions between and within ethnic groups are important contextual factors as are the common values and priorities shared across ethnic lines.

In addition, the specific nature of the services provided by the center for over two decades has been shaped by the needs of the community's families and children. The penetrating presence of poverty and unemployment has required continuing accessibility of emergency services (i.e., food, clothing, financial assistance). The challenges facing immigrant parents in locating and retaining employment, including the need for job skills, English as a second language skills, and child care, prompted the creation of an employment program and have shaped the services provided through the center's community schools programs. The problems faced by the community's youth reinforce the staff's strong commitment to providing a range of educational, socialization, youth development, recreational, and employment programs for children and teens.

Belonging to the community is not without tensions. For example, an article about society's pretending to love its children published in the *New York Times Magazine*, included a sixteen-year-old Sunset Park youth's descriptions of his life on the streets and at home (Rosenblatt 1995). The youth was quoted as saying that Jennifer, a staff member at the Center for Family Life, has been "everything to me" (p. 59). The article also described the center's programs, and the author reported a conversation with Sisters Geraldine and Mary Paul. Sister Mary Paul was quoted as saying, "They came up with the idea of teaching bilingualism, which serves no useful purpose at all for children trying to make it in American society. In Sunset Park, bilingualism is promoted solely to get patronage jobs for Spanish teachers" (p. 90).

In response to concerns about this quote raised by the principal and some of the teachers at P.S. 1, Sister Mary Paul and Sister Geraldine circulated a letter "To All Teachers and Parents in Sunset Park," stating that they were "appalled and dismayed" at the misquote in the article. They clarified that "Sister Mary Paul never said this and it does not represent her views," apologizing for "the hurt this must be causing to many hardworking and underappreciated professionals," and calling for "an early meeting in which we can share our feelings and thoughts about our statements." Some community residents demonstrated at the center; among the accusations was that the center and Sister Mary Paul were racist. Letters of accusation as well as letters of support were forwarded to the center directors. The center directors as well as other staff responded, requesting an opportunity to meet and discuss the article and the topic of bilingual education. Sisters Geraldine and Mary Paul met with the parents of children and youth at P.S. 1. Subsequent to that meeting they distributed a statement of position on the topics of bilingualism and bilingual education, correcting the misstatement but acknowledging concerns about "over-commitment to goals" in the carrying out of bilingual education programs.

In the November 5 edition of the *New York Times Magazine*, a letter from Sisters Mary Paul and Geraldine was published stating:

> We wish . . . to draw your attention to a single sentence in the article: "In Sunset Park, bilingualism is promoted solely to get patronage jobs for Spanish teachers." The sentence as written is a compressed and misleading expression of our opinion of bilingual education. It is no way represents our feelings or thoughts on this issue.

A letter to the center directors from the author of the article acknowledging that he "inadvertently misrepresented your views on bilingualism" was circulated to community teachers and parents.

For some time the center staff, those participating in center programs, and other Sunset Park residents experienced painful conflict, focusing on this issue of central concern to the community, many of whom are first or second generation immigrants. Sister Geraldine believed the incident, while difficult for all involved, was a catalyst for further growth within the center and with the broader community. She observed:

> The misunderstanding of the article and the angry reaction to it by the school administrators and teachers—the anger focused on Sister Mary Paul and me—placed the staff in a position of mediators. Their own intensive relationships with so many in the community resulted in lots of conversations with residents about the center, about us [Sisters Mary Paul and Geraldine], and about our work. Within the center, several intense meetings took place in which staff processed the incident, helping us all to carefully think about and understand our beliefs and feelings. I believe this process facilitated increased staff leadership of the center and greater cohesiveness among us.

Since this incident occurred while we were conducting our research, and we observed many of the meetings to which Sister Geraldine referred, we can confirm her conclusion.

Creating Communities of Interest

The center's commitment to community membership is not limited to geographical definitions. In addition to the center's commitment to be in and belong to the community of Sunset Park, the center also creates opportunities for children, youth, and adults to experience membership in communities created out of shared interests, such as the arts, sports, and parenting.

The undesirable consequences of not providing positive community experiences for children and youth have been stressed by John Kixmiller, one of the leaders of the community school programs. He has emphasized that when children and teens are unsupervised for long periods of time with no structured activity, "they're going to figure out some things to do and will create some kind of a community out on the streets." Yet without involved adults who allocate resources and assist with structure, youth become frustrated and angry. He stressed that "that anger and frustration leaks out in all sorts of destructive behaviors. . . . The anger means that youth are without positive involvement and are angry about it."

Julie Stein Brockway, another of the leaders of the community school programs who was appointed codirector of the center in summer 2000 after the untimely death of Sister Geraldine in April, described the way in which the center attempts to develop community experiences as follows: "We create community through projects that we all engage in together. It's not getting together for the sake of making community, it's being involved in certain things that we all enjoy and value and benefiting from the relationships formed." Sister Mary Paul has also emphasized that "one person alone might find something too daunting . . . but the experience of community and of doing things together is what generates hope."

COMPREHENSIVE, INTEGRATED, HOLISTIC SERVICES

Since its inception, the center has also been consistently committed to providing comprehensive, integrated, and holistic practice and services. For the center staff holistic practice has several meanings. First, it approaches families and communities as interdependent entities. In Sister Geraldine's view, "While we're working with families, we think of them in the context of community, so that both of those contexts educate us. . . . If the school system is accessible and responsive to families, families will do better. The stronger the community context, the better families survive."

Second, integrated, holistic practice means avoiding dichotomies in goals, processes, and method. Sister Geraldine emphasized:

> You don't throw process away on behalf of task and you don't throw task away on behalf of process. We work hard at that integration. You don't throw settlement house away on behalf of clinic; you don't throw social group work away on behalf of casework—it's both. And we're constantly working on the integration of these pieces on behalf of the systems that we are working with, whether it's a family or what have you. It's so much easier to break apart in pieces than to keep the integration going.

This is particularly evident in the center's unique integration of the concrete and therapeutic services typical of family preservation programs (Cole and Duva 1990; Fraser, Nelson, and Rivard 1997; Kinney, Haapala, and Booth 1991; McCroskey and Meezan 1997; Nelson, Landsman, and Deutelbaum 1990) with the continuously available comprehensive neighborhood-based services typical of family support programs (Allen, Brown, and Finlay 1993; Kagan and Weissbourd 1994; Lightburn and Kemp 1994). Over the past two decades these two distinct program models have been developed within the field to address the needs of vulnerable families. Family preservation services are specifically designed to prevent, through intensive brief services, the imminent out-of-home placement of children in families on the verge of breaking apart, while family support services are envisioned as providing a range of continuously available primary prevention services to all families who perceive themselves as needing such support. Yet there are many families whose needs place them somewhere on a continuum between these two extremes: families who are not yet at serious risk of breakdown but whose needs and problems are more complex than can be adequately addressed by family support services. Since its inception, the center's model has combined elements of both family preservation and family support programs to provide a comprehensive yet individualized response to the needs of Sunset Park's families.

To illustrate, Carol Heiney-Gonzalez, a social worker who served as clinical supervisor at the center when it was established, commented that

> we thought we had to use the best of ourselves and of our clients to try out things, all sorts of things. There was no distinction between clinical social work and community social work. It was all one and the same. . . . The center was a place to try out things, not clinical things, not community things, but human things.

Connecting a mother with concrete resources, such as day care, food stamps, and a job, was one part of her practice; helping the same woman with a problematic marital relationship and a developmentally disabled son was another. Linking the mother with other parents interested in relieving crowding at their children's schools was a third. "Nothing our clients wanted was little or big; it was all, very simply, necessary." Throughout the eight years Heiney-Gonzalez worked at the center, she viewed full engagement of individuals, families, groups, and community leadership as "my job and the center's reason for being."

The center's commitment to comprehensive integrated practice continues. Families as well as staff members acknowledge the importance of the comprehensive nature of this service approach. For example, a parent served in the center's preventive program commented:

I was only expecting to find counseling here, like they would help me with the kids, but I didn't think they would care about me personally. I thought they would just care about my son and help him because he was the one with the problem. But once we started going, they really helped me. If you don't have a job, they help you, and they also help with summer camp for the children. If you are a couple and you have problems, you can go there for counseling. And if you don't have food, they give you food. They also have free classes in English for the beginner. I wasn't expecting this.

INCLUSIVE AND NONSTIGMATIZING PROGRAMS AND SERVICES

The center also has always stressed inclusivity. To the center staff inclusivity means that *all* families with children in Sunset Park have access to its free programs and activities. It is assumed all families may at some time have the need for a range of services and that families themselves are able to determine which services are needed and when.

To assure families' ease and comfort in accessing the center's services, the directors and staff have consistently avoided any word or act or funding that would stigmatize families who participate. This commitment is demonstrated through the sources of funding sought and accepted, the nature, location, and names of its programs, and the language used by staff members as they describe their work with Sunset Park residents. Unlike workers at many family service agencies and mental health centers, they *never* refer to their clients as patients. Center staff members actively reject thinking of center clients or program participants as people with special problems.

To illustrate, therapeutic small groups, which are available to children, youth, and parents through the center's preventive services program, are identified not by a problem focus, such as women who are battered or youth who are delinquent, but rather by participants' age and/or gender (e.g., the preadolescent girls' group, the women's group, the men's group). Workers believe this method of grouping clients encourages the engagement of clients who might not participate were the problems with which they were struggling identified in the group's name. A worker noted:

All the women who come to the women's group are there to support their families and improve the level of their functioning for their families. That's their commonality. There doesn't have to be anything else but that—that they want something better for themselves and their families.

John Kixmiller, coordinator of the Beacon School project at P.S. 314, commented that in seeking to offer normalizing rather than marginalizing programs and services, the center's staff has long viewed the public school as a critical service location:

Schools are a vital part of every community's and every family's public space. And public space enables everyone to be on equal footing. That's one of our goals [at the center]: to help expand the public space so that the families we work with establish and know that they are on equal footing with everyone else in the community.

Not only have center staff members aimed to avoid stigmatizing clients, but also, according to Sister Mary Paul, they have sought "to erode people's and the neighborhood's sense of victimization." She suggests this is accomplished over time, first, through staff actively involving people in working partnerships with each other and with social service professionals who value social and personal problem-solving, and, second, through "constantly learning about the possibilities of people and helping them to recognize and realize those possibilities more fully."

WORKING PARTNERSHIPS

The development of partnerships with families, community schools, and others in the community is another defining characteristic of the center's model. As described earlier, the cofounders established the center with a blueprint of the model they wanted to develop. A partnership with community schools was central to this model. However, Sister Geraldine stressed that when the center enters a partnership with another agency or organization neither the center nor its partner gives up its identity, mission, or structure. She emphasized that

we don't become a part of another system, we become a partner. We are a separate entity from the schools—just like we wouldn't move in with a family, even though the family would love for you to. It is important for systems, such as the individual family system or the individual school system, to have their own lives and to be separate from us, but for us to be a partner.

As partners, parents and children share the staff's interest in the continuation of the center's community-based programs. To illustrate, in the mid-nineties, when New York City funds for the Community School Program were threatened, parents and children associated with the center wrote to the city's mayor to argue for continued funding. A content analysis of the letters identified the great value attributed to the center by families. For example, children most frequently noted that the center helps with homework/school, keeps children "off the streets" and "out of trouble," and is "fun." Children also wrote that they make new friends at the center and can "hang out" there. They emphasized that the center encourages dance, art, drama, sports, etc., and that elimination of the center's activities would be like "taking down a part of my life." Children/youth wrote that the center "teaches us how to perform on the job" and helps "prepare for the future," "learn how to work with the younger children," and develop confidence and cooperation.

In their letters parents emphasized that they cannot afford babysitters and that the after-school program keeps their children from becoming latchkey kids; it keeps their children "off the streets." Many parents' comments paralleled their children's regarding the help with homework and opportunities for recreational activities. Parents also noted that the center allows them to meet other parents and gives parents an opportunity to become more involved in the school and the community.

One reason for these enthusiastic endorsements is that staff members invite and foster the participation and partnership of Sunset Park children, teens, and adults in the myriad activities—recreational, artistic, vocational, educational, and therapeutic—that make up the center's programs and services. A parent of two children enrolled in one of the center's Community School Projects commented:

They [center staff] never close the door on me. I could have a question, a disagreement, a concern, and that door was always open, and they always tried to resolve the problem. That in itself is enough. I don't need anything else . . . just having that sense of security, that [knowledge] that they will listen to my concerns, that is enough.

Families served in the center's preventive program also reported highly valuing the sense of partnership in their relationships with their social workers. Family members served in this program consistently described relationships with their social workers in which they feel accepted, not judged, and equal with their counselors.

AN INTERGENERATIONAL AND DEVELOPMENTAL FOCUS: "PEOPLE REALIZING THEIR POSSIBILITIES"

The paradigm of development—of the individual (child, teen, adult), the family, the community—is a theme of center conversation and written materials. The staff members conceptualize the center's programs as interventions designed to address the developmental needs of all family members.

This developmental focus further incorporates a particular understanding of the role of intergenerational contact and interaction in the ongoing development of individual children, youth, and adults, of their families, and of the community. For example, the center's community school programs are designed to involve Sunset Park teens with adult staff in the care of elementary school-aged children and to engage parents and grandparents in various aspects of the children's experiences. Two of the leaders, Kixmiller and Onserud (1995:209–210), have asserted that "the task of creating and maintaining a holistic environment representing the various ages and developmental stages of life is at the heart of any community center model." They describe the school-aged child care program as an integrative component for the center, as it encourages

> a wide range of age groups, activities, roles and responsibilities to overlap and meet around a common purpose. It includes teens who volunteer their time working with children through a counselor-in-training program, and who then become committed to the success of that operation; young adults who have reached the level of maturity needed to become group leaders; and parents who naturally have a stake in the well-being of their children and of the community in which they live. (p. 210)

In discussing the developmental emphases in the center's after-school child care and youth development programs, John Kixmiller, program director, stressed that "teenagers need to feel that they have some mission in life. Most teens are at a stage where they want to imagine and think about playing some role for the [common] good that matters." He further emphasized that teens need to be able to meet and socialize with other people and experience "community life. By community life I mean that the different ages and stages are represented, that there are group activities and communitywide activities, that there's a center where people can become a part of a hub." Kixmiller also pointed out:

> I've never met a Sunset Park kid or adult who wants to fail, who prefers to fail, if given the chance and resources with which to succeed. If we can create structured opportunities and the public space in which people can be full participants in their own development and in school or community life, Sunset Park kids and adults are going to succeed, not fail.

A former counselor-in-training who is now an adult and a center staff member reflected upon her own development, the development of the children she works with, and the experience of becoming a role model for the younger children:

> It's interesting to see how they [the younger children] grow, how they develop, certain stages they go through. You see yourself in them also, like when you were a child, the things you used to do. . . . It's important for them to have positive things to look at and model on. . . . I feel proud of what I do, like I was saying about being a role model. Being a role model is a hard thing to do, but it also brings positive feelings.

Fostering self-expression. The center's commitment to participants'/clients' development has not only involved attention to the individuals' developmental needs but also to making opportunities for self-expression, cultural expression, and creativity fundamental aspects of daily life in Sunset Park. It is not sufficient at the center to help Sunset Park residents with food, housing, jobs, money, schooling, health care, child care, home care, family harmony, and safety; the center staff members place high priority on helping people express their talents and aspirations. For example, each year in the community school programs two musical performances are presented in which all children participate. Each performance is written, designed and produced entirely by the children and staff. A high priority is given to the development of such opportunities. To illustrate, Julie Stein Brockway has devoted her professional life to the proposition that "it is a right, not a privilege, a basic human need to express oneself in a variety of ways. Not just verbally, not just through sports. I think that art belongs to everybody and that everybody should be exposed. Boys and girls, everybody from the youngest to the oldest can do it." She described the benefits of enhancing capacities for self-expression:

> Self-expression, particularly finding one's voice, finding what one has uniquely to say as well as learning to hear from others, is such an incredibly important part of getting one's needs met, resolving conflict creatively, dealing with and managing difficult feelings, finding a way to address difficult feelings without resorting to behaviors that might be detrimental to oneself or to others in the community.

Sister Geraldine was similarly inspired by a deep concern to ensure Sunset Park residents of getting the chance to build literature and the arts into their daily lives: "We had to argue for enrichment to take place [in the school] because it was in that process of enrichment that the children would love school. We got a Reading is Fundamental grant in one school where every child gets three books a year. But we didn't just do that. We created a program around it so that clubs got involved in book swapping."

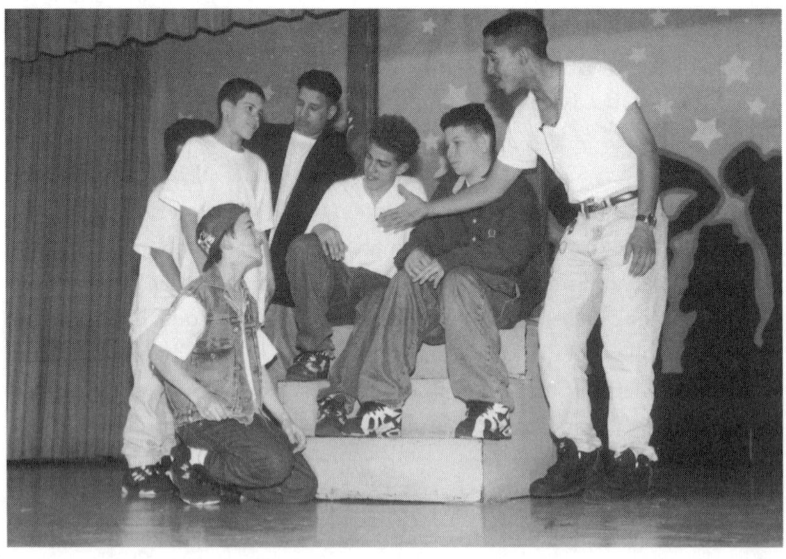

FIGURE 1.3

A performance of the Life Lines improvisational musical *Chillin' to the Sunset Rhythm*

Sister Mary Paul also feels deeply about the importance of nurturing Sunset Park residents' creativity as a part of the center's core work. In describing a Saturday carnival at P.S. 314, she said:

> The music started and they [the children] came down the street, walked all along 4th Avenue and around to 60th Street and came in. They danced their way in. To see 350 children dance their way in and around . . . I know that those children come from homes that have very little, they come from very struggling homes. I know that those children don't come from totally joyous homes. They come from homes with a mix of contentments and lots of love. You see 350 children and young teenagers dancing to a joyous beat and owning this sense of expression, like "I am. I want to say this." It was a transporting experience.

A parent's description of the center's work with each of her children further illustrates the benefits of the programmatic emphases on development and self-expression:

> My son was the first in our family to join the program, and I felt it had an impact on his self-esteem. From a very shy little boy, he sort of grew into this self-assertive person. I was in shock the first time I saw him in a show at the center. For a child who would not even say hello to people, now to be on stage performing. He had counselors who were very positive role models for an Hispanic child. He felt comfortable. He felt he was accepted. That helped him a lot. He became more secure in himself. He learned to express his feelings.
>
> [My daughter] is very artistic, and the center has a wonderful art program. I saw her blossom. . . . She's a very assertive young person and one of the things that used to bother her a lot in her classroom was that the teacher used to send the boys only to do certain jobs, heavy lifting and that kind of thing. She always had a problem with that. One of the things that she used to come home and tell me is that she was allowed to play any sport in the center. It could have been basketball, dodge ball, very physical kinds of things. And she felt she was capable of doing it. . . . She just wanted to play and she was allowed to play. I think that was important for her.

CONTINUITY: A SECURE BASE

Since its inception, the center has enacted its commitment to maintaining continuity in its provision of accessible services to all families in Sunset Park.

The loyalty and longevity of key program coordinators and other center staff, including volunteers and former program participants now on staff, and the ongoing accessibility of the center's programs and services over a lengthy period have enhanced community residents' perception of the center as a "secure base" where a range of needs can be met.

Longevity of Program Staff

Over forty staff members have been with the center for over ten years; many of these have been with the agency for much longer. To illustrate, Edie Crockenberg, the center's office manager, has been with the center since 1979. Anita Cleary, case supervisor for the Preventive Program, and Mary Lou Duggan, computer specialist, have been with the agency since 1980. Julie Stein Brockway and John Kixmiller, leaders of the center's school-based programming, have worked at the center since 1982 and 1983 respectively. A parent's observation highlighted the staff's constancy: "I think there's a lot of commitment, and that's something that's hard to find. They must have something special that makes them want to stay."

Julie Stein Brockway explained some of her reasons for staying since 1982:

> One thing that keeps me here is the building process. . . . At one point, when I considered leaving, I realized that, if I was going to stay, it was going to take me at least another five years to develop the foundation for something that would grow at this middle school. And I had to ask myself the question, Was I going to commit the five years? Five to eight [years] I figured. I knew it was going to take that long for the sixth graders to become junior staff. And I'm in my fifth year, and we are just beginning to reap the benefits. I don't think I was off in my estimate of what it takes, and that was a commitment. . . . I didn't want to start something and not get it to the point where I could leave and others could carry it on.
>
> I feel very rooted here. I feel like this is my community. There's a continuity that I've never experienced anywhere else. Some of my sixth graders are the children of the older teens that I worked with my first year.

During in-depth interviews with the center's staff, the center's mission, philosophy, and program model were described both as "what draws" staff members to the work at the center and what retains them. In addition, center staff members reported greatly valuing the opportunities for professional development, the administrative support for autonomous professional practice, and the supportive relationships with center colleagues. One social worker noted: "What I value about this place is it's the most autonomy I've ever been given. I was told when I was hired that I would have creative freedom—freedom to use yourself in a variety of ways. I have felt respected, and that has supported me. It makes an environment where people grow."

We have concluded that there is a coherence and integrity between the philosophy, definition, and structure of the center's programs and both the personal and professional philosophies and commitments of the staff who implement the programs. This contributes to a synergy that enhances the sense of community experienced throughout the center, the positive experiences and outcomes reported by program participants, and the continuity made possible by the retention of committed staff.

A Philosophy of Continuity in Program Access

Since its establishment, the center has enacted a philosophy of continuity in the provision of accessible services to Sunset Park families. Many have observed that current family support programs have built upon the settlement house movement of the early 1900s (Halpern 1988, 1991; Lightburn and Kemp 1994; Weissbourd and Kagen 1989). In their emphasis on the accessibility of comprehensive, developmentally oriented services to all families in a community, such programs inevitably are characterized by continuity of services. Since its inception the center has shared these commitments. However, it is important to note that the center's inclusion of intensive clinical services designed to prevent the unnecessary placement of children in out-of-home care (the preventive services program) as one of its continuously available and accessible core programs differentiates it from other family support programs and settlement houses, which typically lack a clinical component (Hess, McGowan, and Botsko 2000). Every family served by the center in all its programs, including the preventive services program, is encouraged to access services over time as needed on a voluntary or self-referred basis. We found that many families were using not only school-based child care, parent education, and other family support services over many years as needed but were also accessing therapeutic services both continuously over several years and episodically over time as the need arose.

Center staff members stress the benefits to families of being able to stay involved with the center's programs over long periods of time to maintain the children in the home. In discussing the services to one such family, the social worker emphasized that she will "have to be constantly involved . . . be there as a transitional object, as an authority figure, to kind of keep things in balance. If I leave the situation, you can pretty much be sure it will go down the tubes."

We believe that the strong commitment to continuity in access to services over time and to consistency of staff responses over time contributes to the experience of the center as *like home* or an *anchor* for many community residents. Conceptualizing the center as a secure base to which family members may turn and return as needs arise may be useful. The concept of a child's attachment to a parent as a secure base for exploration was first introduced by Mary Ainsworth (1967:345–346). Although the concept of a secure base typically has been limited to dyadic attachments relationships, including those of parent-child, intimate partners, and therapist-client, the multifaceted patterns of families' service use and interpersonal connections with staff over time would suggest that many family members may in fact experience the center itself as a "secure base." This is consistent with the observation of Lightburn and Kemp (1994) that family support programs provide a "supportive ongoing base" (p. 23) from which services are accessed as

FIGURE 1.4
Participants at a community festival celebrating the center's twentieth anniversary

required. For example, in outlining the many changes made by a single mother over several years, a worker described the center's continuous role as follows: "I think the center has given her a grounding, a place for her and her children." Similarly, a staff member in the community school programs who has participated in center programs "since I was a little girl" observed that "a lot of people from the community consider this like home to them." She further emphasized the depth of her long-term connection to the center both as a child as well as currently:

> As a child the after-school program meant a lot. Whenever I couldn't come, I would cry. I remember that. I remember crying to my mother, begging her to let me stay. It really meant a lot to me. . . . What kept me returning year after year? All these people. They've seen me since I was a little girl. They's always told me, always, come back, help us. [Now as a staff member] I enjoy being with my group, my supervisor and my assistant, you can speak to them when you need them. I guess that those are the only true friends that I have, and I love coming here.

Similarly, a supervisor described a mother as

> attached to her worker and attached to the center as a whole. . . . There have been many times when she would come here and under the pretense that she would have to meet her child here, she would stay quite a bit in the reception area, maybe writing, or finding another excuse to be there. I think it's partly our aggregate involvement. Everybody knows her. . . . The center has a certain amount of resource itself and that represents something to her. I am absolutely positive that she comes here for more than to see her worker alone. . . . The center is her anchor.

The perception of the center as "like home" to many Sunset Park families both reflects and facilitates repeated access to services over time as needs arise. It is most likely that family members' experiences with the center's continuously accessible, responsive, sensitive, and trustworthy staff in all programs makes possible the experience of one parent described as follows by her preventive program worker: "She has a constant sort of knowing that there's a place for her here. Whether I'm here or not, she would see this a place where people respect and understand her and she won't be ridiculed or judged." Experiences such as this are essential to families' willingness and ability to seek services as they identify needs and thus prevent crises, rather than seeking services only when a crisis arises.

PROFESSIONALISM: GROUNDED IN VALUES, KNOWLEDGE AND THEORY, AND SKILLS

A deeply committed community of professionals is at the core of the center's service delivery model. Although this could be said of many community-based agencies, the center has developed an unusual degree of coherence, mutual respect, and support between the professional social workers and performing artists who staff its diverse programs. Both within and across programs one quickly senses staff members' mutual deep respect for each others' professional knowledge, skills, and values, shared commitment to Sunset Park's children and families and to the center's mission, and collective investment in an authentic, dynamic process of creative program design, delivery, and evaluation.

Although the majority of the center's professional staff are social workers (twenty-six), the center also employs eighteen full-time professional staff in other disciplines, including the creative and performing arts. Center cofounders Sisters Mary Paul and Geraldine made a commitment to have at least one professional staff member in each program in whatever discipline is relevant—a social worker with particular expertise, such as group work or family treatment, or a professional artist or dancer. Thus they assure that the daily decisions that must be made about both broad programmatic and specific service issues are consistently informed by professional knowledge. In addition, the presence of at least one professional in each program guarantees that regular supervision and support are available for the center's many paraprofessional and volunteer staff.

Whether one is a social worker or a creative or performing artist, professionalism at the center means being grounded in the knowledge and theory of the profession or discipline, undergirding family and program development with comprehensive professional assessment of needs and resources and purposeful use of professional knowledge and skills in building productive working relationships with people and institutions. The importance of the staff members' ability to draw upon their professional knowledge in their work at the center was stressed by the center's directors. To illustrate, Sister Geraldine emphasized that

> you don't ask young paraprofessionals to teach dance—they flood little five year olds with their own personal style, their own dance. You need at least one minimum professional staff member in whatever discipline is relevant

for the program—professional artist, dancer, social work group worker. We've made that commitment.

Similarly, Sister Mary Paul explained the importance of using professional staff who have "a certain sense of purpose" and are knowledgeable: "We came from the outset with a commitment that we would have people [on the center's staff] who had a knowledge that they could account for and that they could utilize. . . . I can't imagine doing this work with untrained people."

Ongoing collaboration, including questioning of program design and sharing of information and expertise among all center staff about individual and program interventions, is also a critical aspect of the center's professionalism. Helene Onserud, coordinator of Project Youth at P.S. 1 commented:

A piece of the program that's not talked about very much . . . is all of the networking that goes on between myself, the mentors, the supervisors, the tutors, because all of the teenagers who are in the program also do community service in the after school program. . . . There are countless relationships that are very very important in the way the program works. It goes back to being a community center. . . . The reason why this program [Project Youth] works is because it's really connected with the other pieces of the community school project. We work as a team. We need to keep abreast of everything that's going on, and we can work together. And that's, I think, what makes what we do work.

Inclusive Definition of Center Staff

Although the staff members of the numerous programs meet regularly to plan and coordinate their activities, all full-time social work staff members meet together *as a whole* each Monday morning, structurally including staff from all programs in the definition of center staff. At first glance this seems unnecessarily resource intensive, yet the benefits are immediately evident. Staff members are all apprised of current information about center and Sunset Park community activities, staffing needs due to illness or other difficulties, or emergent issues such as a threat to the funding of a specific program. In addition, program challenges and dilemmas are identified and problem-solving occurs. Sister Geraldine emphasized that when she and Sister Mary Paul established the center, "we resolved to have only one name, and whatever program pieces were developed, major players would have to get together regularly in one room." As discussed earlier, in one of the many staff meetings we attended, the staff discussed the community's reaction to the misquote of Sister Mary Paul regarding the topic of bilingualism in a *New York Times Magazine* article about the center's programs. Staff asked questions, shared information, and discussed strategies to respond to Sunset Park's school administrators' and teachers' angry reactions. Coming together weekly as a whole promotes the continuing sense of a professional community engaged in achieving a shared mission through the staff's daily work in distinct but strongly interconnected programs.

The shared sense of mission and of professional community are articulated by staff in a variety of ways, but there is a widely held acknowledgement that what is being achieved collectively through the staff members' diverse professional contributions far exceeds what any one could achieve alone. The following observation from Julie Stein Brockway illustrates: "You set something in motion and it's much better than you ever could have done on your own. . . . I believe that I have talents and skills and things to offer, but I believe the whole is so much greater than the sum of the parts."

The Influence of Professional Social Work on the Center's Services

The professional social work presence at the Center for Family Life is palpable. The center's directors and social work staff are proud of their professional identity and are unusually well able to conceptualize and articulate the theoretical and conceptual bases of the center's programs and their own professional practice. Center social workers assess the needs and resources of individuals, families, and the community, coordinate and implement programs, supervise other professional staff and interns from graduate schools of social work in New York City, supervise, train, and develop leadership among volunteers, paraprofessional, and bachelor-level workers, perform clinical work with families and individuals, and involve themselves in community development, advocacy, group leadership, and other activities.

A common framework and value base. In their discussions with us Sisters Geraldine and Mary Paul consistently emphasized the value they place on their own and other staff members' social work education and their shared commitment to the values of the profession. Sister Mary Paul emphasized that "we never have to argue values with our staff. We don't have to educate staff about our values. They share them." Integral to staff members' discussions about their relationships and work with Sunset Park's families and children are their professional concerns about confidentiality, self-determination, starting "where the client is," and conveying respect.

The shared social work identity and professional education provides a common framework from which staff members think and act. Sister Mary Paul stressed:

> Social work does ground one in a particular knowledge base that is important in building constructive working partnerships with families—knowledge of oneself, knowledge of the psychological bases of professional and personal relationships, knowledge of child development and family relationships, knowledge of organizational dynamics. . . . Also it's imperative to pay attention to the environment, the community, and to the ecology of community.

To illustrate, the profession of social work has always had a primary focus upon the *psychosocial* needs of those one serves (Hamilton 1951; Hollis 1964; Meyer 1970), or, as others have stated, a focus upon the person:environment (Germain 1973, 1978b; Kemp, Whittaker, and Tracy 1997). This dual focus upon psycho- and social is evident in the center's mission statement, in its development of programs that focus upon children's and families' inner and outer worlds, and in staff members' ongoing interventions with individuals, families, and community institutions.

Skillful use of professional self in relationships. Further, the uses and qualities of professional *relationship* and the importance of the *conscious use of professional self* are frequently referenced in staff members' descriptions of their work in all center programs. For example, Sister Mary Paul noted that "helping is not a 'delivery' of some kind. It results from two people or a group of people exchanging their understandings, their life experiences, or a problem or perception at a particular point in time. It's an exchange. Their learning occurs within a relationship. Most change in human beings occurs within a relationship of some kind." Consistent with Sister Mary Paul's observation is Julie Stein Brockway's reflection on the challenge with regard to use of professional self in her work in the community school programs:

> The hardest thing about my job, if I had to define it, is my use of self, my professional use of self, in all the different roles. . . . That's where I struggle the most. Do I respond to my junior staff member as a colleague and friend, because I've known him for years and let my hair down and say 'Look, I'm really disappointed?' Or am I still a professional there and do I still have to call for work in him? Push him to get a full-time job, push him out of the nest, because as a professional I recognize he's having an individuation process with me. I'm his family. I'm the mother. He's the teenager. At what point am I me, and at what point am I me and a professional?

Clients' descriptions of their work with center staff also provide examples of the staff members' skillful use of professional relationship. One single mother stressed the ways in which her worker related to her:

> My worker is always there not to supervise but kind of help and guide me in how to handle a situation. . . . I have the sense that she understands where I'm coming from and what I'm trying to tell her. . . . She says, "I know you have a feeling, can you tell me what kind of feeling? I see it in your eyes."

She continues, "Sometimes I want to run out the door, and she says 'No, that's not the way to go about it. Running away is not going to solve anything.' "

Similarly, youth who have participated in the center's after-school child care and youth development programs emphasized the importance of the staff's use of professional relationship. One reflected, "I depended on them to help me if something was difficult, and I depended on them if I had a problem with the other kids. . . . I depended on them to help me through it." Similarly, another commented, "The social workers, the people who work here. . . . I learned from them. . . . They got some wise people in the center."

Focus on both case and cause. Central to the social work profession is *a commitment to social and economic justice.* In center staff members' work with individual clients and families they often discover needs or problems that also are affecting others in the community. The identification of a problem affecting both the one and the many is often referred to within the profession as moving from "case to cause" (Sunley 1970). Center staff members' willingness and ability to move from case to cause is assumed by the center's directors. Current advocacy efforts are discussed in the Monday morning all-staff meetings along with programmatic and clinical issues.

Both Sister Geraldine and Sister Mary Paul have been role models for staff in their own constant movement from case to cause. A number of issues commanded their attention as advocates during our study, including state efforts to computerize child welfare records, raising widespread concern about clients' privacy. In describing her own advocacy efforts about the computerization of records and the possible effects of this on client privacy, Sister Mary Paul noted that

> I find more recently my letters are much angrier. . . . I protest more vigorously. [The anger comes from] frustration, from actually seeing that the obligations and commitments that have long been respected are being trifled with. Like the value of privacy and confidentiality, the very heart of social work practice. It's a value that has to be central. People act as if they can give it away, compromise it, trade it, negotiate. I'm not sure we have a right to negotiate, confidentiality is a client's right.

The Influence of Theoretical Frameworks on the Center's Programs

The work of the Center for Family Life is theory driven. One hears in the directors' and staff members' discussions elements of the theoretical frameworks that have emerged as particularly influential in shaping the center's practice principles and the staff members' professional interactions with community residents and the center's programs. Staff members' references to various conceptual frameworks are not rhetorical. The center social workers clearly are engaged not only in applying theory to practice but also in examining the application of various social work theories in practice. Thus center staff members differentially draw upon various practice conceptual frameworks and approaches as they struggle with the complex problems facing Sunset Park's families and children. As one staff member noted:

> We have a great flexibility here to work with people in a way that seems best for that particular individual—individualized in terms of what techniques we use and how we work. It's not like we're all behaviorists here or all psychoanalytic here, or that we just do individual work or that we just do family or that we just do group.

Similarly, another stressed, "We have the goal of trying to keep families together. . . . We can use any kind of intervention that we feel comfortable with to achieve that goal." Those theoretical frameworks clearly shaping the center's practice include systems theory and an ecosystem perspective, developmental, attachment, and psychodynamic theories, and developmental group work.

Systems theory. Meyer suggests that general systems theory "makes possible an organized view of the individual in his multiple interactions; it provides a convenient form for viewing the parts of things in an interrelated way so as to avoid fragmentation and disparateness" (1976:136). Any question to the center's directors and staff regarding the theories that undergird the center's work yields a discussion of social systems, including family systems. Sister Geraldine has stated that

I can't emphasize enough how much all of Mary Paul's deep embeddedness in systems theory has been the life of the center. Here was another system you had to look at—the school, family systems. How do you bring those systems together? Where do you find those places where they meet and have common goals and common agendas?

An understanding of the relationships between systems within the community and within the family and the constantly changing and interacting nature of systems shapes center staff members' short- and long-term assessment, planning, intervention, and use of self. The integration of an ecosystems framework into the staff's understanding of the Sunset Park neighborhood, the center's mission and service delivery model, program activities, and specific interventions is immediately evident to any visitor. The following observation by Sister Geraldine is illustrative:

The center has to be more than just a counseling service for this family or that. It has to be a part of a dynamic process that values the life at any level, the individual person, the family unit, and the processes among families and the people they live with. It's that dynamic between schools and parents and their children.

She further stressed that "we couldn't help any one individual child without being part of the process of stimulating the schools' interest in the social life of the children, the family life of the children, the community life of the children. I think it produces change in the schools. It is a constant dynamic process.

In remembering her first exposure to systems theory Sister Mary Paul recalls that her masters degree education had grounded her in psychodynamic theory. Later in the sixties, while working on her doctorate in social work at Columbia University, she had a "wonderful, wonderful" class with Robert Merton, the renowned sociologist. Sister Mary Paul emphasized that her introduction to systems theory expanded her understanding of process and created an awareness of "additional realities": "Once you understand the power of the unconscious and of the mind, you look for and recognize things that flow from that reality. But Robert Merton really helped me to see process, social process, and additional realities in an interactional kind of frame." The ways in which the systems way of thinking were integrated into her own are illustrated in several publications, including "Systems Concepts in Casework Theory and Practice" (Janchill 1969).

Developmental theories. The center's mission to promote and support the development of the individuals, families, groups, and institutions within the Sunset Park community, and thus the community itself, requires that staff members rely daily on developmental theories. A book chapter by staff members John Kixmiller and Helene Onserud (1995) exemplifies staff members' ability to conceptualize the relevance of developmental theory to center programming. They stress the "major psychological assumption" that healthy individual identity is nourished by an environment in which a community of different age groups come together (p. 209). They describe the center's school-age child care program as an integrative component that allows for a wide range of "age groups, activities, roles and responsibilities to overlap and meet around common purpose" (p. 210). Specifically, they state that

> children need to have a context in which they can play, or come together around activities as well as acquire and practice the skills that will allow them to gain mastery and feel competent in the accomplishment of a variety of tasks. . . .
>
> Adolescents' developmental needs dictate a wider variety of options. In addition to the counselor-in-training program, which provides the link for teens to the school-age child care program and to the rest of the community, there have to be other forms of peer groups in which young people can acquire skills and struggle with identity issues in various ways. Teens need to be able to choose a group based on their interests, level of skills, or their attraction to a group worker who can become a suitable role model for them. (pp. 209–211)

Attention to developmental theories, particularly ego psychology and the concepts of autonomy, drive for mastery, and competence (Erikson 1969; Hartmann 1958; Maluccio 1981; White 1959, 1963), is also evident in center staff members' assessments. For example, staff members consider an individual child's, youth's, or adult's physical, social, intellectual, and emotional development in developing plans for his or her participation in center programs—whether the individual is engaged in counseling, recreational, vocational, educational, or other types of program activities.

Sister Mary Paul stressed that "the developmental is at least as important as looking after the remediation. Unless we touch the process of development, remediation won't come. They go hand in hand. . . . For parents it's a second chance at development." Developmental tasks are supported through center policy as well. For example, the center's policy is not to take a parent out of work or a child out of school for meetings and appointments.

Attachment theory. Supporting the development and maintenance of parent-child attachments and making every effort to prevent unnecessary parent-child separation and loss are center philosophical commitments that are supported by attachment theory. As defined by Bowlby (1958, 1969, 1973, 1988) and Ainsworth, Blehar, Waters, and Wall (1978), attachment is the affectional bond that an infant forms with another person, usually a parent. Attachment theorists have emphasized the severe distress experienced by children when they are separated against their will from a person to whom they are attached.

Perhaps the clearest example of the center's incorporation of theory regarding attachment, separation, and loss into its practice is the neighborhood foster care program, initiated in 1988. This program's objectives are to maximize foster family care as a resource for protecting children while "offsetting trauma that follows radical ruptures of bonds with parents, relatives, school, friends, or other primary attachments" (Janchill 1997:1). Proximity of the foster home to the family while the child is in care facilitates frequent visiting, essential to support the parent-child attachment during placement, and ongoing parent involvement with foster parents and the center's assigned social worker.

The attachment related concepts of continuity, accessibility, and mutuality are interwoven into the fabric of the center's programs. Social workers not only engage in therapeutic work that supports the development and maintenance of strong parent-child relationships, they also provide the range of comprehensive services that prevent family break-up and the placement of children outside their homes. Staff in all programs are attentive to the impact of separation and loss upon the children and youth who participate—loss due to divorce, AIDS related deaths, incarceration of a parent, and immigration. In addition, the development of attachments between program staff and family members is encouraged.

Psychodynamic theories. Although it is evident that the center's Directors and staff draw upon psychodynamic theories, particularly ego psychology, the impact of these theories on their practice is less explicit, more subtle. For example, center practitioners' discussions regarding their therapeutic work with families and children often incorporate references to the impact of clients' personal histories upon their current situations, feelings, and behaviors. Although practitioners state that their clients' early life experiences may become an appropriate focus for counseling, it is not expected that early internal conflicts would be resolved through the therapeutic relationship. For example, we heard no reference to therapeutic efforts aimed at creating a transference relationship. As a consequence of the center directors' and staff members' strong commitment to avoid labeling and its attendant stigma, their spoken and written clinical hypotheses and conclusions with regard to psychopathology rarely incorporate diagnostic categories. Yet Sister Mary Paul stressed that "we're very conscious of pathology, we're not Pollyanish."

Developmental group work theory. The center staff members incorporate the use of group work in a range of programs for multiple purposes: therapeutic, educational, socialization, and task completion. Staff members work from the assumption that family members effectively enhance their social functioning through specific types of group experiences and that, through attempting to accomplish a group goal, peer relationships are established (Tropp 1976:200). This approach is viewed by staff as imminently useful in supporting the ongoing development of individual children, youth, and parents as well as of a sense of community (Kixmiller and Onserud 1995). The list of groups developed over the years at the center is extensive and inclusive. Groups are typically defined by gender and age (adolescent girls group, latency aged boys group, parents/infants/toddlers group) or by focus (library group, tutoring group, adult fitness group, father-son activity group). Groups are also extensively integrated into ongoing programming, such as the focused activity groups in the after-school child care program.

A number of staff have specialized in group work in their professional education. However, in our discussions regarding the application of theory in the

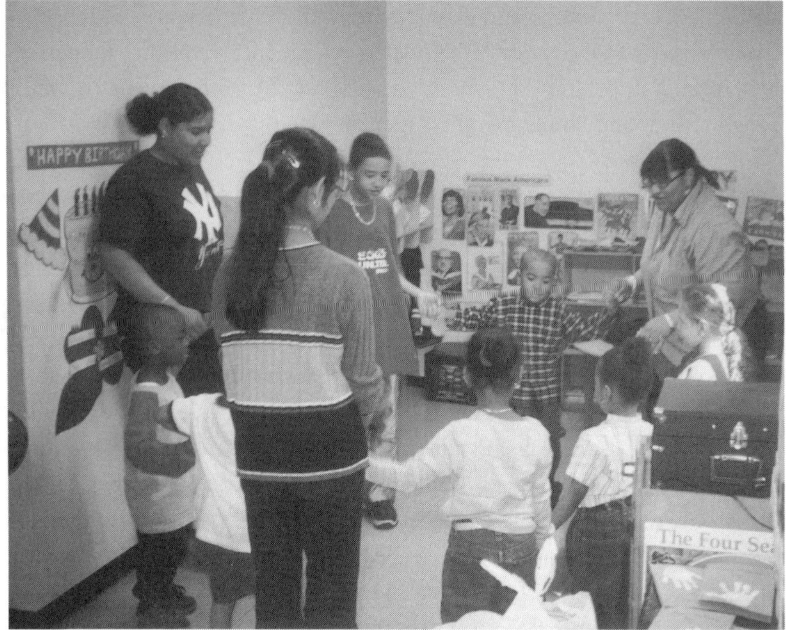

FIGURE 1.5

After-school activity group

center's programs, Sister Geraldine expressed the concern that increasingly in social work education "the real skills of group work have gotten diluted down to none. . . . There are actual skills that one must learn." Therefore, staff members have been strongly encouraged to develop their knowledge and skills through the center's ongoing weekly seminar on social group work.

Theology

Sisters Mary Paul and Geraldine have maintained the center's fiscal and political separation from the religious order of the Sisters of the Good Shepherd, from the Roman Catholic Diocese of Brooklyn, and from neighborhood churches in Sunset Park. However, because the center was cofounded by women who were both members of a religious order as well as professional social workers, the question often is posed: Where does religion fit in what they do? Sister Mary Paul commented that "the motto of my religious order, Sisters of the Good Shepherd, is that 'one person is of more value than a world.' This belief gives unity to my personal life and my work at the Center for Family Life." She elaborated:

> I believe in a personal God who loves each person, even more than we could love, and who invites us to live a response; that time itself is a gift, and the present moment, in which my life is an encounter with another, has the possibility for divine grace to take form in both of us.

She further observed that she finds that while her coworkers at the center "are of different religious denominations and come from different practice traditions, we each have a spirituality that appreciates the individual as centerpiece of God's work."

In discussions with Sisters Mary Paul and Geraldine on theories that inform their practice, references to "process theology" (Cobb and Griffin 1939; Cousins 1971; Pittenger 1971) were not uncommon. Sister Mary Paul emphasized that "wherever we were looking, we were really looking at change and development, at becoming, at the human person, not finished, not determined, genetically or otherwise. It all flowed."

Sisters Geraldine and Mary Paul identified many "points of congruence and interception" in process theology and the professional and social sciences theories upon which they draw. They emphasized that there is a synergy between these ideas and ways of understanding change, development, and becoming.

A FLEXIBLE, LEARNING, AND EVOLVING ORGANIZATION

Although continuity and stability have been essential to the center's development of the strong connections with community residents, the center as an organization and its staff are also flexible, reflective, self-evaluative, and responsive to community and broader change. A learning organization has been defined as "an organization that is continually expanding its capacity to create its future" (Senge 1990:14). Senge identifies five dimensions essential to building organizations that can truly "learn." As discussed in various sections of this chapter, all are present in the center. These include systems thinking, which permeates the center, personal mastery, the commitment of the individuals in the organization to their own lifelong learning, essential to "reciprocal commitments between individual and organization" (ibid., p. 8); mental models, making explicit, scrutinizing, and discussing people's assumptions and conceptual frameworks; building shared vision, "a set of principles and guiding practices" (ibid., p. 9); and team learning and dialogue.

In addition to possessing these interactive dimensions within the center as an organization, the center's historical record indicates that the directors and program coordinators have created many forums for ongoing dialogue among program participants, parents, school personnel, and community leaders about the nature and quality of the programs and services being offered. Many center programs, such as the advocacy clinic and the thrift shop and service center, the basketball league, and the annual community carnival, have emerged from careful listening and entering into a dialogue with Sunset Park residents' about their daily lives. The center directors' active monthly participation in the Human Services Cabinet, convened by Community Board 7 in 1979 and composed of representatives of public and voluntary agencies and community groups in the neighborhood, is further evidence of the directors' desire to gain regular feedback and new ideas from colleagues in other Sunset Park agencies and organizations.

Each year the enter publishes an extensive *Progress Report* that describes the center's activities, staffing patterns, programmatic initiatives and changes, and findings regarding a range of outcomes. A careful reading of these reports indicates that the center's directors, program coordinators, and staff have consistently extended themselves to gain feedback and suggestions on a regular basis from children, teens, and adults involved in their programs, from parents of children enrolled in center activities, and from community and public school leaders. Over the years such feedback and suggestions clearly have shaped the development of the center's programs and other initiatives.

MAINTAINING CONTROL OVER PURPOSE AND SIZE WHILE RESPONDING TO NEEDS AND OPPORTUNITIES

Although the Center for Family Life draws upon and is influenced by its experiences and interactions with its community, policy, and professional environments, the center remains true to its mission. In this regard it is versatile but pragmatic. It does not permit its programs, services, or practice approaches to be fully defined by changes in any aspect of its environment. Rather the center actively participates in and pragmatically selects from those contextual shifts those that support and enhance its capacity to achieve its central purposes: to provide "an integrated and full range of personal and social services to sustain Sunset Park's children and families in their own homes, to counter the forces or marginalization and disequilibrium which impact on families, to prevent delinquency, and to prevent inappropriate uses of foster care and institutionalization" (Center for Family Life 1979:1). Peters and Waterman would say that the center, like successful American companies, is "hands-on, value-driven," and "sticks to the knitting" (1982).

The center's purposes ground its responses to environmental changes. The center's leadership and staff critically and collectively weigh changes in the center's relevant contexts against the center's mission and primary purposes, integrating what supports and enhances these purposes and setting aside or actively disregarding that which would undermine its work with Sunset Park's families and children. Through this ongoing iterative process the center enacts its deep commitment to developing and providing a continuum of integrated comprehensive services that promote the well-being and development of the community's families and children and of the community as a whole. The center's cofounders' and staff members' tenacious commitment to control the center's purpose and size while responding to community needs and funding opportunities has also shaped the center's development. Few organizational leaders in New York City have persisted in proceeding on their own terms as long, as vigorously, or as successfully as Sisters Mary Paul and Geraldine. Their fierce independence has taken several forms. For example, they have refused to employ categorical terminology or to take categorical funding. As stated previously, they maintain the center's fiscal and political separation from the religious order of the Sisters of the Good Shepherd, from the Roman Catholic Diocese of Brooklyn, and from neighborhood churches in Sunset Park. Additionally, they have resisted turning their school-based group leaders into home-visiting school guidance counselors, as some school principals sought in the 1980s.

Organizational Structure

The ingenious administrative structure within which the center for Family Life operates has assisted the center in protecting its independence while contributing to its cost effectiveness. The center is technically a satellite program of St. Christopher-Ottilie Services for Children and Families, a large voluntary agency based in Sea Cliff, Long Island. However, it functions in programmatic terms with autonomy. The Diocese of Brooklyn has a representative on the St. Christopher-Ottilie board of directors and therefore participates in oversight of the mission, fiscal, and legal operations of the parent agency. As the sponsor and parent organization for the center, St. Christopher-Ottilie and its executive director, Robert McMahon, have provided indispensable administrative services. Billing, disbursement, auditing, purchasing, payroll, insurance, personnel tasks, and accounting procedures are all administered for the center by St. Christopher-Ottilie's staff. Additionally, the license issued to St. Christopher-Ottilie for its foster care activities covers the neighborhood foster care homes of the center.

St. Christopher-Ottilie's administrators are also resources to the center. For example, St. Christopher-Ottilie administrators negotiated the lease for CFL's building on 43d Street and have managed the fiscal end of CFL programs. The center's codirectors meet with the comptroller semiannually regarding budget. The director of computing services assisted the center in establishing its management information system, and Mr. McMahon's assistant director was a resource for the center in consultations with an architect regarding a recently completed building expansion.

Substantively, however, in mission, program development, hiring, professional practice, and service obligations, the Center for Family Life functions autonomously. The center directors maintain frequent contact with St. Christopher-Ottilie's executive director, who is a member of the center's advisory board, in order to keep him abreast of center work and concerns. St. Christopher-Ottilie's staff manages many of the financial and regulatory aspects of the center without interfering in program direction, emphasis, staffing, or community relations. Few community-based organizations have managed to devise as beneficial an arrangement with a larger sponsoring agency as this one has proved to be for the center.

Both historically and currently, the Center for Family Life's programs have been found to demonstrate its consistent commitments to focusing on the family as the unit of attention, belonging to the Sunset Park community, providing comprehensive, integrated and holistic services that are both inclusive and nonstigmatizing, developing working partnerships with families, schools, and the community, integrating an intergenerational, developmental focus in program design, maintaining professionalism and grounding the center's work in theory, maintaining a flexible learning stance organizationally, sustaining continuity, and exerting control over focus and size while remaining responsive to needs and opportunities. The ways in which these commitments are specifically elaborated and enacted in various services and programs are further described in the subsequent chapters.

2

THE DEVELOPMENT OF THE CENTER IN THE CONTEXT OF CHILD WELFARE POLICY AND PROGRAMMING

■

Since its founding in 1978, the developments at the Center for Family Life have been shaped by many of the forces in the larger child welfare environment at the local, state, and federal levels. And the programmatic developments at the center have anticipated and contributed to some of the recent shifts in family and child service policy and programming. To illustrate, its core satellite model of foster home care has been widely replicated in different sites around the country, and this model has recently been adopted as the preferred model of foster care for agencies funded by New York City's Administration for Children's Services (New York City Administration for Children's Services 1999:4, 8).

In this chapter we shall review the policy shifts that have shaped the center's development and the structural, political, and programming issues in the city's child welfare system that have impacted on the center's delivery of services.

AN EVOLVING PUBLIC POLICY GOAL: TO KEEP FAMILIES TOGETHER

The delegates to the first White House Conference on Children, organized in 1909 to consider the needs of dependent children, went on record as supporting the principle of maintaining children in their own homes whenever possible and not depriving them of home life "except for urgent and compelling reasons" (Bremner 1971:365.) Yet for over fifty years after this conference the child welfare system maintained its primary focus on child rescue and child protection through removing children from troubled families and placing them in out-of-home care. It was only in the 1970s that child advocates began to call for the provision of services to children in their own homes (Temporary State Commission on Child Welfare 1975; Knitzer, Allen, and McGowan 1978; Persico 1979). This occurred as a consequence of repeated reports highlighting the problem of children growing up in foster care without a plan for their future and the potential negative consequences of separating children from their parents (Maas and Engler 1959; Goldstein, Freud, and Solnit 1973, 1979; Bernstein, Snider, and Meezan 1975). At the same time, programs throughout the country began to experiment with different types of services designed to enhance family functioning and prevent foster placement. Somewhat paralleling these developments, the founders of the center, who had spent many years working in residential institutions for "wayward girls," began to question the efficacy of treating children and adolescents apart from their families. Convinced that the healthy development of vulnerable children would be better supported by neighborhood-based family services than by even excellent institutional care, they and other members of their religious order began to experiment with community services designed to promote family and community functioning at the Family Reception Center, opened in Park Slope, Brooklyn in 1972. As described earlier, after several years (1978) Sisters Mary Paul and Geraldine left the program in Park Slope to start the Center for Family Life in Sunset Park. Because Barbara Blum, the commissioner of social services in New York at that time, was also exploring the viability of services designed to prevent foster placement, Sisters Geraldine and Mary Paul were able to obtain a demonstration grant from the state to fund this initiative. In 1979 New York State passed the Child Welfare Reform Act, which predated and in many ways served as a model for the federal Adoption Assistance and Child Welfare Act of 1980, P.L. 96–272. With the passage of these two laws, the center was assured continued funding for community-based services for high-risk families and public support for the staff's efforts to keep families together.

The Adoption Assistance and Child Welfare Act was initiated in response to 1. repeated studies documenting the fiscal and human costs of the child welfare system's failure to offer services to children and parents in their own homes and to secure permanent homes for children languishing in foster care (Fanshel and Shinn 1972; Gruber 1978; Knitzer, Allen, and McGowan

1978; Persico 1979) and 2. reports of cost-effective demonstration programs that helped to prevent placement and/or secure early discharge from care (Emlen, L'Ahti, and Downs 1976; Jones, Neuman, and Shyne 1976; Stein, Gambrill, and Wiltse 1978). This law made prevention of placement and permanency planning explicit objectives of federal child welfare policy and created incentives for more widespread development of the different types of prevention or family preservation services that had been initiated in various locations.

P.L. 96–272 created great expectations that programs such as the Center for Family Life would be expanded. However, the law's implementation has been marred by three major problems. First, it has never been funded at the level originally anticipated, so preventive services have not expanded as fully as needed. Second, the law has been implemented during a thirty-year period best characterized by widespread dismantling of federal social programs established to strengthen family life and to provide the financial resources required to provide an adequate standard of living for low-income families. As a result, increasing numbers of families began to require services that could not be obtained.

And third, because of limited federal funding, state child welfare administrators quickly became preoccupied with limiting the numbers of families eligible for "preventive" services. Consequently, family-centered service programs such as the center have been instructed to provide services only to families in which children were at "imminent risk" of placement. Prevention of out-of-home placement quickly became the ultimate criterion of success rather than the enhancement of family and child functioning. This meant that no federal or state funding has been available to serve all families in Sunset Park because technically the center is expected to give sole priority to families in which children are at imminent risk of placement.

THE EXPANSION OF FAMILY PRESERVATION AND FAMILY SUPPORT SERVICES

Despite these difficulties, during the past two decades the country has witnessed rapid expansion of both family preservation and family support services. Family preservation services are directed toward implementing the federal mandate enunciated in the Adoption Assistance and Child Welfare Act of 1980 to make "reasonable efforts" to prevent placement and/or reunite families. They are specifically targeted to families in which children are at imminent risk of placement or are in placement and generally involve a combination of counseling, concrete, and advocacy services provided to the family as a whole. These services attempt to build on the skills of individual family members and to enhance families' support systems. They are usually intensive and time-limited, aiming to restore balance by intervening during crisis periods. Family preservation services draw on a range of theoretical orientations including family systems, crisis, ecology, and social learning theories, but they all aim to empower families by drawing on the strengths of individual members, respecting cultural differences, providing extensive services in the home, and emphasizing strong, supportive, flexible relationships between workers and clients (Hess, McGowan, and Botsko, 2000; McCroskey and Meezan 1998; Fraser, Nelson, and Rivard 1997).

The best known and most widely studied of these programs, Homebuilders, limits service to three months, provides constant availability (twenty-four hours a day, seven days a week), and limits caseloads to two families per worker (Whittaker and Tracy 1990; Kinney, Haapala, and Booth 1991). Homebuilders, which is aimed primarily at preventing placement, is the prototypical model of what is now known as intensive family preservation services.

In contrast, family support services, sometimes called family resource services, have developed independently of the child welfare system. They are neighborhood-based programs that provide comprehensive services aimed at promoting healthy child development, parental competence, family stability, and the development of neighborhood networks of support. These programs have been initiated primarily by experts in early child development, drawing on lessons learned from Head Start as well as other mutual aid and parent education initiatives. They are also modeled in part on the early settlement houses. Family support programs typically have a universalist perspective, making them open to all families in their catchment areas, and they emphasize primary prevention rather than the secondary and tertiary prevention emphasized in family preservation services (Lightburn and Kemp 1994; Weissbourd 1994). Kagan defines the fundamental premises of family support services as "a focus on prevention and a recognition of the importance of the early years . . . an ecological approach to service delivery . . . a developmental view of parents . . . [and] the universal value of support" (1994:379).

Although both these service streams have been subject to extensive research, findings concerning their effectiveness have not been definitive. The early studies of Homebuilders and other intensive family preservation services were very promising, showing decreased rates of child placement in comparison to traditional child welfare services (Fraser, Pecora, and Haapala 1991). However, recent, more carefully designed experimental studies have raised questions about their targeting and subsequent effectiveness because so few of the children in the control groups entered placement either (Rossi 1992; Schuerman, Rzepnicki, and Littell 1994). Others have raised questions about the applicability of intensive family preservation services, which emphasize crisis intervention, to families with chronic problems such as substance abuse and mental illness (Besharov 1994; Dore 1993). At the same time, many experts in the field argue that family preservation services are a critical component of any continuum of child welfare services (Nelson 1997; Wells and Tracy 1996; McCroskey and Meezan 1998; Schuerman 1997).

The results of most of the research on family support services are equally indeterminate. Although many programs have had positive effects on child development and family functioning, others have demonstrated little impact. It is generally argued that program impact is extremely difficult to measure when goals are amorphous and complex and there are wide variations in target population and program foci (Weiss and Jacobs 1988; McCroskey and Meezan 1998:60.) Questions have been raised about the applicability of this universal model to families with severe emotional and/or social problems as well (Roditti 1995). But, again, most experts in the field agree that family support services should be part of any meaningful continuum of child welfare services.

THE CENTER FOR FAMILY LIFE: ELEMENTS OF BOTH FAMILY PRESERVATION AND FAMILY SUPPORT

What has not been reported previously in the literature is a systematic attempt to combine these two models of intervention. We found that the Center for Family Life model combines elements of both family preservation and family support services (Hess, McGowan, and Botsko 2000). Program elements that correspond with those typically identified as characterizing family preservation programs include a family focus and orientation, the development of a client-centered relationship between family and worker, staff accessibility day-to-day, and flexibility in service planning and delivery. Many agencies throughout the country have shifted to providing only short-term services to families with children at risk for placement, modeling their programs on the Homebuilders approach; however, the center has determinedly retained its range of crisis intervention, short-term services, and long-term services to at-risk families.

Thus the center's flexibility in service duration and two other program elements—broad and inclusive access to noncategorical services and service comprehensiveness—differentiate its service model from typical family preservation programs and reflect the center's adherence to family support principles. Since its establishment the center's services have continued to serve families in which the out-of-home placement of children is imminent, families who need continuously available primary prevention services, and families whose needs place them somewhere on a continuum between these two extremes.

ONGOING CHILD WELFARE POLICY CHANGE

In 1993, in recognition of the increasing demands for services created by rising rates of child maltreatment and foster care entry and of the widespread interest in family preservation and support services at the state level, Congress created a new Family Preservation and Support Services Program and approved $930 million over five years for this program under the Omnibus Reconciliation Act. However, negative research findings about intensive family preservation services were beginning to emerge, child abuse and foster placement rates continued to rise, and a rash of stories were reported in the media about children being injured or killed by their parents after overzealous caseworkers tried to "save" families at risk (MacDonald 1994; Murphy 1993; Weisman 1994). Together these forces precipitated widespread questioning about the potential conflict between the goals of child protection and family support and a backlash against the concept of family preservation, especially among conservative commentators (Kamerman and Kahn 1997:45).

Congress, as a consequence, essentially reversed the pro-family policy stance implied in the Omnibus Budget Reconciliation Act of 1993 and passed the Adoption and Safe Families Act of 1997 (P.L. 105–89). Although this law reaffirms the concept of permanency planning established under the Adoption Assistance and Child Welfare Act of 1980, it makes the safety of children a clear priority in all child welfare decision making. It emphasizes adoption as the means of achieving permanency for children, not services directed toward family support, family preservation, or family reunification. Instead, it expedites consideration of termination of parental rights, provides bonuses to states that increase adoptions of children waiting in foster care, and requires that all caseworkers for children in foster care engage in "concurrent planning." Concurrent planning means that while caseworkers provide services intended to achieve family reunification they simultaneously make plans for termination of parental rights and adoption in case their efforts to return children home are not successful. Although it is too early to determine how this law will impact preventive programs such as the Center for Family Life, it is highly unlikely that the shift in federal child welfare policy will be paralleled by a shift in the center's emphasis on preventing unnecessary out-of-home placement by providing services to sustain children in their own homes.

NEW YORK CITY'S CHILD WELFARE SYSTEM

Historically, New York City could be characterized as one of the few American cities that pursued a liberal social policy for children and families. However, that picture began to shift in the mid-1970s, shortly before the establishment of the center, and that decline has continued to the present as a consequence of major economic, social, and political changes that have made it increasingly difficult for poor families and children to thrive (Kamerman 1996). To illustrate, it is now estimated that every day in New York City approximately 760,00 children are living in poverty, nearly 8,000 are homeless and living in shelters, 146 are reported as being abused or neglected, and nearly half of all elementary and middle school children are reading below grade level (Citizen's Committee for Children of New York 2000).

The city's child welfare system serves large numbers; in fiscal year 1999 38,440 children were in foster care, 54,673 complaints of child abuse or neglect were investigated, 27,124 families received preventive services, and 3,806 children were adopted (Watching the numbers 2000). It also spends many millions on these services. The New York City Adopted Budget for the

Administration for Children's Services (ACS) for Fiscal Year 2001 totals S1.552 billion: $155.2 million for preventive services, $109.3 for protective services, and $930.1 million for foster care services (Citizen's Committee for Children of New York 2000). Yet no one would argue that the system is working effectively. The many deficits in its child welfare system have been documented repeatedly for over fifty years. As one of the authors commented in 1986:

> What is now often referred to as the current crisis in child welfare services cannot really be defined as a crisis. It is rather the inevitable, quite predictable outcome of the repeated tendency of City officials to look for "quick-fix" solutions to the very complex legal, moral, and social questions posed by public recognition of the inability or unwillingness of large numbers of parents to care adequately for their children. Inadequacies in the City's child welfare system have been documented repeatedly for at least 40 years.
>
> (McGowan, Bertrand, Kohn, and Lombard 1987:11)

For the past thirty years the city's child welfare system has maintained the same broad mission to protect children from abuse and neglect, prevent the unnecessary breakup of families at risk, provide appropriate substitute care for children who cannot remain at home, and ensure permanency planning for children who cannot be reunited with their biological families. However, there have been dramatic shifts in emphasis during the center's relatively brief existence. Since the center was founded, the city child welfare agency's name has been changed three times. There have been at least seven different commissioners of children's services. And at least twenty class action suits have been filed against the city's child welfare system (Scoppetta 1996:29).

When the center was founded in 1978, great attention was being given at both the local and national levels to the need for increased services to children and families in their own homes in order to prevent placement. By 1984 stories of mishandling of child abuse cases by the city agency, then named Special Services for Children (SSC), hit the media. As a consequence, more funding was allocated to expand child protection services, the city's Board of Estimate passed a resolution creating a new academy to train mandated reporters to identify child maltreatment, and a new panel was established to examine the structure and functioning of SSC and its umbrella agency, the Human Resources Administration (HRA). The report of this commission, commonly known as the Beattie Commission, recommended that SSC be combined with other HRA divisions into a new Family and Children's Services Agency (FACSA). This agency was to integrate the full range of family services and decentralize delivery of services to the neighborhood, community district level. Such a change would have, of course, been very beneficial for the center, which was already attempting to provide integrated services at the community level. However, the recommendations of this commission were never fully implemented (Scoppetta 1996).

Instead, a dramatic increase in the demand for foster care due to increasing poverty, homelessness, and the crack-cocaine epidemic led to another media scandal regarding the numbers of infants being kept for extended periods in hospital maternity wards because of the lack of appropriate foster homes. The city quickly turned its attention to recruitment of special foster homes for these children, a new, higher reimbursement rate for special needs foster homes was established, new, tighter monitoring and management procedures were introduced, and, in 1989, the name of SSC was changed to Child Welfare Administration (CWA).

While this foster home crisis was being addressed, still another child abuse scandal hit the media in the late 1980s regarding the failure of city agencies to prevent the deaths of three children, Lisa Steinberg, Jessica Cortez, and Michael Baker. In response, another major reorganization of the agency was announced in 1990, eliminating the newly formed multipurpose agency, FACSA. Yet little really changed; because of budget cuts in the city, many CWA caseworkers were laid off.

Shortly after the well-publicized death of another child, Elisa Izquierdo, in 1995, the new mayor announced a systematic reorganization of CWA and the creation of a new freestanding agency, the Administration for Children's Services (ACS), that would report directly to him and be charged primarily with child protection. Also in 1995 a major class action lawsuit, *Marisol v. Giuliani*, was filed by Children's Rights, Inc., seeking to place the whole child welfare system into receivership. Both these actions reflected the frustrations of the many child welfare practitioners, administrators, public interest attorneys, and concerned citizens about the ongoing failure of city officials over several different administrations to implement and sustain an effective child and family service system.

As the commissioner of the new agency wrote in this plan of action (1996):

> In the past 20 years, there have been at least four dozen studies, audits, reviews, analyses, and evaluations of the perceived disarray in the City's child welfare policies and programs. Indeed, analyzing the city's child welfare agency has become a veritable industry in itself. Numerous boards, committees, and commissions have been formed by several mayors, the Courts, the City and State Comptrollers, Borough Presidents, the Public Advocate, the City Council, other officials and non-government entities to study, monitor and/or reform all or parts of the system. (Scoppetta 1996:54)

He went on to note that the recommendations of these various bodies were strikingly similar and tended to emphasize decentralized, community-based services, retention of capable, dedicated personnel, higher-quality staff training and supervision, lower caseloads, separation of protective/investigative functions from long-term case management, and reduction of excessive and redundant paperwork (Scoppetta 1996:54–55). These recommendations were all quite consistent with the practice orientation at the center.

The plan of action laid out in this report regarding protective and foster care services was greeted with approval by most of the actors who had written the many earlier critical reports of the system, and the new ACS has been making real strides in achieving the objectives and timelines set out in the report. However, concern has been expressed about what is perceived as overemphasis on the agency's investigatory and protective functions and inadequate attention to preventive services that could protect children at risk and eliminate the need for placement.

This problem has been accentuated by the passage in 1995 of New York State's Family and Children's Services Block Grant that capped funding for child welfare services and reduced state spending by 25 percent in the first year. Although the grant promised to reduce mandates to counties by eliminating restrictive regulatory and statutory requirements, its effect has been to reduce overall state support for protective, preventive, and foster care services in the City. With its increased emphasis on child protection, ACS inevitably responded by maintaining spending on protective services and reducing funding for foster care and preventive services. These cutbacks were passed on to voluntary agencies such as the Center for Family Life and resulted in a drastic reduction of preventive services (Citizens' Committee for Children of New York 1998).

During this same period, perhaps in an effort to move forward with this plan rather than spending endless resources in litigation as had been done with the preceding lawsuits, the city agreed to a consent decree in the *Marisol v. Giuliani* class action lawsuit that was filed in U.S. District Court in 1995. This consent decree established a Special Child Welfare Advisory Panel composed of child welfare experts from different parts of the country to advise ACS on how best to achieve critical goals for improving the child welfare system. The advisory reports issued by this panel have noted marked achievements in the structure of services and the effort to move toward neighborhood services. Yet the work of this group has also been criticized for operating within the framework imposed by the ACS Reform Plan and failing to give adequate attention to issues of early intervention and prevention (Child Welfare Fund 1999).

What is interesting is that one of the Special Child Welfare Advisory Panel's most recent reports (March 9, 2000) concluded that "front line and supervisory practice in New York City are in need of substantial improvement" (p. 7). Ultimately, this report, although noting some important exceptions, is a damning indictment of the quality of practice, supervision, and training in the city's child welfare system and the lack of professionalism in the family court system. Sadly, it also noted that "judges see themselves as powerless victims of the system rather than as powerful change agents" (p. 48). Unfortunately, despite the success of the center and the city's recent effort to develop community-based services, no real attempt has been made to replicate the center or to draw on its resources in designing and implementing the city's new reform plan.

These contradictions in child welfare policy and deficiencies and shifts in the city's child welfare system have all been described in some depth in order to convey the complex environment in which the center has had to function and the challenges it has confronted in pursuing its mission of serving children in their families and in their communities. Outside commentators occasionally dismiss the center's achievements on the grounds that it is much easier to operate from a voluntary agency base than the public sector, and New York City offers resources not available in other locations. It is true that since the center is a voluntary agency it does not have to cope with some of the bureaucratic rigidities and personnel deficiencies that characterize many large, public child welfare agencies. However, it operates under contract to the City of New York, has no endowment, and has to endure all the contradictions in public policy and cutbacks in public funding that plague child welfare agencies throughout the country. What is different about the center, as will be elaborated in subsequent chapters, is that it has met these challenges with creativity, enthusiasm, and a determination to continue pursuing its mission despite the obstacles.

3

THE CORE: FAMILY COUNSELING SERVICES

■

A single mother of five, whom we'll call Carmen, had used the center's preventive services for two years when we first met her. Like a third of the families served by the preventive program, Carmen was not referred by an agency but rather called the preventive program on her own at the suggestion of a friend. She had a completed a drug treatment program and was living with relatives. The father of the older children was uninvolved with the family; the father of the younger children was incarcerated.

Carmen began to describe her experience with this center program by recalling that "I knew about the center, that it was in the area, but when my children were taken away from me [by the public child welfare agency], I had nobody to talk to. A friend recommended that I come here. So I called and made an appointment and talked to Sister Mary Paul." Like other Sunset Park residents whom we interviewed about the preventive program's services, she emphasized the importance of her open relationship with her worker:

Then I met my worker [in the preventive services program]. I thought I was going to hate her . . . but she is just like a big sister to me, the sister I never had. I could just . . . lay everything on the table and be myself—I don't have to hide anything—and from there we discuss and we try to compromise, to

Portions of chapter 3 were previously reported in P. Hess, B. McGowan, and M. Botsko (2000), "A Preventive Services Model for Preserving and Supporting Families Over Time," *Child Welfare* 79:227–265; and in P. Hess, B. McGowan, and C. Meyer, "Practitioners' Perspectives on Family and Child Services," in A. Kahn and S. Kamerman, eds. (1996), *Children and Their Families in Big Cities*, pp. 121–137 (New York: Columbia University School of Social Work), and are included here by permission.

find ways to deal with me, the children, any problems that might occur. . . . My worker is always here, not to supervise, but kind of help and guide me in how to handle a situation.

The range of services used by Carmen and her children is similar to the range of services used by other families served in this program:

All my kids go to the center's programs. My daughter goes to a teen group, which I like because she is able to talk with kids her age about how her mom gets on her nerves, and "Mom doesn't understand me," and problems that occur in the house with her brothers and sister.

My eleven year old still has the mind of a child, but yet he wants to be grown up. He goes to a semi-teen group, and there they help him to find his identity, how to get along with other children because he likes to fight a lot. Through sports at the center and other activities they help him to share and respect other people's feelings.

My other son is going through changes himself because he was in foster care and when he was returned to me he was very rebellious. He's in a lot of pain, and that's very stressful to me. The center helped me to set one day of the week to spend quality time with him at the center. . . . I needed a space where I could go to spend time with him. I can't do it at home because then the other kids would distract me. That's kind of helped.

I've used the thrift shop. When I had my newborn I had no income at all and I was homeless and I had just got the apartment and was in a very stressful situation where I had nothing at all. The ladies in the center support group knew I was going through changes, so they all chipped in and they got me Pampers, clothes, crib sheets, a carriage. I got a shopping bag of food from the thrift shop. I got some clothes. And that held me over until I could stand on my feet.

In addition, Carmen completed her GED, secured a part-time job, and began to attend college. Her reflections upon her own progress during the two-year period she had worked with her preventive program worker convey both her learning and her tenacity: "I have come a long way in how to deal with my children, but I have three different stages of kids. . . . It helps me to learn that there is a different way of parenting without using violence or anger. I was always subjected to that, and I don't want to do that to them because I know how that feels." She stated emphatically that "the most important thing I learned in the center is never, never talk *at* your children.

Talk *to* your children. . . . When I go home I practice those skills. It doesn't get easier overnight, but some day . . . "

Carmen summarized her feelings about the center's preventive program as follows:

I believe that you can't keep what you have learned unless you give it away. And I want to do that in turn to a newcomer to the center, to give her a sense of family, and say, "Hey, I've been there, I know what it is like. Trust these people. They know what they are doing. Just give them a chance. Don't quit."

The purpose of the preventive program. The center's family counseling program, referred to by staff and families as the "preventive program," is designed to prevent the unnecessary placement of children in out-of-home care. It has been a core program component since the center was established in 1978. In New York City the phrase *preventive services* is widely used to identify services provided by various agencies to prevent unnecessary foster care with the support of city funding and in accordance with the state's Child Welfare Reform Act of 1979.

Soon after the center was established Sister Mary Paul wrote about the issues in the use of the term *preventive* to describe such programs: "There is widespread agreement that the term is an unfortunate one, because of the vagueness of the term 'preventive' in relation to the social problems which the services are intended to address" (Janchill 1981:20). She emphasized the importance of a program's focus upon *both* the psychological and environmental aspects of families' situations as follows:

> Whatever the reader's opinion of the comparative values in working with change in the individual vs. change in the conditions which affect individuals, it is here proposed that "preventive services" *should* encompass the creation of conditions, *psychological and environmental*, which promote the well-being of families and protect the capacity of parents to sustain their children. Case management (that is, selection, coordination and integration) of the tasks necessary for this, in situations referred to preventive service programs, will usually consist of certain personal social services directly provided by an agency, along with advocacy, brokering of needed resources, and/or environmental change. (1981:20)

In addition, she stressed that a preventive program must collaborate with other organizations in service delivery and development, "sometimes to stimulate the development of new services in the community. Sometimes too these new 'services' will be informal social arrangements, self-help groups, involvement of college/university internships in developmental activities, etc." (1981:20).

In providing the clinical leadership that has shaped this program since its inception, Sister Mary Paul has been true to her own early prescription regarding the provision of "preventive services." Staff members diligently maintain the program's dual focus upon the psychological and environmental aspects of families' needs and difficulties and actively coordinate services to families with other center programs as well as with other community resources.

A unique approach. Our findings document the program's effectiveness in implementing a coherent philosophy, mission, and approach to preventive services through rigorous adherence to key principles and through creative, flexible social work practice. We believe that these findings provide ample information to suggest that further professional and public attention should be given to the center's approach to preventive services. As described in chapter 2 and reported elsewhere (Hess, McGowan, and Botsko 2000), the center's preventive services program has combined elements of both family preservation and family support services to provide a comprehensive yet individualized response to families in need. The center's preventive program has consistently incorporated program elements that correspond with those typically identified as characterizing family preservation programs, including a family focus and orientation, the development of a client-centered relationship between family and worker, staff accessibility day-to-day, and flexibility in service planning and delivery. Yet, as documented by our findings regarding services to a study sample of 301 caregivers and 423 children in 189 families, the center's program also is characterized by its service comprehensiveness, flexibility in service duration, and broad and inclusive access to noncategorical services. These characteristics differentiate this program from typical family preservation programs and reflect the program's enactment of family support principles. We found that the center's program model provides for individualized, comprehensive, often intensive, short- and long-term services that address families' extensive service needs and are associated with identifiable positive changes, particularly in children's problems and behaviors.

Our findings also strongly suggest that the center's preventive service program model addresses the limitations of current family preservation programs. In contrast to these programs, described in chapter 2, the center's program provides "opportunities for ongoing supportive therapy for depressed, maltreating parents" (Dore 1993:552), "coherent and coordinated long-term services to disadvantaged and at-risk families" (Besharov 1994:448), and "a continuum of family and services" that are less narrowly targeted (McGowan 1990:82). It must be noted that the practice principles that are foundational to the center's preventive service model have long been associated with social work services to families with multiple problems and needs.

Access to the preventive program. In contrast to the other programs at the Center for Family Life, which are accessed by "open enrollment," the preventive program is accessed through an intake interview that is conducted at the center. Families are scheduled for an interview without regard to the nature of their need or problems either with Sister Mary Paul, who conducts the interviews with English-speaking clients, with the casework supervisor, who conducts the interviews with Spanish-speaking clients, or with Sister Mary Paul and a preventive program staff member who is bilingual in Chinese and English. Sister Mary Paul described the program's approach to scheduling intake appointments:

> If a parent were to call me today [a Friday] I would offer an appointment tonight or over the weekend. Sometimes, if there's reluctance, they're not jumping to come in, they'll say, "I have an appointment, I can't do it until next week." If they put it off, I do not pressure them. I accept their own timing. If I see that they are uncertain, I would ask if they want to wait. . . . When we get a referral call [for preventive services], I don't make an appointment unless I'm in contact with the actual prospective client. My response to a referral source is "Have them call me." If parents want it, we offer an intake appointment.

Thus, whatever the referral source, preventive program services are not initiated until the clients schedule and complete an intake interview. In the interview the intake interviewer explores a family's needs and problems, explains the services, and confirms the family's willingness to enter voluntarily into a relationship with the program. The limited number of families that are not willing to work voluntarily with the center are not accepted for service but are encouraged to contact the center should family members change their minds. Forms that identify who in the family will be involved with the center are completed. The intake interviewer explains the only exceptions to confidentiality, e.g., if a family is reported for abuse, or a child is placed in foster care, the center will have to provide certain information to the New York City and State child welfare agencies. Sister Mary Paul described her intake interviews as follows:

> First I hear their problem, and then I tell them, "Now I have to explain to you more about the Center for Family Life. The counseling is free because we are funded by the city." I tell them that three-fourths of our funding comes from CWA [the New York City Child Welfare Administration] and that by the city we are classified as a preventive service program. That doesn't mean a lot to some of the families, and I have to explain again that there are certain programs that the city [of New York] funds so that they can help keep the family together and prevent any out of home care or any further breakdown if they step in early.
>
> I tell them that what goes on in this building is just the counseling of families and that families come here with every sort of problem. I tell them about the other services, and then I go back to the preventive service idea. I tell them that I consider counseling an umbrella service. Everything that we encompass here is encompassed in counseling, whether it's advocacy or direct service.

Sister Mary Paul stressed two purposes for the intake interview: "To get a sense of the problem and what the person's expectations would be about coming here and to prepare them and motivate them." She described her intakes as "fairly skimpy. They're not an intake study by any means. I purposely do not do that. I try not to get too much information because it's hard for families to have to repeat it when they are assigned to a worker. . . . [But] you need to get a projected sense of the task before you make an assignment." Information from the intake interview is routinely recorded by the interviewer on an Intake Recording Form.

Following this interview, families are assigned to a preventive services worker. According to Sister Mary Paul, cases are assigned based on the complexity of the case, worker's experience and current availability, and the client's language fluency. The worker contacts the family immediately to schedule an appointment by telephone, or by letter if the family does not have a telephone. The family and the assigned worker subsequently further explore and define the family members' needs and problems. Together they develop a service plan. Families' service plans are individualized and vary with regard to service goals, the involvement of family members at different points in time, the treatment approaches used by the worker, and the nature, sequence, and duration of services.

In this chapter we describe the key characteristics of the center's preventive service program, drawing upon the voices of families and staff. We also identity the program staff members' responsibilities and experiences with the program. In addition, throughout this chapter we report selected characteristics of a study sample of 423 children in 189 families and the services they received in the center's preventive program.

SOURCES OF INFORMATION REGARDING THE PREVENTIVE PROGRAM

Because the preventive program is viewed by the agency as the "core" of its work, we emphasized this program in our study design. In order to understand the program we gathered extensive case-specific information about services provided to a prospective sample of families whose cases were opened during a thirty-month period. Center codirectors and staff were actively involved in the decisions regarding data collection and instruments to be used (Weiss and Horsch 1998). In addition, we collected in-depth information from families whose cases had been open in the preventive program for at least two years when our study began. Finally, over a three-year period we met frequently with supervisors and staff to explore their perceptions of the program's philosophy, services, and outcomes and their own experiences as staff in the program.

Case-specific information about the 189 study sample families. Extensive case-specific information was collected on 301 caregivers and 423 children in 189 families whose cases were opened for service in the preventive program during the study's data collection phase. Data sources included standardized case data collected at the initiation of services to a prospective sample of families, at six-month intervals, and at case closing. Information was collected from each family's preventive program worker using the Family Assessment Form (FAF; McCroskey, Nishimoto, and Subramanian 1991), preventive services program forms, and a service needs/service utilization instrument developed for the study. Our sampling strategy allowed us to follow all cases for at least one year and up to thirty months subsequent to case initiation. In addition, in 1999 we collected follow-up data regarding the case status of the 189 study sample families.

We learned that just over half (51 percent) of the families had at least two adult caregivers residing in the household. Almost half (49 percent) had a single caregiver, most commonly a biological mother (44 percent) living alone with her minor children. A caregiver was defined as an adult family member having "significant child care responsibilities," in the family's worker's judgment, and did not necessarily have a biological or legal relationship with a child in the household. A biological mother resided in almost all (92 percent) of the households and a biological father in almost 40 percent. The majority (83 percent) of the primary caregivers were Latina(o), 4 percent were Caucasian, 7 percent were African American, 4 percent were Asian, and 2 percent were other. Over half of the families (54 percent) were receiving public assistance.

Family size ranged from 2 to 11 members, including caregivers, noncaregiving adults, and children, with a mean family size of 4.2. The mean number of children was 2.3 and ranged from 0 (a mother and her adult daughter who was expecting her first child) to 9. The largest percent of the 423 children (44 percent) were ages 5 through 11, 33 percent were 12 or older, and slightly less than one-fourth (23 percent) were less than 5 years old. The mean age was 8.8 years (see figure 3.1.).

Cases in the study sample were referred to the preventive program from six sources (see figure 3.2). Formal social service agencies, including the New York City public child welfare agency, accounted for the largest source of referrals (35.4 percent, 67). Self-referral was the second largest referral source (27 percent, 51). Of the self-referred families, 45.1 percent (23) had previously been served in the center's preventive program.

Almost 10 percent (9.7 percent) of the children were known to have been placed in foster care at one time prior to the current opening of their case in the preventive program. The 41 previously placed children lived in 17 families and had spent a mean of 28 months in care, ranging from less than one month to 72 months. Preventive program workers were unable to determine whether an additional 31 children in 18 families had ever been placed in care.

The problem category most frequently identified at the intake interview for study sample families was problems between caregivers and their children (60 percent). This category includes problems of caregiver-child con-

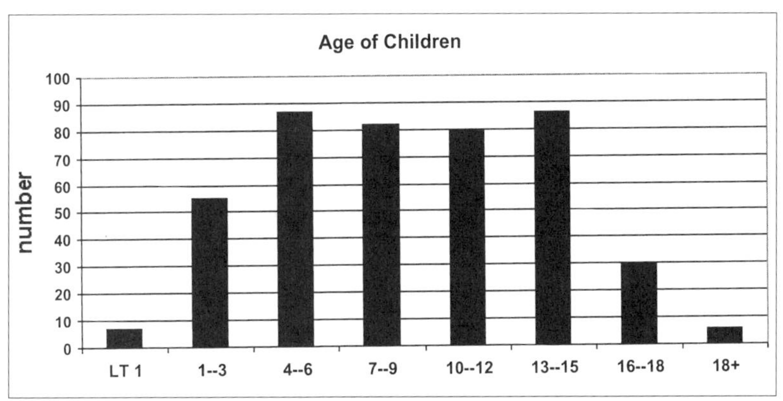

FIGURE 3.1
Number of Children in Study Sample by Age

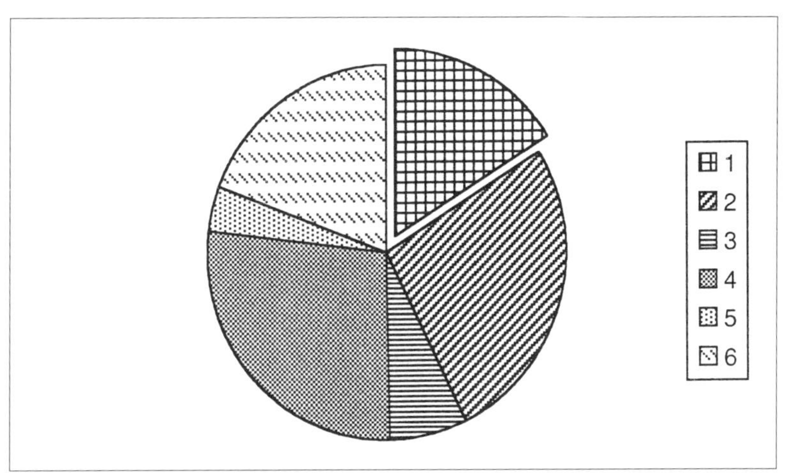

1. Public Child Welfare Agency
2. School Personnel
3. Other Informal
4. Self-referred
5. Internal CFL
6. Other formal

FIGURE 3.2
Referral Sources of Study Sample Cases

flict (42 percent), caregiver role (33 percent), caregiver-child communication (29 percent), and visiting between children and noncustodial parents (4 percent). Child-centered problems followed in frequency, with children's school and behavior problems identified in 41 percent of the families and children's personal problems identified in 38 percent. Problems related to the relationship of the caregivers/adults in the household were identified in over a third (36 percent) of the families. Information collected subsequent to the intake interview indicated that a total of 102 caregivers (34 percent) were identified as having problems, or behaviors that placed a child at serious risk for placement, with a problem in emotional control the most likely problem to present such risk. Within the total sample of 189 families, 65 percent had at least one caregiver, child, or environmental problem identified as requiring immediate intervention to prevent placement. Selected findings about the families' needs and about the services they received are reported throughout this chapter.

Additional sources of case-specific and program data. In addition to the case-specific information gathered about the families in the study sample, we conducted in-depth semistructured interviews with selected family members and their preventive program workers. These interviews focused on the families' and workers' separate perceptions of the purpose, process, and outcomes of their work together. We also analyzed data from the center's management information system regarding the total center service utilization of almost six hundred families using the preventive program during the twenty-four months between January 1, 1994 and December 31, 1995.

In addition, we conducted in-depth semistructured interviews with program administrators, supervisors, and practitioners regarding the program's organization, characteristics, service approaches, and desired outcomes, and their professional experiences in the program. Finally, we conducted extensive interviews and program observations with staff and participants in other center programs in which preventive program families were served. Thus, as described in greater detail in appendix A, over a three-year period we collected extensive qualitative and quantitative data about the preventive services program from different sources using multiple methods.

To identify and understand the service model used in the center's preventive program, transcripts of interviews and the data from all other sources were analyzed. In interviews concerning the program, staff responses regarding its key characteristics were strikingly consistent. Case-specific interviews with family members and their workers echoed the same themes. These emergent categories and themes were compared with and further confirmed by findings based upon analysis of the case-specific quantitative data. The consistency among the findings derived from the analysis of data from multiple sources provides us with a high degree of confidence regarding the characteristics of the center's preventive program.

Although these themes are consistent with the center's commitments, philosophies, and interests as described in chapter 1, we found that emphases vary somewhat from program to program. For example, in the preventive program practitioners place great emphasis on the development of a trusting relationship with family members and on engaging the parent(s) and all family members in service use. Thus, while the focus on the family as the unit of attention is an overall center commitment, this focus is particularly explicit in the preventive program's work.

KEY CHARACTERISTICS OF THE PREVENTIVE PROGRAM

The description of the preventive program in the center's annual progress reports emphasizes that the family counseling services are "a core component" encompassing "individual, group and family counseling services" (Center for Family Life 2000:3–1). Written by the center directors and staff, these reports serve as its official statement of mission and philosophy and provide a record of services provided to Sunset Park families each year. Consistent with Sister Mary Paul's previously cited description of preventive services in 1981, the 2000 *Progress Report* emphasizes the inclusion within family "counseling" of advocacy and community linkages and the family focus of the program's clinical social workers:

> The center does not split the tasks of therapy from those that may be classified as case management. A single therapist is assigned to each family and works with the family to develop a plan that may include individual and family counseling, participation in one of the center's group therapy modalities, connection of families to resources within the center and in the community and advocacy on behalf of the family. The service plan encompasses the family, and in each instance there is individuation based on the receptivity of the members and perception of what is needed. (ibid.)

The *Progress Report* stresses the program's inclusion of a broad range of developmentally focused interventions in addition to family counseling, a program characteristic that differentiates the center's program from many placement prevention programs: "It is the center's belief that a service model based on a single modality or on remediation alone often fails to bring families to a better level of competence, that to see growth in personal functioning requires a more developmental approach and enhancement of positive life experiences." The wide range of interventive methods and approaches were also stressed: "Accordingly, there is a blending of individual and group methods, of the formal and informal, and of the center's activities with those of other opportunities for socialization, employment and other developing experiences" (ibid).

Historical and current sources have yielded a coherent image of the characteristics of the center's preventive services program. We describe each key program characteristic in the following sections.

Comprehensive, Holistic, Integrated Services Grounded in the Community

Without exception, staff members describe "counseling, plus" a range of other within-center community-based services as comprising the preventive program. They identify as both essential and unique the comprehensive, holistic nature of the services available through the center's preventive program. This model allows preventive program social workers to reach multiple aspects of each family member's life, and to do so over time as family members develop and their needs change.

The structured linkages between center programs assure that intra-agency referrals and connections support the work of practitioners and meet the needs of families in a timely way. Through these within-center service connections, family members have frequent contact both concurrently and sequentially with professional staff in multiple programs and receive services that address their clinical, developmental, educational, and recreational needs. One worker stressed: "The preventive service program here gives the workers a foundation. I have a whole center to back me up."

The information collected about the 189 study sample families confirms the comprehensive nature of the services provided. The families' service needs were extensive. On average, families had 10.6 service needs, ranging from 1 to 29 (i.e., at least one family member had a particular service need).

Over 80 percent of the families needed individual and family counseling, and over half (57.7 percent) needed parent education. Caregivers most often had difficulties in the area of emotional problems (77.5 percent). Similarly, over two-thirds (69.2 percent) of the children had an emotional problem, and almost two-thirds (62.8 percent) a behavioral problem. Other specific counseling (i.e., marital and group) and family support (i.e., child recreation, summer day camp, and after-school child care) service needs were identified for more than one-third of the families.

In response to these service needs, families received a range of 1 to 27 services through the preventive program (mean = 9.4 services, SD = 5.8). Seventy-five percent of the families received six or more services. It is important to note that the majority of services were provided to study sample families *within* the Center for Family Life and thus within the neighborhood. Over half received three particular within-center services: individual counseling (80 percent), family counseling (76 percent), and parent education (53 percent) (see table 3.1). On average, 4 services per family were provided through referrals to resources outside the center, including medical and dental care and special education evaluations.

Thus, the extensive case-specific data we collected confirmed staff members' observations regarding the center's comprehensive approach to preventive service. Two staff members' observations further illustrate:

The preventive services program encompasses a lot of different components. . . . There are lots of different ways to engage people, not just the traditional one-on-one counseling. I worked in preventive services before where they only had the counseling component. It was a less effective way of working with families and engaging them. Everybody doesn't get help in the same way. For some counseling's effective and for some it's not.

From one case to the next, it's almost 100 percent sure that I'm going to be relying on the employment center or I'm going to be calling a center staff member in the school to work with me with the client. If there's a young mother and an infant, I'm thinking of the infant-toddler program. If she's unemployed and there's no pressure for her to be employed until the child is a little older, I encourage her to go to the employment program. Or I suggest the women's group to women who are just beginning a divorce, because their peers and social group have changed dramatically. . . . Some women are not ready and some are. But if they are saying "I want," we set up a meeting [with the staff of one of the programs]. It's an intervention. . . . Sometimes I feel like

TABLE 3.1 Services Needed by and Provided to Study Sample Families

	All families needing (n = 189)		Percent of families needing services that received it	Services Received				Service Not Received	
				At CFL		Elsewhere			
	n	%	%	*n*	%	*n*	%	*n*	%
Individual counseling	156	82.6	98.1	151	96.8	2	1.3	3	1.9
Family counseling	153	81.4	94.8	143	93.5	2	1.3	8	5.2
Parent education	109	57.7	94.5	100	91.7	3	2.8	6	5.5
Child recreation	90	47.6	83.3	51	56.7	24	26.7	15	16.7
Crisis counseling	84	44.4	94.0	76	90.5	3	3.6	5	6.0
Group counseling	77	41.2	71.8	42	53.8	14	17.9	22	28.2
Marital counseling	75	39.5	81.3	57	76.0	4	5.3	14	18.7
After-school care	72	38.1	80.6	31	43.1	27	37.5	14	19.4
Summer day camp	70	37.1	85.7	50	71.4	10	14.3	10	14.3
*Dental care**	59	31.2	10.2	0	0.0	6	10.2	53	89.8
*Medical care**	50	26.5	94.0	0	0.0	47	94.0	3	6.0
Diagnostic assessment	49	25.9	83.7	25	51.0	16	32.7	8	16.3
Food assistance	33	17.5	100.0	27	81.8	6	18.2	0	0.0
Sex abuse counseling	33	17.5	93.9	28	84.8	3	9.1	2	6.1
*Special-ed evaluation**	31	16.4	87.1	0	0.0	27	87.1	4	12.9
Employment services	30	15.9	66.7	13	43.3	7	23.3	10	33.3
Financial assistance	27	14.7	100.0	11	40.7	16	59.3	0	0.0
Domestic violence counseling	27	14.7	66.7	11	40.7	7	25.9	9	33.3
Drug/alcohol counseling	26	13.7	65.4	5	19.2	12	46.2	9	34.6
Housing assistance	26	13.7	96.2	16	61.5	9	34.6	1	3.8
Tutoring	25	13.2	64.0	10	40.0	6	24.0	9	36.0
*Day care**	25	13.2	84.0	0	0.0	21	84.0	4	16.0
Legal assistance	25	13.2	100.0	2	8.0	23	92.0	0	0.0
Clothing	25	13.2	96.0	24	96.0	1	4.0	0	0.0
Job referral	24	12.8	62.5	6	25.0	9	37.5	9	37.5
Self-help groups	21	11.0	61.9	1	4.8	12	57.1	8	38.1
Family planning	17	8.9	70.6	4	23.5	8	47.1	5	29.4
*Headstart**	16	8.5	87.5	0	0.0	14	87.5	2	12.5
Money management	15	7.9	93.3	13	86.7	1	6.7	1	6.7
Household goods	14	7.4	100.0	10	71.4	4	28.6	0	0.0
Project Youth	11	5.9	100.0	11	100.0	0	0.0	0	0.0
*Psychotropic medication**	11	5.9	81.8	0	0.0	9	81.8	3	18.2
Transportation	7	3.7	85.7	4	57.1	2	28.6	1	14.3
*Emergency shelter**	6	3.1	100.0	0	0.0	6	100.0	0	0.0
Utility assistance	6	3.1	100.0	1	16.7	5	83.3	0	0.0
*Temporary respite care**	6	3.1	83.3	0	0.0	5	83.3	1	16.7
*Homemaker services**	3	1.6	66.7	0	0.0	2	66.7	1	33.3

* Service not available at the Center for Family Life.

Note: Since ninety-seven families' cases were still open when data collection ended, some families may have subsequently received additional services.

I'm writing a prescription: "This child needs to be in a preadolescent girls group." Then you're working in a team with that group worker.

Workers particularly value being able to access the services that families need without having to "refer out to a whole other agency where we might lose touch with what's going on." They described the importance of integrating a family's services through teamwork with staff in different center programs: "You know who they are, and you can talk to them and be open. You know what to expect from them, and that's a real security."

Workers consistently emphasized that the center's comprehensive services model attracted them to the center's preventive program and keeps them there. For example, a worker stressed: "The support systems for the families I see—groups, the after-school program, the employment program—are one of the most important pieces of the work. . . . That is what draws me here—the model itself. Without the other services so many of my cases wouldn't be moving. It gives such a roundness to the worker." As illustrated by the single mother's statement at the beginning of this chapter, families similarly acknowledged the importance of the wide range of services they receive as clients in the preventive program.

The preventive program staff members clearly value their professional relationships with others in the community and the program's goal of connecting families more positively with the community. Many of these connections are forged through helping families become involved with center community-based services, such as the after-school child care program. One staff member emphasized: "We serve one community as opposed to being scattered across the borough. You get to know the community well, and they get to know you."

Family Focus and Orientation

The preventive program staff members consistently apply a family-centered approach to assessment and to intervention. The multiple services provided to both caregivers and children reflect the program's emphases on 1. meeting the needs of all family members and 2. viewing the family as a system. We found that, from the first contact, the majority of study sample family members participated in identifying the family's needs and problems and in establishing an intervention plan. Intake interviews were attended by 70 percent of the 301 study sample caregivers and over half (54.5 percent) of the 423 children.

Staff members articulated the importance of engaging all family members, understanding family systems, and identifying and supporting each family's strengths. Sister Geraldine, who served families in the preventive program in addition to her other responsibilities, reflected on the importance of helping families recognize their strengths: "There is a strain here that is very strong, that there is something in every family that you meet that has something to get from the center and something to give. In the early days we would always say 'in the assessment you are responsible for looking for the strength as well as what the presenting problem might be—looking at the whole person.'" She further stressed: "I find that the hardest thing to get clients to do with you is to recognize their own strengths."

Both workers and families described interventions with multiple family members individually, in dyads, and with the family as a whole. Staff members identified positive changes in family relationships and preserving families as important case outcomes. The following are illustrative of staff observations:

You can work on different aspects of the family. Depending on the situation, you'll see different pieces in different ways. For example, if the largest stressor is the marital relationship, then maybe what you would work on is the marital relationship. Depending on how the kids were reacting or if they needed extra support, you might see them individually or the siblings together. Or for a time you might work on the marital piece and then switch to something else like the parent-child relationship, depending on where the client's at and where they want to move.

[I try to provide] as many opportunities as I can for family members to be able to reflect on who they are, to do that with each other as a family. That's what family counseling will do, just getting that open communication of feelings and forming those attachments to each other.

Clients similarly both understand and value the family-centered nature of their work with the preventive program staff. For example, three different single mothers described their families' problems as follows:

Many of the problems between me and my daughter were trivial, but they had built up and had become a big problem. My counselor helped us to look at our whole relationship and not let little things become so important that they destroy everything. Since I was referred here, the relationship between me and my daughter has changed. She's changed. I've changed.

Sometimes I'll slip and I'll say, "You're so dumb," or "You get me sick" [to the children]. They'll tell me in the family group meeting, "Hey, Mom, you told me this and I don't like it. I think you're a bad mom." It hurts, but it's reality, and I have to take it. And then it's my turn. I tell them, "Listen you could help me around the house . . ." And I say, "Why is it my job? Isn't it a team effort? Remember, we work as a team." And we get to the point [in the family meeting with the worker] where we write a contract, including me.

I started coming for services because I needed to work on myself in order to deal with the kids. The reality is that my son was acting the way he was because I was upset—the crying, he couldn't deal with it. He suffered along with me. As long as his mother is fine, he's fine. Life is fine.

Staff identify a family-centered orientation as essential to their work in the preventive program. Sister Geraldine commented that "the mission is to really be available to families in the community to either provide directly or provide the linkages with the services that would help a family be supported and sustained. That's our mission. We do that. That focus is in every role we have in the community." She emphasized that any new staff member in the preventive program would have to "definitely buy into" a family-centered orientation.

The inability to engage in family-focused work was identified by staff as a common characteristic of families who "don't work out" in the preventive program. In an observation consistent with that made by other program staff, one practitioner noted:

[Some] parents want the social worker to take care of their acting-out child. It's quite a different thing when you start to focus on "why is the child acting out?" They're not really here for themselves. They're here for you to fix their child, and when you tell them that you can't fix their child unless they take part in the process, they step off.

Development of a Client-Centered Relationship Between Family and Worker

Program staff and clients also view the development of a client-centered helping relationship between the worker and family members as an essential program characteristic. Important relationship dimensions include the expectation that clients voluntarily enter the helping relationship and remain active over time in determining the treatment goals, the services that are needed, the outcomes desired, and the point at which services will end. Workers noted that the concept of shared parenting (Gabinet 1983), in which the agency partially assumes some parental tasks, often shapes their relationships with parents, particularly those who have severe difficulties in maintaining their children at home.

Relational components particularly valued by families include the focus on family members' strengths as well as difficulties, the experience of being respected, the frequency of worker-family contact, and the sense of worker-family partnership. In their interviews with us, clients conveyed strong positive feelings about the mutuality they experience as participants in this process. Family members consistently described staff members' accessibility, responsiveness, sensitivity, and trustworthiness as integral to their positive experiences with the program. They emphasized that they feel free to communicate their thoughts and feelings without being judged. As one mother commented: "I don't have to hide anything." From the clients' perspective, feeling respected is perhaps the most important dimension of their experience. One recalled the respect she experienced in her intake interview:

> Sister Mary Paul has been wonderful. The first time she saw me she reached out her hand to me, and for someone to reach out to a perfect stranger and you don't know where you are coming from—from the street—that made me feel very comfortable. Nobody pushed me away because of my reputation.

Others described the ways in which they felt they were partners in the relationship from the beginning and the ways in which they were encouraged or permitted to shape the experience. For example, "[At intake] Sister Mary Paul really wanted to make sure I wasn't being forced to come. . . . She wanted to make sure that this is what me and my daughter wanted to do." Clients also described a relationship in which they felt accepted and equal with their counselor. Two different clients' comments illustrate:

> [How would you describe your relationship with your worker?] Like my equal person. I am not embarrassed to cry in front of her. . . . I was upset and she told me, If you don't want to do this, if it gets to be too much, you just let her know. When I leave I feel good because she tells me that I'm OK, that what I'm feeling is OK. You don't need somebody to judge and say "Don't say that" or "That's silly."
>
> She did not judge me at all. When I told her I had had an abortion, not from my husband but from another man, I thought she was going to judge

me, but she didn't. In my identity crisis, when I told her my confusion [about sexual orientation], surprisingly enough she was "OK—and?"

The importance of this relationship to the clients' willingness and ability to persevere with the work when it became difficult was also articulated. For example, one single mother described her ambivalence about discussing certain topics and, periodically, about continuing with counseling generally. She stressed that her worker taught her about and helped her stay with the process:

My worker will say "How are you doing?" And I'll say "OK." And then she'll say, "You are not talking to me." And then she'll say, "Do you want to talk about anything specific?" and I'll explain to her the situation. Right now we are going to start on a log I've been writing about my childhood, being a victim of abuse. So it's hard for me to talk. . . . I have the sense that she understands where I'm coming from and what I'm trying to tell her. . . . She says, "I know you have a feeling. Can you tell me what kind of feeling? I see it in your eyes." . . . Sometimes I want to run out the door, and she says, "No, that's not the way to go about it. Running away is not going to solve anything."

But sometimes I've said, "Why am I doing this? Why am I going for counseling? Why am I putting these kids through counseling?" . . . I wanted to see results right away. I would say, "I'm going to stop going." And then I would stop coming. I wouldn't call. My worker would call me: "What's going on? Why aren't you coming? Do you want to stop coming? Why do you want to stop coming?" I said, "I don't feel like talking right now, I just want to be left alone." So I just kind of listened, and after I talked with her, that same day I came back . . .

I got into the habit if something scares me I don't want to face it, and my worker doesn't allow me to do it. She says, "No, you have to face your problems, you cannot hide. You are teaching your kids to face responsibility, not to hide, you have to do the same thing. If the kids see you doing that, then they'll do it."

A secure base for exploration. Bowlby describes therapeutic relationships in which the characteristics portrayed above are achieved as providing a "secure base from which he [the client] can explore the various unhappy and painful aspects of his life, past and present, many of which he finds it difficult or perhaps impossible to think about and reconsider without a trusted companion to provide support, encouragement, sympathy, and, on occasion, guidance" (1988:138). The concept of a child's attachment to a parent as a secure base for exploration was first introduced by Mary Ainsworth (1967:345–346). Bowlby emphasizes that the practitioner's role is "analogous to that of a mother who provides her child with a secure base from which to explore the world" (1988:140).

Bowlby further stresses,

> Throughout adult life the availability of a responsive attachment figure remains the source of a person's feeling secure. All of us, from the cradle to the grave, are happiest when life is organized as a series of excursions, long or short, from the secure base provided by our attachment figure(s). (1988:62)

Ainsworth similarly describes affectional bonds that develop throughout the life span (1991) including attachments to parents, surrogate parent figures, intimate partners, mentors, and therapists.

We believe that the concept of a secure relational base from which to explore is very useful for understanding the centrality of family members' relationships with preventive program practitioners in their ongoing development and change over time. Workers' and clients' descriptions of their work together amply illustrate the characteristics of accessibility, individualized responsiveness, and sensitivity identified by Bowlby as essential to providing a secure base for therapeutic exploration. From this relational base family members explore developmental and/or therapeutic tasks, issues, and problems. Practitioners extend themselves as resources that may be used by families for a brief period, over the children's childhood and adolescence, or periodically over time as needed.

Shared parenting Lightening the load. Program practitioners described developing close relationships with children's parents and other caregivers as a goal of the work. This goal is consistent with the recognition that the emotional support or lack of it that caregivers receive affects the quality of their parenting (Bowlby 1988:126). Program staff members also often referenced Gabinet's concept of "shared parenting." Gabinet (1983) proposed a model that extends the notion of emotional support of parents to include ongoing supportive neighborhood services to parents and their children, a "series of services which could be offered to protect rather than disrupt family functioning" (p. 405). She elaborates:

> Shared parenting is the term which describes a new kind of service designed to compensate for parental inadequacy and at the same time to prevent the child abuse that in many instances results from these inadequacies.... Families need facilities within walking distance of their homes, where they can feel they belong, can find trustworthy friends and can receive assistance when necessary.... What is new in these recommendations is the basic concept: that institutions would be viewed as vehicles for improving the parenting experience of children, that where parents are inadequate, parental responsibilities would be shared or augmented but not supplanted by the institutions. These facilities would also be viewed as providing supportive services to parents because these supports will relieve some of the parental stresses which increase the risk of abuse and neglect of children. (pp. 405–406)

The benefits of a parent's therapeutic attachment to a center preventive program practitioner and the related experience of "shared parenting" were frequently identified. To illustrate, one worker described her relationship with a chronically depressed mother and her five children, four of whom have serious special education needs. The family had been referred to the center by the city public child welfare agency. Although an allegation of sexual abuse of one of the children by another was unsubstantiated, the child welfare agency felt the family could benefit from center services. At the time of our interviews with the worker and the family, the family had been receiving multiple center services for over three years. The mother, whom we will call Marla, had been hospitalized as an adolescent for over a year following a suicide attempt. The worker observed:

> Her contact at the center over the past three years has been really important in keeping her level of depression from overwhelming her. She usually walks in like the weight of the world is on her shoulders, and you can see it sitting there. Sometimes it takes a while for us to get into an issue in any kind of depth or length. . . . You have to ask a lot of questions, you have to be more active. . . . She was evaluated here by our psychiatrist, and he thinks her limitations are much greater than we had thought.

Marla's responsibilities as a mother are central in her life. The worker stressed: "She really tries, she really struggles in wanting something better for her kids, although not always knowing what to do about that. I have a real sense that life has always been a struggle for her, and yet she still manages. I have a lot of respect for that." The worker described changes that she had observed in Marla and their shared success in maintaining the children at home: "She's now able to look at a problem and think it through a little bit more, to better trust herself and her ability to make the right choices. The struggle is always whether she is able to follow through. We have been able to keep the kids in school and make sure that they are safe in the family."

Like many immigrants in Sunset Park, Marla has limited contact with her family in another country. She relies heavily upon her relationship with her preventive program worker for emotional support and assistance with her own and the children's relationships with special education, health, and legal professionals and with connections to other center services and staff. The worker emphasized Marla's isolation and the necessity for shared parenting: "She doesn't have anybody in her life that believes in her, that understands her—her family is far away, she has no friends. . . . Her husband refuses to work with us on her problems. She tried to separate from him a few years ago, and he told her that he would go to court, prove her incompetent, and keep the children." The worker described the way in which Marla perceives their relationship and some of the ways in which they share parenting:

> She sees me as somebody like one of her sisters who she would be able to go to and discuss things that she wouldn't discuss with other people, somebody that she would trust, like family. She knows the distinction between me being a friend or family member and somebody from the helping profession. She and her children can engage with me and utilize our work effectively. The relationship has been significant to her even though there have been so many referrals to other resources. The negotiation of the systems has been an ongoing task for both of us—school, legal, camp, employment, or training programs for the children. At some point I've had to intervene or help her make the connections with all the systems that impact upon the family.

Marla: Now she is strong. In a separate interview Marla and one of her daughters described the significance of the worker-client relationship and the three-year connection with center services. The mother related that a typical meeting with her worker would include talking about her problems, outlining steps to solve the problems, and then talking again about whether she could take the steps and what supports she would need to take them. She noted that at the beginning of a meeting, the "weight is heavy. When I leave the weight is light." Marla openly described her thoughts about suicide and that with her worker's help she has been able to tell herself to "hold on, be strong, hold your ground." Her daughter interjected that "my mother was weak, now she is strong. We used to walk all over her. Now she is strong. What [my mother's worker] does for Mom, Mom now does for me." Both mother and daughter commented that they could not imagine a time in life when they would not need the center's services.

Some will read this and other case descriptions throughout this volume and express concern about the center's "encouragement" of a family's "dependency" upon a worker and upon the center's services. It is here that we find the concepts of attachment and of shared parenting to be particularly useful. In her initial description of the concept of a secure base, Ainsworth wrote that when babies are able to crawl, rather than staying close to the mother they make "little excursions" to explore other objects and interact with other people, returning to the mother "from time to time. The mother seems to provide a secure base from which these excursions may be made without anxiety" (p. 345). Developmental theorists consistently stress that continuous close relationships across the life span are essential to the development and maintenance of autonomous functioning, competence, and positive self-esteem. "Dependence" upon such relationships is recognized as integral to the development of the abilities that are required for successful interpersonal relationships, including those of parent, partner/spouse, and employee. Thus, through close relationships with center practitioners, family members are able to explore, plan, and carry out "excursions" with increasing degrees of autonomy and confidence. As they do so, they rely on center staff and programs for emotional support and nurturing, role modeling and learning, problem solving and advice.

This approach to practice is consistent with the implications for child welfare drawn from studies of the helping alliance by Dore and Alexander (1996), who stress that "for families with significantly impaired psychosocial functioning alliance formation should become an end in itself, at least in the beginning phase of treatment" (p. 357). They suggest, in instances when clients' difficulties in interpersonal functioning are serious, that the initial focus should be "developing relational capacity in the client" rather than on changes related to the presenting problem (ibid.).

Workers' general and case-specific discussions with us about their relationships with families conveyed authentic respect for their clients' tenacity, spirit, and courage. For example, when asked what has drawn them to the work, one worker responded: "The clients. I like them and enjoy working with them over time. I like their commitment and their spirit." Another stressed her respect for clients' courage: "I see them handling hard things. That takes a lot of courage. It takes a lot of courage to be a little kid and say out loud these things that you're afraid of or that have been worrying you and to say it to somebody who isn't your family." In response to the same question, another worker emphasized the satisfaction derived from establishing productive and meaningful professional relationships with family members:

I like the chance to make those relationships with people . . . helping them figure out what they want to be doing. . . . Just that sense of working together with a family on things that really matter to them. Doing what I can do, what needs to be done, helping them do what they need to do, and getting them on surer ground.

Flexibility to Individualize Services

Essential to the preventive services program is flexibility to vary the work in ways that respond to families' needs over time. This permits highly individualized, client-centered service. Staff greatly value this flexibility. For example, one worker stated:

Here there is a great level of freedom to do what you think needs to be done with the family. There are certain basic requirements related to home visits and contacts, those kinds of things. But if a family needs you to be in the home much more, that's fine. I feel trusted to do what I think would meet their needs. There are different ways you can become involved in their lives.

Another preventive service social worker similarly states: "We have the goal of trying to keep families together, but we don't have a strict guideline that says I must see the child, I must see the mother, or I must see the family together. We can use any kind of intervention that we feel comfortable with to achieve that goal." Another noted the freedom to apply various treatment approaches:

We have a great flexibility here to work with people in a way that seems best for that particular individual—individualized in terms of what techniques we use and how we work. It's not like we're all behaviorists here or all psychoanalytic here, or that we just do individual or that we just do family or that we just do group. That is a tremendous difference from programs that are set up much more like a mental health clinic.

Therefore, although similarities can be identified in services provided to different families, workers develop an unique service plan with each family, providing services in the family's home, the worker's office, and elsewhere in the community. Service plans also vary in the frequency of meetings with family members, which family members are included in sessions at various points in time, and which additional services are accessed both within the center (i.e., after school, employment center, emergency food, etc.) and outside the center (i.e., preschool child care, medical care, psychotropic medication, etc.).

Flexibility in Service Duration and Access to Services Over Time

One characteristic that distinguishes family preservation services currently provided throughout the country from other services to families is their brief nature, typically limited in duration from one to five months (Fraser, Nelson, and Rivard 1997). Thus in using such programs families are not empowered to access them over time in ways that would be consistent with their problems and needs. Due to the definition of service as time limited, a family with chronic problems that require continuous or episodic service over time, such as a parent's or child's severe mental illness, would not be eligible for extended services.

The limitations of a brief service model in addressing many families' needs have been described (McGowan 1990; Dore 1993; Dore and Alexander 1996; Besharov 1994). For example, Dore has stressed that "current family preservation programs are unlikely to succeed with families whose characteristics typify depressed, maltreating families living in poverty" (1993:551) and states, "It is imperative that family preservation services include opportunities for ongoing supportive therapy for depressed, maltreating parents" (1993:552). Consistent with others' recognition of these limitations, the authors of a recent review of studies of family preservation programs raised as a question for further study "Can a brief intervention be expected to offer protection against complex problems like child maltreatment [child abuse or neglect]? . . . Should the duration of service be extended?" (Fraser, Nelson, and Rivard 1997:150). The center's answer to this second question is a definite "yes."

Flexible service duration. Findings regarding the center's preventive program's provision of both short- and long-term service emerged early in our study from in-depth interviews with preventive program workers. When asked whether case "types" or "categories" could be identified in the program's client population, workers primarily identified types of cases based on service duration. A "short-term" case was described by workers as a "higher functioning family with specific needs or problems." In contrast, a "long-term" or "maintenance" case was defined as "someone who for years will need that constant support in order to make it. Most of my clients live on the edge of a lot things, and they are dealing with very bread-and-butter issues. There are some clients where there will always be an immediate issue that's too much for them to solve on their own." The worker then illustrated this definition by describing a family that needed and used a number of concrete, therapeutic, recreational, and other supportive services over time:

For example, I have a client who had her children in foster care multiple times, an alcoholic. She has three children at home, one in a residential treatment facility. I've referred her to the women's group here, so she's attempting to build other supports besides myself. She greatly depends on the other [Center for Family Life] resources like after-school child care and summer camp. Those things are definitely crucial to help her to survive daily. . . . Meanwhile, while she's getting this together, the kids still have their feelings about foster care. Two are in special education. They have a lot of needs themselves that Mom isn't ready to meet. She's ready to meet their basic physical needs in her own way. She needed basic things—how to manage a budget, how to buy food—those were the issues for a long time. Now we've kind of moved beyond that to relationship issues. But it's very hard for her because she doesn't have supports, her judgment is poor, and her own capacity to deal with the kids and with her feelings is limited.

Another worker further elaborated that in long-term cases

the progress may be very minimal, and you're really just trying to maintain the family in some way or support the functioning of the children until they grow up. There's not necessarily the expectation that things are going to improve dramatically—there might be very small progress here and there—but it's really to allow the children and the family to have the support that it needs to maintain its level—to not get worse.

Similarly, when asked how she would know that her work at the center is ended, a single mother of five reflected, "To be honest with you, I think I will always need the center. . . . This has become my second home."

However, long-term services are provided only with a clear rationale. Each case is regularly reviewed by a clinical supervisor to determine whether the case should remain open. In addition, at least every six months the center's preventive program is required to account to the New York City public child welfare agency for service goals, goal attainment, and the need for continued services in each case. If family members believe that continued services are necessary and the practitioner's and clinical supervisor's assessment differs, the family members' concerns are thoroughly reviewed. Then either extended service is provided, with the objectives for continued service clearly defined, or a "trial" termination is attempted, with periodic meetings for ongoing review.

Previously reported case-specific findings regarding the duration of services to the study families (Hess, McGowan, and Botsko 2000) support the program staff's conceptualization of general types of families whose presenting problems can be addressed more immediately and those for whom lengthy and extensive service efforts are necessary to assist the family in reaching and maintaining an adequate level of functioning. In examining the length of service to study sample families, we found that of the 182 cases closed by summer 1999, service duration ranged from less than 6 months (25 percent of the study sample) to over 3.5 years (6 percent), with an average service duration of 17.5 months (SD = 13.5 months). Greater service duration was associated with a higher number of presenting problems at intake, a higher mean service need, and children's health/mental health problems, parent's health/mental health problems, and children's needs, problems, and behaviors that were identified by the family's worker as sufficiently severe to place the child at high risk of out-of-home care. An open-ended approach to establishing service duration permits the center's preventive program to serve differentially clients with problems that vary in nature, number, and severity.

Multiple service episodes over time. When preventive program services are concluded, workers encourage families to return for service if the need arises. Preventive program workers view a family's self-referred return for service as positive. Workers believe that when a family identifies a service need it should be able to initiate continued access to the program before the onset of severe difficulties or family breakdown. The following staff member's observation regarding desired case outcomes illustrates this philosophy:

> My general [desired service] outcome is to hopefully help the family resolve the one thing they came in with. That one thing might change over the course of three months or in the course of three years. If they leave feeling better about themselves—I don't care how small it is—and have made a change in some of the destructive patterns that brought them here, then it's completed for now.
>
> A lot of times they come back and work on something else. . . . I don't think everyone can work on all the issues at one time. What I might perceive as something they really need to work on, they may not see it that way, and I have to respect that. I have to throw it out, but if they don't pick it up then the work is done. The hope is that they will come back when they are ready to discuss more issues.

Through content analysis of summary statements included in the preventive program workers' Case Closing Form for the 189 study sample families, we found that workers frequently reminded families about the continuing availability of the center staff. A typical closing summary indicated that "Mrs. R. is aware that the Center for Family Life services are available to her in the future if she wants to work on other family issues."

Possible effects of flexible service duration on workers' satisfaction. The center's preventive service program practitioners view the accessibility of the services over time and the flexibility with regard to service duration as empowering not only to families but also to them. "There is a great deal of freedom to do what you think needs to be done with the family. . . . I feel trusted to do what I think will meet their needs." Practitioners described the value of being able to take time to build trust with clients as well as the benefit to families of being able to maintain the children in the home by staying involved with the program over long periods of time. In discussing one such family, the worker emphasized that she will "have to be constantly involved . . . to kind of keep things in balance. If I leave that situation, you can pretty much be sure it will go down the tubes."

Preventive program workers also emphasized the satisfaction that they themselves derived from serving families with a variety of needs and problems and from having both short-term and long-term relationships with clients: "I like working with clients over time . . . I like their commitment and their spirit. . . . I like the long term aspect. . . . You get the chance to know them, and to see change over time . . . to see the growth and the changes."

Although limited information is available about the effects of different program models on practitioners' stress and job satisfaction, the center preventive program workers' strong positive observations about the center's model and about the relationship between the model and their satisfaction differ from those of thirty-six family preservation workers surveyed in a pilot study reported by Tracy, Bean, Gwatkin, and Hill (1992). Most of the respondents worked in programs in which the length of the treatment model was ninety days. Tracey and colleagues report that

> Workers' responses to the question "From your experience, what are the major stressors in family preservation work?" yielded 42 instances in which the structure of the program, the limited or intensive time factor . . . were mentioned as major stressors. Workers stated such things as . . . (c) "the time factor of 90 days to make a change" . . . (e) "short amount of time to work on goals that will take longer" . . . (h) "going into people's homes where there are deplorable situations that cannot be solved" (in the time allotted). (p. 473)

Although these comparative findings must be viewed with caution, they do suggest that program models may not only affect outcomes with various client populations but also affect practitioner job satisfaction and retention.

Staff Accessibility

Associated with the program's flexible and individualized approach to service provision is the physical and emotional accessibility of staff. Workers accommodate to family needs with regard to immediacy and to the timing and location of the work. The location of services in the neighborhood and the center's commitment to round-the-clock accessibility increase the ease with which family members can access preventive program workers. Access is further enhanced by scheduling preventive program staff to work at least two evenings each week. The workers' availability and willingness to hold sessions in the clients' homes further assure accessibility for single parents without child care, for parents with a child who is ill, and for clients unable to come to the center for other reasons.

Practitioners emphasize that making themselves easily accessible promotes family members' engagement in services. In discussing services to preventive program families, a worker emphasized that "you cannot just sit there and be a desk person. You really have to be out there, and your clients need to know that you're with them." Another worker similarly stressed that home visits are an important part of the work, "not just a requirement. . . . The home visit can be a way of reconnecting and reengaging for somebody who's having trouble making it in each week because of depression, young children, anger at the worker, frustration. It provides them with a sense that there is a caring and a willingness for us to do our part too—that they're not totally alone in it.

Many of the examples given by workers as they described their work with families demonstrate the range of ways in which they are accessible both physically and emotionally:

We're allowed to enter the families' lives in a very different way than in some other programs. [A key program characteristic is] our ability to see our clients, not just weekly, but if something comes up, in the daytime or the night time, we're able to see clients several times a week or to accompany them if there's some issue going on in school or with welfare or some health-related thing. I think that makes a really strong connection with the clients, and they join more quickly when they are offered that service.

Similarly, another worker reported that "his [an adolescent's] mother didn't want him spending the night at Riker's [New York City jail and detention center], so I offered to go with her. So we went and spent hours waiting for him together, waiting to get him out at three in the morning."

We found that the staff members' accessibility is particularly important to clients. For example, an adolescent commented:

I meet with her every Wednesday after school. If I can't make it, I call her. If there is an emergency, she comes to the house. If I'm having a problem, like now and then, I would just run there. If she's with someone, she says, "Can you give me a half an hour so I can finish with this person?"

Similarly a mother described her worker's responsiveness and accessibility as follows:

If I have an urge to have a drug, I will call her up and say, "I can't go over there, can you come here because I don't trust myself to go outside." Or, "Right now, I'm so angry I'm afraid I'm going to hurt one of my children, because I just want to hit them or yell at them or shake them. Please come over and help me." She'll come over and she'll stay with me until I can deal with them.

Inclusive Access to Noncategorical Services

Developed to provide intensive, effective intervention in families in which placement of a child appears to be imminent, family preservation programs are typically accessed only through a referral following a report of child abuse and neglect (Cole and Duva 1990; Dore and Alexander 1996; Fraser, Nelson, and Rivard 1997; Kinney, Haapala, and Booth 1991; Nelson, Landsman, and Deutelbaum 1990; McCroskey and Meezan 1997). Such services are typically categorical and focus on specific problems contributing to the risk of placement. Thus in most communities these programs are not available to all families, and families are rarely self-referred. As a consequence, a family that has not yet been identified by someone outside the family as needing specific services (such as a family with problems that have not yet been detected or are not sufficiently serious to warrant consideration of placement or a family with needs or problems not typically associated with risk for placement) would be unable to access them.

In contrast, we found that the Center for Family Life is committed to inclusivity in serving all families in Sunset Park. Consistent with this philosophy, families who themselves identify a need for the comprehensive services provided through the center's preventive program may access the program through self-referral. The intake criteria regarding imminence of placement or the presence or absence of specific problems that are typically used in family preservation programs are not applied by the center. In this regard the center's inclusive approach to service access differs markedly from models of placement prevention services in which the population served is narrowly targeted to the category of families at imminent risk of child placement (McGowan 1990) and whose primary goal is tertiary prevention (Nelson, Landsman, and Deutelbaum 1990).

Continuous voluntary accessibility. Thus it is important to note that 51 of the 189 study families (27 percent) were self-referred and 13 (6.9 percent) were referred by relatives and friends. Of the 51 percent who were self-referred, 23 (45.1 percent) had previously been served in the center's preventive program. The service needs of the self-referred families were serious. Almost 60 percent (58.8 percent) had at least one caregiver, child, or environmental problem that was identified by their worker on the FAF as requiring immediate intervention to prevent out-of-home placement. These findings strongly suggest that when families are empowered to use easily accessible, continuously available neighborhood services to prevent family break-up *voluntarily*, they are able and willing to do so.

Prior access to other center services. Our study of the patterns of families' use of various center programs further strongly indicates that for some families self-referral to the preventive service program may be eased by having previously established a relationship with another center program and other center staff. We found that almost one-third of the families using any center service between January 1, 1994, and December 31, 1995, and receiving preventive services either during that two-year period or previously, had used at least one other center service before using preventive services. The service most frequently used by families prior to receiving preventive services was one of the center's summer day camp programs, followed by participation in one of the after-school child care programs. These programs provide opportunities for socialization, educational support, and recreation for children and youth as well as summer and after-school child care that permits parents to work and/or attend school. They also provide parents support in and respite from child care responsibilities as well as opportunities to meet and socialize with other parents.

Not labeling clients or services. The center's philosophy also emphasizes not labeling clients or services by client problem. In responding to the researchers' efforts to identify whether preventive staff identified client "types" or "categories," one worker's comments are illustrative of the majority, noting, "There are similarities with the problem, but not with the person. I see every single family [as] unique in its characteristics. . . . People react differently." Although workers noted that different client-families required different approaches, none identified a specific plan that would be applied to all clients with a particular problem. Moreover, in the preventive program, therapeutic small groups are identified not by a problem focus, such as women who are battered or youth who are delinquent, but rather by participants' age and/or gender (e.g., the preadolescent girls' group, the women's group, the men's group). Workers believe this method of grouping clients encourages the engagement of clients who might not participate were the problems with which they were struggling identified in the group's name.

Supportive Professional Community

Preventive program practitioners described a supportive professional community both within the preventive program and through the staff's programmatic connections to other components of the center. It is evident this professional community is a significant variable in recruiting and retaining preventive program staff.

The workers' respect for each other's knowledge and skills is readily apparent. One worker noted that a key characteristic of the center's preventive program is "professionalism. That's number one. . . . They are very highly skilled." Consistently including not only the preventive program staff but the center staff as a whole, workers refer to the "community of colleagues," "camaraderie" with colleagues, and "professional and personal affinity" with colleagues. One described a source of support as "the workers. Their commitment and sense of community. . . . This is a community place. It helps me feel more confident."

Within the context of a supportive professional community, the preventive program staff implement the program as described above, with each key program characteristic functioning as an integral aspect of the whole. We observed many ways in which the preventive program staff function interdependently with staff in other center programs. Thus central to the model's implementation are the staff of the preventive service program as well as their colleagues in other center programs, working together as a professional community.

THE PREVENTIVE PROGRAM STAFF

Staff Characteristics and Responsibilities

Throughout the research project and since, the number and responsibilities of the staff in the preventive program have remained fairly constant. Most staff members are assigned to the preventive program exclusively; some also carry assignments in other center programs. In late 2000 twenty-one practitioners (eighteen females and three males) serve families in the preventive program, with a full-time equivalent of nineteen staff. Nine workers are bilingual (seven in Spanish and English and two in Chinese and English). Seventy-six percent (sixteen) of the preventive program staff members have served families in the program for over three years, and twelve of these for over six years. Eighteen have master's degrees in social work, and one is completing an MSW, one has a master's in divinity, and two have BSW degrees, one of whom is entering an MSW program. Each year, from September through May, the staff expands to include approximately six social work interns completing the final year of a master's degree education.

Full-time preventive program staff serve an average caseload of sixteen to eighteen families at any point in time. Because of the long-term nature of the service to many families, the average annual caseload is only slightly higher. Staff work a minimum of seventy hours in a two-week period, thirty-five hours per week. Most report working several more hours per week, particularly during the school year (September-June) when the caseloads are higher, client groups are meeting regularly, and family members are available. Workers report that their time is allocated primarily to direct service with families. Supervision, staff meetings, and other collateral meetings require four to eight hours per week. Clinical case supervision is provided by Sister Mary Paul, who has a doctorate in social work and who conducts intake interviews but does not carry a caseload, and by three MSW supervisors who are also assigned cases. Paperwork requires two hours to one day per week or more, depending on the cycle of forms due.

To better understand the staff members' experiences with the preventive program, we asked them to identify what drew them to and retains them in the program, the characteristics that enhance effectiveness as a CFL preventive service worker, and their responsibilities, stresses, and supports.

Preventive Program Workers Are Drawn to the Program By . . .

As illustrated in previously cited excerpts from workers' interviews, the philosophy, model, and services available through the Center for Family Life's preventive program both draw social workers to and retain them in the program. In addition, preventive program workers greatly value the opportunities for professional development, the administrative support for autonomous professional practice, and, as described above, the supportive relationships with center colleagues.

The program's staff members emphasize the strong appeal of both the community-based, comprehensive, holistic services model and the program's focus on the family as the unit of attention. Many commented that the model contributes to their being and feeling effective and emphasized the congruity of the center's philosophy with their own values and beliefs. To illustrate, one worker described being particularly drawn to the community-based nature of the center's approach:

It's a community approach where the community sees the center as a helpful place, not only just for counseling but in a lot of other ways. That's important because it's more part of the community as opposed to a little building where the people come once in a while. I like the community part of it, the building of the community, and the building of the family, and supporting all the things they already have going for them.

Preventive program workers also consistently identified being drawn to the opportunities for professional guidance, support, and learning balanced with a respect for their competence, a respect that translates into a comfortable degree of staff autonomy. An experienced staff member elaborated:

They [Sister Mary Paul and Sister Geraldine] let you do your job. You don't have anybody on your back telling you what to do or checking on you. They know that you're doing the best you can. When I encounter situations where I feel I have to consult, I go and do it. I think the sisters particularly trust that I would never go overboard. . . . The bottom line is that you're on your own, but not on your own, because you have supervision but they trust your judgment, and that's a great feeling. That's why I love this place.

Another, in describing her professional growth since joining the program staff, identified the multiple benefits derived from the relationship with her supervisor Sister Mary Paul:

I have never had a learning experience with a supervisor before this. . . . She provides very strong guidance and support. And she is a resource. She has the power connection to say "I know someone, I'll make a phone call for you." Probably in almost every case I have she's intervened in a way that has really helped move things along, or she's put in a good word, or she's signed her name to a letter. . . . You know your back is always covered. I think sometimes in this profession you can feel very isolated. I feel very secure with her.

Perceptions of Characteristics That Enhance Practitioners' Effectiveness

We also asked the preventive program practitioners to describe the characteristics of social workers who are effective in the center's preventive services program. Their responses emphasized a broad range of professional and personal characteristics. Not surprisingly, the characteristic most frequently identified was flexibility—particularly with regard to using multiple practice approaches and being open to differences: "Flexibility—being able to adapt and pitch in and change—from the concrete to the more abstract. Being willing to look at things from different angles—people's behavior and expectations."

Workers also consistently identified the importance of a practitioner's commitment to the center's mission and comprehensive services model, to the program's clients, and to the family as the unit of attention. Respect for clients and a nonjudgmental attitude were also stressed. For example, one worker explained: "The cases run the gamut, and you really have to have a broadness of scope. You have to be constantly willing to learn about a variety of things and expect to hear a variety of things and be willing to want to try to understand." Professional knowledge and skill were also frequently reported to be important worker characteristics. Workers emphasized the necessity of sophisticated assessment skills, clear professional and personal boundaries, and skills in the professional use of self, in working with children, and as a team member.

In addition, numerous personal qualities were identified as important. These included having strength, problem-solving ability, hopefulness, "not being fazed by different kinds of things that come up," compassion, "a thick skin," energy, independence, and sensitivity. One worker emphasized the personal characteristic of consistency:

Families come to depend on you. They need to know that you always follow through on what you say. A lot of our families don't have that in their life. They have someone they depend on and that person falls through. It's integral to their trust of you that you act on everything you say. That takes a lot of time when you're very, very busy. But consistency is number one.

Stresses

As one would expect, the preventive program workers identified a number of stresses associated with their work. In reflecting upon these, three words were spoken again and again: *responsibility*, *ambiguity*, and *unpredictability*. Practitioners described the stress associated with the responsibility conferred upon them by referring sources in cases where child abuse or neglect had occurred and recurrence was to be prevented and by parents and children who desperately want their difficulties to be resolved quickly. They also described the obligations they placed on themselves in making professional decisions associated with serving families and children who are at risk daily for suicide, family and street violence, teen pregnancy, dropping out of school, and other serious problems with life-long consequences. One worker commented: "It feels like a lot of responsibility sometimes—knowing when you can handle it [the case] on your own and when you should really be alarmed." Another similarly reflected: "Thinking back over the years, the greatest stress is the worry of not knowing what might be occurring in the family, such as child abuse and neglect. Sometimes you just don't know. You put faith in the parent, and you don't know if it's been misplaced or not." Another related: "In some of the riskier cases, there's always a sense of frustration, the worries about whether there's going to be enough change or enough progress, worries about the children in general, about how they're going to develop. Having to make choices you don't want to make."

Practitioners also identified as stressful what they described as an inherent ambiguity and unpredictability in implementing a service approach that involves continual interactions with family members and others in many community settings—in families' homes, in practitioners' offices, in schools, on the streets. Cases in which family members are seriously depressed or angry were noted as particularly stressful because of the amount of energy required to manage one's own reactions to the client's emotions and behaviors when with them. One worker noted: "It's stressful trying to stay focused with all that's going on. Some clients are very disturbed, and you have to be careful how you step and how you negotiate. There's always an element of unpredictability, volatility, or potential conflict wherever you are."

Practitioners also underscored the burden related to the enormity of many families' needs. For example, one worker explained: "There are some days when you feel like you can never meet this family's needs. It is so overwhelming because there is so much to do, and you only can do this much. It isn't even possible to do all that you could do if you spent every single hour." Another elaborated:

There are a lot of demands. You can't get this degree of commitment to clients without demands. You have the success that the center has, and success is built upon what you are offering in the program. To build that success there are an awful lot of demands on the workers, and it can at times be a big stress. Sometimes the cases that come in are very stressful, very involved, sometimes difficult because of the nature of what you're seeing, and that can be stressful.

The quantity of paperwork also was identified as a stress, as were difficulties in accessing resources needed to help families, personal safety, and low salaries.

Supports and Benefits

As illustrated by interview excerpts in this chapter, workers identified the center's preventive program model and the resources of the center as major sources of support and security: "I have the whole center to help me." Workers stressed that the structured linkages to comprehensive services available within the center itself were critical to their own effectiveness with clients. Accessible supervision was also consistently identified as very important, providing guidance, emotional support, options, and power—"My supervisor opens doors for me."

One worker reflected upon the importance of "not being alone with it" in managing the case-related stresses:

What helps me with the cases where I worry is supervision and talking with other staff about similar situations. . . . Not being alone with it—everybody has or has had worries. My supervisor might be worrying with me about a particular case or she may have put it in perspective for me so that I'm not worrying as much. Or other staff members may have had a similar case in the past and say, "This is what I did, this is how I handled that." Or they might make suggestions.

It is noteworthy that the workers' description of supports are echoed in a comment made by Sister Mary Paul as she discussed what helped her, as a clinical supervisor, manage the risk in a difficult case carried by one of the social workers she supervises:

I think partly in this agency it's our joint and aggregate involvement in it [managing risks], it's not myself taking risks. It's others making contributions to the management of that risk. . . . Everybody is a part of this client's care. It's an aggregate situation. I don't bear it on my shoulders alone.

As discussed earlier, the preventive program social workers also are supported by a "community of colleagues." In describing resources essential to managing the stress, several phrases repeatedly emerged: *collegial support*, *a sense of community*, *camaraderie*, and *friendship*. From colleagues, practitioners reported receiving respect, acceptance, validation, ideas, and encouragement.

Despite the stresses they identify, we found that the preventive program practitioners' sense of pride in the work they do collectively is readily apparent, as are their energy, enthusiasm, and commitment to the center, its preventive program, and their clients. It is evident that they are deeply engaged by both the specific nature of the work with families and the agency and community environment in which the work is occurring. As the following response to the question "What holds you with the program?" suggests, from the preventive program practitioners' perspective, with the challenges come the benefits: "I'm in it because there are problems—I sort of like to deal with the problems. Now and then there are cases that I've been assigned to that are for some reason a little different, that have a twist to them that challenges me in a different way than other cases in the past." The worker illustrated this point as follows:

I just got a new case that's got me interested, challenged. I just started to work with her a few weeks ago. Depression, maybe hostility from a parent towards a child, I wonder what's behind that. She has this enormous anger, and it comes out toward her child. She says things that are kind of shocking. But I can see that behind it there's a sadness, and she's been deeply hurt. I'd like to be able to get past that anger to the vulnerability and some of the other feelings there.

As the worker continued, she noted that her own professional growth was among the benefits that led her stay with the program: "I've had some satisfaction from a sense that there have been sessions I've had with this woman that I know that when I first came here I wouldn't have been able to have because I would have been too shocked by the level of hostility in her. I feel pleased that I see some growth on my part."

Through the analysis of the qualitative data we have collected, we have found striking parallels in the experiences described by the clients served in the center's preventive program and the experiences described by their workers. The parallels include their experiences of feeling respected, of finding the family focus and the flexibility valuable, and of being supported as they grow and change. Thus the center's preventive program philosophy and model not only meet the needs of clients but also support the staff who serve them.

PROGRAM RESULTS

In addition to findings reported throughout this chapter, our analysis of the study data in three areas strongly suggests that the center's preventive service program is accomplishing its goals.

The Extent to Which Families' Service Needs Were Addressed

As described earlier, workers identified the service needs of a prospective sample of 189 families and over time reported whether and how these needs were addressed through center services. Almost 90 percent (87.9 percent) of the families' identified service needs had been addressed at the study's end. The workers' reports were corroborated by service information available through the center's management information system. The importance of this finding is underscored by the findings described earlier regarding the *extent* of service provision required to meet families' service needs. Seventy-five percent of the total sample received 6 or more services, and families received a range of 1–27 services through the program (see table 3.1).

Preventive program workers identified a mean of 1.4 services per family as needed but not provided. Reasons for lack of service provision included a family member's refusal to use the service, a waiting list, the unavailability of a service, such as day care, in the geographic area, and ineligibility of family members(s) for a service (e.g., age).

Information is also available for the study sample regarding two additional indicators of the intensity of service provided by the family's preventive worker: monthly home visits and monthly clinical contacts. These two somewhat overlapping service contacts are reported by the preventive program to New York City's public child welfare agency. Overall, the study sample families received a monthly average of .5 (SD = .5) home visits, ranging from 0–2.6, and a monthly average of 2.99 (SD = 1.5) clinical contacts, ranging from 0–8.9 per month. Thus, on average, families received approximately 3.5 monthly service contacts. The total number of home visits provided to the families ranged from 0–50, and the total number of clinical contacts ranged from 3–229. It should be noted that the intensity of total Center for Family Life service (i.e., the frequency of contact in all programs in which a family participated) provided to the study families is not known. However, findings regarding families' service needs and the range and extent of center and community services provided to address these needs indicate that preventive program workers' contacts represent only one of several components of service intensity. These findings, together with those related to type and number of services provided, document the delivery of comprehensive and individualized services to the study sample families.

Changes in Final Family Assessment Form (FAF) Scores

As described earlier in this chapter, extensive case-specific information was collected on the study sample families. Workers reported this information using the Family Assessment Form (FAF) developed by the Children's Bureau of Los Angeles (McCroskey, Nishimoto, and Subramanian 1991; McCroskey and Meezan 1997). The FAF incorporates an ecological approach to assessing family functioning and requires the family's worker to provide characteristics of caregivers, children, and others in the household, sources of income and housing, and assessment of family members and of family interactions on numerous dimensions. The FAF was completed at the third session with each family, and repeated measures were administered at six-month intervals and at case closing on all families whose cases were closed prior to the conclusion of data collection.

Changes in the initial and final Family Assessment Form (FAF) scores were computed for four family environment factors, six caregiver-centered factors, and eight child-centered factors. For the ninety-two cases closed prior to the end of the study's data collection phase, slight changes of FAF scores in the desired direction were found in 61.1 percent of the factors (see appendix C). The degree of score change is statistically significant in six of the child-centered factors. Positive change is found in the areas of children's behavioral difficulties, developmental difficulties, relating difficulties, learning difficulties, and serious emotional disturbance. Negative change is found in the area of child health difficulties. Our conversations with workers suggest that this finding can be explained by the increased information gained over time from families about children's health problems, which are often not directly observable. As workers completed the FAF, their greater awareness of health problems was reported. Although this change in children's health problems appears to be a real one, it is more likely only a change in the information available to the workers.

In the six caregiver-centered factors, changes in the desired direction were found in five, though not at a statistically significant level. In one factor, caregiver responsibility, the change was in a negative direction. In three of the four family environment factors, changes were in the desired direction, but not statistically significant. In the fourth, the community environment, changes were in a negative direction, but again not statistically significant.

It is not clear why statistically significant positive changes were found only in child-centered scores. Both caregivers and children were typically receiving multiple services. However, neither our study data nor the center's management information system data can determine the full intensity of service for each family member (i.e., number of hours of service per week in various center programs). It is possible that a greater number of children were involved in multiple frequent or high-intensity interventions (i.e., daily attendance in an after-school child care program, summer camp) than were the caregivers, and, if so, that this difference affected service results. Children's difficulties may have been less intractable than those of their caregivers and than those in the families' environment. It is also possible that changes in the closed cases were more immediately observable to the families' workers in the children than in the adults.

In the ninety-seven open cases, statistically significant change between the initial and final (at study's end) FAF scores was found in the desired direction in the area of financial stress as well as in five child-centered factors: child behavioral difficulties, developmental difficulties, emotional disturbance, relating difficulties, and learning difficulties (see appendix C).

Study Sample Children Placed Outside the Home

A primary goal of the center's preventive program is to prevent unnecessary placement of children in care. At the conclusion of the data collection phase of the study, 98.6 percent (417) of the 423 study sample children remained with their families. Six children (1.4 percent) in 5 (2.6 percent) of the study sample families were either placed in foster family or group care or in the custody of the criminal justice system. Thus placement was avoided for the children in 96 percent (118) of the 123 study sample families identified as having at least one caregiver, child, or environmental problem requiring immediate intervention to prevent placement.

All five families in which a child was placed, however, continued to receive center services, one through continuing in the preventive program, one through the children's placement in the center's neighborhood foster care program described in chapter 4, and three through services in other center programs to various family members, including those children remaining in the family. The five families' situations, the nature of their needs and problems, and preventive program interventions, were as follows.

The first family was Latina/o and headed by a single working mother, with a history of being battered and with serious emotional and behavioral problems, living with two teen-aged boys. The family was referred to the center's preventive program by the police because of both boys' gang activity, including robbery. The family had not received any services in the center prior to this referral. On the Family Assessment Form both boys were identified by the worker as having a strong risk of placement. The family received extensive services, including diagnostic assessment, drug/alcohol services, individual, family, and crisis counseling, services regarding domestic violence and sex abuse, parent education, self-help group, employment and job referral services, the summer youth employment program, housing assistance, and medical care. The family received three home visits and twenty-six clinical sessions. Within the first six months of service the older boy was sent to a juvenile delinquency facility and at the end of the study was still awaiting placement in a group home. The family received service in the preventive program for fourteen months; at the time of the closing of the case in preventive services, the younger son was still living with his mother and continuing to use the Center for Family Life's Teen Center.

The second family, also Latina/o, included three children, two boys ages seventeen and fifteen and a thirteen-year-old girl, living with their maternal grandmother. The family was supported by public assistance. The family was referred to the center's preventive program by family court as part of a Juvenile Intensive Services Project after the fifteen-year-old boy was arrested for possession of drugs. None of the three children had received services in the Center for Family Life prior to this referral. The children's biological mother, who was known to have had a severe drug problem, had surrendered custody of the three to the maternal grandmother "many years ago." All children were identified by the worker as having emotional, behavioral, drug/alcohol, and/or learning problems and all were in special education classes. The worker indicated on the Family Assessment Form that there was severe risk of placement. The family received individual and family counseling, parent education, summer youth employment program, after-school child care, recreation, and food assistance. Within the first six months of service the oldest child was arrested on drug-related charges and subsequently sent to prison. The family was served for an additional six months, receiving a total of twenty home visits, many at the time of the youth's arrest, and forty-two clinical contacts. At the time of case closing in the preventive program, the two younger teens continued to live with the grandmother and to use several of the center's community school-based services, including Life Lines, the Learning Center, and the Teen Center.

The third family was also Latina/o, headed by the children's biological mother, and a stepfather, both of whom were identified as having emotional problems and prior histories of in-patient drug/alcohol treatment. The five children (all male, ages twenty-one, eighteen, fourteen, thirteen, and five) had three different biological fathers, all with histories of substance abuse and one of whom was in prison. None were in contact with the family. The family's income sources included AFDC and wages. This family was referred by the Child Welfare Administration at the time of the discharge of the three youngest children from foster care, one of whom had been placed in kinship care with the maternal grandmother. Scores on the Family Assessment Form indicated problems sufficiently severe to warrant intervention to prevent placement in all three problem areas: environmental, caregiver-centered, and child-centered. The family received diagnostic assessment, individual, marital, crisis, and group counseling, drug/alcohol services, self-help group, job referral services, summer youth employment program, after-school child care, project youth, special education, tutoring, legal services, and medical care. The fourteen year old was placed in a group home after twelve months of service, and services were provided for another twelve months.

When the case was closed in the preventive program, all other children remained in the home with both caregivers. The family continued to use after-school child care in a center community school program.

The fourth family was Jamaican and was headed by the biological father and a stepmother. The biological mother of the two children, females ages fourteen and twelve, was deceased. This family was referred to the preventive program by the children's school. The children had been separated from their father for two years following their mother's death when he came to the U.S. and left them in Jamaica. The oldest girl was alleged to be a participant in a prostitution ring at the school, and the father had previously filed a status offender complaint on this child. Both children had been placed in a residential treatment facility for two weeks approximately two years prior to their referral to the center's preventive program and had received no previous center services. The Family Assessment Form indicated child-centered problems (emotional and behavioral) requiring immediate intervention to prevent placement. Both girls were also identified as having learning disabilities. The stepmother refused to participate in services. Services provided to the father and his daughters included diagnostic assessment, individual, crisis, family, and group counseling, drug/alcohol services, domestic violence and sex abuse services, parent education, summer youth employment services, after-school child care, recreation services, legal services, medical care, and assistance with housing, food, finances, clothing, household goods, and utilities. After approximately six months of service the oldest girl was placed in a group home, but ran away soon after placement. The case, which was still open in the preventive program at the conclusion of this study, had been open for twenty-three months. At the conclusion of the study the younger girl still remained with her father and stepmother. The family was continuing to access multiple other center services subsequent to case closing in the preventive program.

The fifth family was African American and included one girl, age eight, and one boy, age six, living with their biological mother. The children were referred by the Child Welfare Administration at the time of the children's discharge from a foster care placement lasting 31 months. Although neither child was identified as having serious problems, the worker scored the mother on the Family Assessment Form as having caregiver-centered and environmental problems requiring immediate intervention to prevent placement. The mother had a history of in-patient alcohol treatment and was participating in AA at the time of intake. The family's income source was AFDC. During 3.2 months of service the family received three home visits and thirteen clinical sessions from its preventive services worker. Services identified as received included crisis, individual, and family counseling, drug/alcohol services, parent education, after-school child care, domestic violence services, recreation, and medical care. The case was closed in the preventive program when the mother began drinking again and it became necessary for both children to reenter foster care. However, the availability of the center's neighborhood foster care program, in which the two children were placed, permitted the children to avoid the additional trauma of leaving their neighborhood and school and to continue to access center services, including summer day camp.

The service results for these five families are clearly mixed. Although in all five families the placement of a child was not prevented, in four of the five all the other children remained in their homes, and family members continued to use at least one center service. In one case the family was continuing to receive preventive services at the end of the study period. Therefore, the extensive services provided appeared to decrease the extent of family breakup in four of the five cases. In the fifth family the severity of the mother's addiction, as indicated both by past and current behaviors, resulted in another placement for both children. In this case, however, the availability of the center's neighborhood foster care program allowed the children to remain in their neighborhood and school and to continue to access center services.

As described in this chapter, the Center for Family Life's preventive program uniquely integrates concrete and therapeutic services typical of family preservation programs with continuously available, intra-agency, comprehensive, neighborhood-based family support services. The center's preventive program model exemplifies a particular blend of individual, family, and group counseling, services historically provided by clinical social workers, with community-based family support services, echoing the social work profession's settlement house history.

An important finding of this study that the center's preventive program staff members consistently emphasize is the community-based comprehensive nature of the services model and the experience of a supportive professional community within the program and the center as a whole as both strongly contributing to their sense of effectiveness, work satisfaction, and retention with the program. Thus the service supports inherent in the model for the families also support the *workers* in their helping role. The sense of isolation that can be experienced by practitioners who serve families that need a wide range of community services was not found here. Rather, the brokering of services within the center itself becomes an experience of shared responsibility for the families' care and service: "I have a whole center to back me up." Preventive program workers consistently acknowledge the support of their center colleagues' expertise and guidance. That these programmatic and collegial supports are balanced with a mutual respect for competence and a comfortable degree of staff autonomy assures professionals' complementary needs are met: freedom to do one's best work, while at the same time, "you know your back is always covered." There is no question that within the context of this supportive professional community the professionally and personally committed, flexible, tenacious, and competent preventive program's staff members are central to the model's implementation.

The focus on the family as the unit of attention also strongly appeals not only to families but also to staff. Many staff members highlighted the congruity of the center's philosophy with their own personal and professional philosophies and values. The program's focus on the family is again uniquely supported by the comprehensive service resources of the center. Workers can, as one described, "write a prescription" for services for various family members—services such as the center's employment program, after-school child care program, and the wide range of performing arts and recreational programs that encourage developmentally appropriate engagement with peers, professionals, and others in the community. Thus, at the same time that family members are engaged in therapeutic and problem-solving efforts with a preventive services program worker, other center services to which they have been referred supplement these efforts with important challenges and supports to their individual developmental tasks.

Other key characteristics of the preventive services model echo the methods used in the Minneapolis–St. Paul Family-Centered Project over forty years ago (Overton and Tinker 1957; Compton 1981). These parallels do not detract from the innovative nature of the center's preventive service program, but rather underline both the feasibility and the productive nature of serving families through a program with these key characteristics. For example, the "one-family-one-worker" concept was central to the family-centered project and is central to the center's preventive services program model. Compton, in "revisiting" the family-centered project, asserts that to be helpful to families

> we must work to maintain and or restore the family's sense of competent control of its own destiny. To be helpful, the case management concept needs to be viewed as supplying the family with a "captain of a helping team" in which the case manager carries the central involvement with the family helping them to continuously regulate the forces that cross their boundaries and to evaluate the impact of such services. . . . Case management can work only if it is seen as a brokering, mediating, caring, and advocating service for the family to be used by this one central worker with full and continuing participation of the family. (p. 6)

Other striking parallels to these two successful models evaluated at an almost fifty-year interval should also be acknowledged. These include what Compton calls "the stance of the worker" as "hopeful, open, honest, concerned and actively accepting" (p. 9). She further notes, in words that very much parallel those used by the center families to describe their workers, that "active acceptance means an active search for the strength of the client: an active seeking to understand the position and feelings of the client; *not just a refusal to judge*" (p. 10; emphasis ours). Other parallels include the heavy emphasis by both staffs on the client and worker being active partners in the process, the acceptance of the role of the worker in meeting dependency needs in the service of enhancing interdependence and independence, and the willingness to devote "an inordinate amount of time" (p. 9) to serving families. Finally, Compton notes that in the family-centered project "families riddled by pathologies of all kinds were able to make tremendous gains in social functioning without the workers addressing themselves, even by implication, to the pathology." She continues, in a description uncannily similar to one accurate for the center prevention workers, "The FCP workers addressed themselves not to illness but to the strength of people, not to internal conflict but to active coping with the social problems of their lives, not to client change but to change in the interaction between systems, and things happened" (Compton 1981:17). The practice principles underlying the Center for Family Life's approach to preventive services are firmly grounded in social work practice, both historically and in the present, and warrant broader application and continued study in these times, when brief and increasingly specialized service models are highly valued. As emphasized in this chapter, we found that the needs and problems of the families served by the preventive program are complex, extensive, and significantly reflect the effects of poverty. Many of the 189 study sample families' psychosocial problems were also severe: in almost two-thirds (65.1 percent) of the families, at least one caregiver, child, or environmental problem was identified by the family's preventive program worker on the FAF as requiring immediate intervention to prevent placement. Yet, despite the extent and severity of many families' problems, the preventive program services had addressed the majority of their service needs. Perhaps of greatest interest is the finding that out-of-home placement was prevented in almost all (97 percent) of the total study sample families. Moreover, placement was prevented in 96 percent (118) of the 123 study sample families identified over time by the family's worker as having at least one caregiver, child, or environmental problem requiring immediate intervention to prevent placement. In addition, in those five families in which a child's or adolescent's placement was necessary, the family continued to receive supportive and therapeutic services from the center.

As noted previously, inherent in the program's flexibility is the option for long-term service. The results of the longer-term services could not, however, be fully evaluated through this study. Even at thirty months the data collection phase was too brief to capture the services provided and service results to over half the study families who continued to receive services in the program at the study's conclusion. Of the ninety-seven families' cases still receiving services at the study's end, over half (53 percent) had received twenty-two or more months of service. As described, families receiving services for longer periods of time differed from those receiving briefer services with regard to the nature and number of problems and to service need. It does appear that those study sample families who as self-referred clients voluntarily accessed preventive program services repeatedly over many years have actively joined with center staff in preventing the escalation of their families' problems and thus preventing family breakup. It is difficult to disregard the extent to which placement was prevented in a study sample with families experiencing such chronic and severe difficulties.

In a discussion of family support and the prevention of child maltreatment, Garbarino (1987) asks, "Who has custody of the children?" He suggests that the "answer most likely to preserve and protect children while supporting and encouraging parents is to say that parents and the community have joint custody," offering "a level of community commitment to child welfare that children in high-risk families cannot live without" (p. 112). Our findings regarding the results of the Center for Family Life's preventive program services support the wisdom of locating, developing, and maintaining a continuum of comprehensive, continuously accessible services in the community for families who either self-identify or are recognized by others as needing such services. Through its preventive services program and the program's integral connections to the center as a whole, the center offers families an opportunity for shared responsibility and success in parenting and offers the field a programmatic model for preserving and supporting families over time.

4

THE CENTER'S NEIGHBORHOOD FOSTER CARE PROGRAM

■

In March 1988 the Center for Family Life admitted the first two children into its neighborhood foster care program. This program is an extension of the center's mission to sustain children in their own homes. At the time of the program's establishment, Sister Mary Paul asserted that " 'we are determined to make foster care an integral part of the neighborhood and a form of family support' " (Lerner 1990:14). The program's objectives are to maximize foster family care as a resource for protecting children while "offsetting trauma that follows radical ruptures of bonds with parents, relatives, school, friends or other primary attachments" (Janchill 1997:1). Proximity of the foster home to the child's family facilitates frequent visiting and ongoing parent involvement with foster parents while the center provides the child and the family the intensive preventive program services described in chapter 3. Thus the center staff and foster parents are able to assist families in resolving the difficulties that resulted in the need for a placement while helping the child maintain his or her neighborhood relationships.

In addition, the foster family's geographic proximity to the child's family facilitates the foster family's continued active support of the child and family when reunification is achieved. Upon the child's return to his or her family, all center services continue to be available as needed over time. In some instances the child cannot be returned home safely; adoption or long-term care with the foster family then become options through which the child's relationships with family, friends, and significant others in the neighborhood can be maintained.

Sister Mary Paul reported that for many years she and Sister Geraldine had tried to interest a foster care agency in providing homes that could function as "satellites" of the center, using the center's comprehensive family support and clinical services to assist families in achieving family reunification. When the decision was made to expand center services to include neighborhood foster family care, the license issued to St. Christopher-Ottilie, the center's parent organization, for its foster care activities covered the foster care homes.

Since the center opened its neighborhood foster care program, it has served 146 children in 77 families. Many of these families are still receiving center services. At any point in time the foster care program has about 20–25 children in care in 10–15 foster family homes. This number represents only approximately 10 percent of the children in Sunset Park who are placed in out-of-home care (Citizen's Committee for Children of New York 1999). Since New York City has not taken the family address as a criterion for selection of a foster care provider until recently, Sunset Park children typically have been placed in care outside the neighborhood.

KEY CHARACTERISTICS OF THE CENTER'S NEIGHBORHOOD FOSTER CARE PROGRAM

SERVING FAMILIES IN THE NEIGHBORHOOD

The defining characteristic of the neighborhood foster care program model is its geographic location. Only children from the Sunset Park community are accepted into care and only foster families from the neighborhood are licensed for the center's program. When the neighborhood foster care program was established, the center was immediately recognized as "a pioneer organization in providing neighborhood foster care worthy of being copied" (Lerner 1990:49). Within a year after the opening of the program, the Foundation for Child Development funded a study of the center's new foster care program model. The foundation subsequently published a monograph that examined the provision of foster care services within New York City, the rationale for and characteristics of the center's model, and the "compelling reasons for moving toward community-based foster care" (ibid.).

The location of foster care in the Sunset Park community has a number of tangible benefits for children and families, including the reduction of trauma to children at separation by maintaining important neighborhood relationships—those with their parents, relatives, school, friends, and other primary attachments. Neighborhood foster care with the goal of family reunification also facilitates immediate services to all family members, access to all services within the Center for Family Life and the community, frequent visitation between the child and other family members (at least weekly), and services provided by the foster parent to the child and his or her parents. For example, foster parents join with agency staff in the assessment of the parents' capacity to manage the child and how best to negotiate ongoing parent-child contact. Foster families and the parents of the children in their homes arrange visits together, informally and flexibly. Sister Mary Paul has noted that only in a few situations has there been the need for a worker to be involved in supervising visits.

Other benefits of neighborhood foster care include the increased likelihood of ethnic, racial, and cultural matches that enhance continuity and understanding in the children's care. Neighborhood-based care also assures the accessibility of after-care services to children and their families by both center staff and the foster parents for an indefinite period of time (Janchill 1997; Lerner 1990). In addition, Lerner emphasizes that

> even if one looks at placement from the cold perspective of economy, efficiency, and logistics, it makes sense for social workers and clients to be in the same community. For one thing it cuts down on the time and expense of inter-borough travel. Neighborhood foster care is also more efficient in the deployment of social workers because it permits one social worker to monitor an entire family. Under the current system that divides some sibling groups among a number of agencies, not infrequently several social workers must be assigned to a single family. Given the shortage of social workers, the weight of their caseload, and the critical choices they must make on where to focus their energies, this duplication of effort is tragically wasteful. (1990:12)

Implementing neighborhood-based foster care, however, has been challenging. Public agency placement workers typically have not taken geography into account in placement decisions. Within the first year of program operations, 45 percent of all referrals to the center's foster care program came from sources other than the public child welfare agency (Lerner 1990:38). The Administration for Children's Services (ACS) has included among its recent reforms the initiation of a neighborhood-based system of child welfare services. Sister Mary Paul noted that "there seems to be an increased commitment [by ACS] to preventive services and a reduction in foster care throughout the city. But in terms of the city's very limited utilization of our neighborhood foster care program, I have no way to know whether the city is making foster care referrals by community district." To illustrate, in 1999 only one new referral for the center's foster care program came from ACS. The child was reunited with the parents within two months and subsequently received services through the center's preventive services program. By October 2000 only one new referral had been received from ACS. In this case the children were reunited with their parents within three days and also subsequently received services through the center's preventive services program.

Recruiting Foster Parents Committed to Preserving Family Relationships

In a recent description of the neighborhood foster family care program, Sister Mary Paul noted that the center seeks foster parents who are committed to family reunification and "strengthening of parent-child relationship, rather than rescue of a child as the totality of purpose" (1997:2). She further stressed,

> We seek foster parents who can understand and support parent-child bonding needs and who can provide empathic support to parents who have to conquer dysfunctional behaviors or particular stressors. In turn, foster parents are regularly in contact with the center's assigned clinical social worker and participate in joint planning. Foster parents and birth parents are strongly encouraged to maintain a friendship which may continue beyond the time of placement. (ibid.)

Sister Mary Paul emphasized that working with families in the community can be continuous work in that the geographic location of the foster family home accelerates the level of contact feasible between the agency and the family as well as between the child in care, the child's family, and the foster family. She stated,

> Neighborhood care is less frightening and difficult for the foster mother. She sees the parents in the neighborhood. There is a different level of knowing between foster parents and parents that reduces the adversarial posture. It reduces the bitterness on the part of the child's parents and reduces the fear on the part of the foster parents.

Comprehensive, Community-Based, Family-Centered Services During and After Placement

All the center's services are available to children in neighborhood foster care and their families on an "open-ended" basis during and following the child's placement. In discussing the services to families with a child in care, Sister Mary Paul emphasized "We would never say to a family, 'We're here until the day you leave foster care.' It really is opened-ended. We have to be careful not to infantilize, not to have people dependent on us, not to say, 'Now you're going to need us for another year.' We don't define that for them." She continued, "Whether it's long-term or shorter-term, professionals sometimes minimize the significance of joining families in the very heart of their struggles—in the very heart of it. It's important to be fully present to that family, not available in some legalistic framework of timing."

During our study, we followed the services provided to a family whose initial referral in 1992 by the public child welfare agency had been for neighborhood foster care for a seven year old. The services provided to this family over a five-year period illustrate the open-ended approach to services during and following placement. The child's mother described a personal history of childhood abuse and neglect and fear that she was or would become mentally ill and might commit suicide. The father acknowledged heavy use of drugs and alcohol. After three months in a neighborhood foster home, the child and mother were reunified with the agreement that both parents, who were divorced, would continue to work with the center, using individual and joint counseling. In addition, the parents agreed to permit their child to participate in individual work and a weekly therapy group. In our first interview about this family's experiences with the center, which occurred about one year after the child had been reunified with her mother, Sister Mary Paul described the following dilemma:

> For the long term, I find the proper path in this case very confusing. It's a question of the right institutional arrangements. As the child gets older, it will get harder and harder. It's a chronic situation that will require long-term management in some service system for years to come. Some would say this is a mentally ill woman and you are trying to manage without sufficient medical resources. And yet, I don't feel there is another institutional setting for which we could advocate that would really work long term from a practical point of view . . .

> We've continually thought about hospitalizing her. We've had a psychiatric evaluation and on that day there was no pathology evident. At another time, a psychiatrist who saw her said the child should be removed and she should be hospitalized. The changes in her status are dramatic.
>
> If we were to take the responsibility to hospitalize her on a given day, she would most likely, based on our experiences in other cases, be discharged in a day. And with what gain? She would likely feel that she had lost the anchor of the agency. What would replace the resources and relationships of our agency for her? The hospital would not share the parenting of her child. . . .
>
> We've also considered foster placement, although everything we know about this case suggests that this is a long-term issue. Foster care won't work long-term for a seven-year-old, because the system is not set up that way.
>
> Somewhere this mother and child are going to need help for a long time to come. If not at our agency, they will need it in another. The mother is working with us and attached to the agency. The child is fundamentally important to this mother, and the child needs her mother. They are attached to each other. But when she really decompensates, it is pretty glaring. When the worker says, "This is what happened today," it doesn't feel very good. Many of us contribute to the management of the risk. But we're taking chances. (Hess 1995:69)

Several months later the child was placed for a second time with the same Sunset Park foster family in the center's foster care program. During the placement, services included individual counseling with the child's mother, the child, and the child's father; counseling with the parents together; counseling with the child and each parent; planning and when necessary supervising separate visits with the mother and the father; and referral of the child to other center services, including a latency aged girls' group, after-school child care, and summer day camp. The father was referred to and completed residential treatment for substance abuse. As he began to maintain himself as drug free, he was permitted daylong visiting on the weekends. In his individual counseling sessions he began to talk with the worker about his life experiences, including his childhood as an orphan, the effects of his wife's mental illness on him and on their marriage, his work, and his other interests. Gradually his parenting became more adequate, and he and his daughter became closer.

The worker stated that, as services progressed, the child became more verbal. During a visit with her mother she was "able to tell her mother 'I want to live with my father.' She didn't even ask for my help or my presence, I was just sitting outside the room during the visit." It was becoming clear that the father would be able to provide the consistent parental care that the mother was not yet able to provide.

Subsequently, planning for the child's return to the father progressed. The worker noted that

> at one point I had to say, "Do you want to take your daughter or not?" For a long time I wasn't sure he was ready. We made tentative time lines, like from November to June, focusing on what he had to do—find an apartment, buy the furniture, work out child care, arrange visiting between his daughter and his wife.

Discussions between the worker and the father also focused on the shifts in center services that could occur following reunification:

> We discussed timing on the day that the father got his apartment, and we could seriously plan for his daughter's return to him. I said, "I just want to let you know that what usually happens is that you go to court, and, after a few weekends with your daughter spending the weekend, we'll try a trial discharge. The day is coming soon that you will not need to meet with me." And you could just kind of see his face, like his life was back again somehow. He would be the captain of his ship.

The child was reunified with her father in the spring of 1996. The father was living with his mother, who assisted in the child's care. The center continued to provide services through the preventive program to the child, the father and his mother, and the child's mother. Later that year the mother and father reunited, with center services continuing. Toward the end of 1997 the center and the family agreed that preventive program services were no longer needed. In a conversation with Sister Mary Paul in late 2000, she noted that "we see the child periodically in the neighborhood, and we know that she is doing very well." Thus, through the availability of neighborhood foster family care—providing the same foster family for both placements—and of continuous services following both reunifications, the center was able to provide intensive individualized services to this family. In this situation, as in many others, the foster family also has maintained contact with the child and the child's family, providing additional support. Being there, as

Sister Mary Paul stressed, "through the ups and downs," the center staff members and foster family provided services that culminated initially in a reunification between the child and her father and, later, between the parents as well.

Program Results

Results for Sunset Park families. Of the 146 children served in the center's foster care program, 128 have been discharged from care. Seventy-two percent (102) of those discharged have been reunified with their parents or with other family members. This compares with an average 60 percent discharge to reunification throughout New York City between 1991 and 1997 (Citizens Committee for Children of New York 1999:143). Twenty have been adopted. Of those adopted, 12 were adopted by the neighborhood foster family that provided care and 8 were adopted by another family. Six children were transferred to another agency.

All 18 children in care in late 2000 had been in care for some time. Sister Mary Paul noted that 13 of them had either been or were being freed for adoption. Eight children in two sibling groups were to be adopted by family members, 2 others by the neighborhood foster family that provided their care, and 3 by families that could meet their special needs. Due to the serious nature of their parents' incapacities, the other 3 children in care at that time were expected to continue in long-term neighborhood foster care with extensive ongoing contact with their families.

While in care in the center's neighborhood foster care program, only 13 of the 146 children were placed in more than one foster home. Of these, Sister Mary Paul identified 3 who had been transferred to another neighborhood foster family in order to reunite siblings; 4 had been transferred to another home in the neighborhood that could better meet their special needs. Six were transferred to a foster family home or residential facility that could better meet their special needs. None of the 149 children was placed in more than two homes prior to discharge.

In our study data were collected regarding services to families with children in the center's foster care program through interviews with center administrators and social workers serving families with a child in care. In those instances in which a child in one of the 189 study sample families (six children in five families, as reported in chapter 3) entered care in the center's foster care program or another program or facility, case-specific data were collected through the same methods as described in chapter 3 for all study sample families. The services provided to these families were described in chapter 3. For undetermined reasons, the city referred few new cases to the center's neighborhood foster care program during the study period (1993–1996), thereby limiting the number of foster care cases included in the study sample.

Neither the center nor the research team has had access to the public child welfare case data required to determine the long-term outcomes for children served through this program (i.e., whether further reports of abuse/neglect were made, whether children reentered care, etc.). However, placement history data for about eleven thousand children admitted to foster care for the first time in 1990 from the Child Care Review Service (CCRS), New York's automated child tracking system, are available (Wulczyn 1996:201). From these data, findings regarding foster care admissions and discharges by poverty rate for first placements of children occurring in the 1990 calendar year were provided to the authors by Fred Wulczyn, who noted that these findings suggest children from Sunset Park "do have a different experience" (personal communication).

As presented in table 4.1, only 12.9 percent of the children from Sunset Park were still in care after four years, compared with 34.0 percent of children from communities with a lower poverty rate than Sunset Park and 37.9 percent of children from communities with a higher poverty rate. Children from Sunset Park were much more likely to be discharged from care before one month (27.4 percent versus 17.4 percent and 14.0 percent) and before twelve months (70.2 percent vs. 42.2 percent and 38.3 percent). These data do not distinguish between children from Sunset Park placed in the center's neighborhood foster care program and those placed elsewhere in the city. However, it should be noted that families with a child placed elsewhere might have received preventive program and/or other services from the center either during or subsequent to their children's placement.

Although a specific relationship between these placement outcomes and a families' participation in the center's foster care, preventive program, and/or other family support programs cannot be established, these data suggest that there are variables operating in the Sunset Park children's experiences that are contributing to more frequent and earlier discharge outcomes than those experienced by children from other New York City neighborhoods.

TABLE 4.1

Admissions and Discharges by Poverty Rates for Children with First Placements in 1990: Comparison of Sunset Park with Communities with Lower and Higher Poverty Rates

	Lower Poverty Rate		Sunset Park		Higher Poverty Rate		Total	
Admitted to care	3,751		124		7,304		11179	
Still in care, 2/1994	1,277	34.0%	16	12.9%	2,768	37.9%	4,061	36.2%
Discharged from care	no.	%	no.	%	no.	%	no.	%
Before 1 month	652	17.4	34	27.4	1,019	14.0	1,705	15.3
Before 3 months	325	8.7	25	20.2	633	8.7	983	8.8
Before 6 months	329	8.8	11	8.9	562	7.7	902	8.1
Before 12 months	274	7.3	17	13.7	575	7.9	866	7.7
Before 18 months	222	5.9	10	8.1	455	6.2	687	6.1
Before 36 months	553	14.7	10	8.1	985	13.5	1,548	13.8
After 36 months	119	3.2	1	0.8	307	4.2	427	3.8

Source: Wulczyn 1996.

Results with regard to program replication. In 1992 the Annie E. Casey Foundation announced its Family to Family initiative. The initiative has a number of systemwide goals, the first of which is "to develop a network of family foster care that is more neighborhood-based, culturally sensitive, and located primarily in the communities where the children live" (*Family to Family: Reconstructing Foster Care* 1998). Family to Family was developed in consultation with community leaders, with national experts in child welfare, and with public agencies in the states of Alabama, Maryland, New Mexico, Ohio, and Pennsylvania, five counties in Georgia, Los Angeles County, and New York City.

When the foundation staff learned the Center for Family Life had developed neighborhood foster family homes as part of its broader family support efforts in the Sunset Park community, they visited the center, spoke with Sister Mary Paul and Sister Mary Geraldine, and toured the community with them. John Mattingly, senior consultant with the foundation, noted that

the center's focus on supporting families, including families caught up in the child welfare system, seemed to be a good fit with staffs' experience of what works best to keep families together safely. The center's development of a small neighborhood-based foster family network to help families reunify safely and in a timely manner fit with the foundation's belief that major changes were necessary in the nation's foster care system—changes that were family-centered and at the same time neighborhood-based.

Mattingly further noted that, with this in mind, the center was brought into the Family to Family initiative to "serve as a guiding light as to what good practice in reformed child welfare systems needed to look like on the front lines—to model this practice for sometimes skeptical public child welfare administrators." Through this initiative, leaders from child welfare systems as far away as New Mexico, Alabama, Maryland, Georgia, and Pennsylvania have visited the center, spending days and evenings learning what neighborhood-based, family-centered practice looks like.

The permanence achieved for almost all the 146 children served by the center's neighborhood foster care program by either family reunification or adoption since its creation in 1988 attests to the model's possibilities. It is a poignant irony that this program continues to receive few referrals for placement from the local public child welfare agency and yet is widely recognized and emulated nationwide.

5

SUPPORTING FAMILIES, BUILDING COMMUNITY, AND DEVELOPING CHILDREN AND YOUTH: THE COMMUNITY SCHOOL PROGRAMS

■

> Some of the kids whom I met in that first year [1982] are people who have grown up to become the staff of the center. The little boys who were in the second grade group are now men and the staff of the center . . .
>
> One of the teens we've really struggled with said to me the other day, "I want to be like you when I grow up." He always teases, so I said, "Sure." He said "No, I am serious. They're going to call me Billie Brockway." The day before we had had a sort of intimate discussion about his family situation and what was really going on with him. I have always been very demanding with him, and he comes back because he wants those demands. So then he said, "I mean it. I think I want to have a center for kids." I think you build those hopes and possibilities, but you have to stay with them. Would I be thrilled if he accomplished it and took my role? Yes, indeed. . . . I always say to the kids, "You go on with your studies, you will always have a place here. You can do your high school internships here. You can do your college internships here. You can do whatever you want to do here and we'll promote that."
>
> Julie Brockway, program director,
> Life Lines community arts project at Middle School 136

Establishing a partnership with the Sunset Park schools was a critical component of the directors' original plan for the center. The agency's first community school program opened within a year of the center's establishment, in 1979. It is located at P.S. 1, a large public elementary school in School District 15.[1] A sec-

[1]Another elementary school program was opened at P.S. 172 in 1980, but it was closed in 1985 to concentrate center resources and open a full-time after-school program at P.S. 1, a larger school. Prior to that time neither program could remain open five days a week because of limited staff resources.

ond community school program, opened in 1983, is located at P.S. 314 in School District 20, another of Sunset Park's five elementary schools. The center's third program for students in grades 6–8 was opened in 1990. It is located at Sunset Park's only school for this age group, Middle School 136.

The three community school programs are a direct reflection of the Center for Family Life's philosophy of service and an integral part of its program operations. Approximately twenty-six hundred youths and almost six hundred parents participate in one or more of the community school program activities each year. In this chapter we describe the various components of the center's community school programs, drawing upon the perspectives of both participants and staff with regard to the program's benefits.

The center's commitment to these programs derives from the knowledge that public schools, together with the family and community, have a critical influence on current and future youth functioning. (See, for example, Dryfoos 1990, 1994; Comer 1996.) Yet schools are frequently defined as the private province of school personnel and function to isolate children from the multiple relationships with older youth and adults in the community that could support their healthy development. Hence, similar to the settlement houses of old, the community school programs are designed to serve as places where youth and adults of different ages and from diverse ethnic, religious, and socioeconomic backgrounds can come together to engage in a range of normalizing and mutually enriching activities. The overall goal of the programs is to support individual, family, and community development through processes of mutual engagement and activity.

The two elementary school programs at P.S. 1 and P.S. 314 offer a similar range of services. These include after-school child care for elementary school children, tutoring, summer day camp, teen evening centers, parent councils, parent groups and workshops, and English as a Second Language (ESL) classes. In addition, under a program entitled Youth to Work (formerly Project Youth), the center provides comprehensive youth development services to the teenagers who serve as counselors-in-training (CITs) in the community school programs at P.S. 1 and P.S. 314. The CITs volunteer to work with younger children in the center's two after-school child care programs and in its two summer camp programs. Youth to Work itself has three main components: mentoring by individual staff members, tutoring for those who need extra academic help, and family life and sex education groups.

FIGURE 5.1

An outdoor performance at a community festival by students in an after-school program at P.S. 314

Because of the ages of the youth involved, the community school program at Middle School 136 is somewhat different; it builds on a strategy that introduces group work and the arts into the classroom to improve student achievement, creating cohesive units of teachers and youth.

The Life Lines community arts project at Middle School 136 has five key components:

1. an in-school arts partnership with teachers and students that provides interdisciplinary learning projects aimed at integrating the arts, community services, and social group work into formal academic instruction;
2. a five-day-a-week after-school arts program and summer arts camp that provide instruction in dance, acting, vocals/rhythm, visual arts, creative writing, photography, and computer skills, along with special events, exhibitions, and three annual original productions;
3. traveling theater and dance troupes that are trained to conduct interactive workshops and performances on family and commu-

nity issues for children, parents, senior citizens, and professionals in the New York area;

4. an internship and mentoring program that offers volunteer work experiences, as well as individual academic and personal support, for high school and college students;
5. a parent participation and leadership program that includes a parent advisory council, parent-youth arts events and projects, family cultural outings, and volunteer support for annual productions.

In 1998 the center was designated the lead arts agency for a grant to Middle School 136 from the Center for Arts Education, commonly known as the New York City Annenberg Challenge for Arts Education.

These community school programs were formerly under the overall direction of the center's codirector, Sister Geraldine, but each had a separate program director. They are now under the supervision of the center's codirector, Julie Brockway, who also directs the Life Lines community arts project. The three program directors are professional social workers who are long-term employees of the center. They are assisted by 4.5 full-time equivalent social workers and 9 full-time and 7 part-time professionals in art, drama, dance, music, education, and sports. The community school programs also employ college students as unit leaders, assistant teachers, and performing arts specialists. In addition, many high school youth work as assistant unit leaders and summer camp counselors. The staff is supplemented during the summer months by approximately 200 teenagers who participate in the center's Summer Youth Employment Program and work as CITs in the two summer camp programs.

The average daily attendance at the community school programs during the 1997–1998 school year was 815. The total annual budget for these programs for the same fiscal year was approximately $1.2 million. This indicates an average annual cost of approximately $1,472 per daily participant, but actual costs are much higher for those receiving intensive service, such as daily after-school child care, and lower for participants in activities that are offered less frequently and require less staff time, such as Teen Center. Program funding is derived primarily from contracts with the New York City Department of Youth and Community Services. These funds are supplemented by a grant from the Department of Employment for the Summer Youth Employment Program (SYEP) and matching funds from the New York State Department of Social Services and the New York City Administration for Children's Services (ACS; formerly the Child Welfare Administration). In addition, approximately one third of the total is supported by private funds derived from foundation grants and contributions.

KEY COMMUNITY SCHOOL PROGRAM CHARACTERISTICS

Many of the characteristics identified as central to the nature of the preventive services program also emerged as critical to the success of the community school programs. These include the *holistic nature of the services*, the *close coordination and integration of staff members*, the *continuity and long-term involvement of staff and clients* in the program, *dynamic professional leadership*, a *strong common conviction about program mission* expressed by all staff members, *emphasis on client and community empowerment*, and *flexibility* in adapting to changing individual and community needs. However, there are additional characteristics that particularly contribute to the success of this program. These characteristics can be detected to varying degrees in each of the community school's multiple program activities.

Intergenerational Integration

One central theme is the heavy emphasis on age integration and parental and community involvement with youth in addressing the developmental needs of Sunset Park's children and teenagers. As the former director of the program at P.S.1, Tom Randall, commented:

> This aims to be a community enterprise where we try to engage the kids who come to the after-school program, their parents, their older siblings, and other teenagers in the community, and we try to build in, through special events or special activities, ways in which they can interact so they will see themselves as members of an intergenerational community.

Developmental Focus

A second core characteristic is that program activities are designed to meet the developmental needs of children and youth. As described by John Kixmiller, program director, at P.S. 314 and Helene Onserud, director of Project Youth at P.S. 1, in a paper presented to a national group work conference:

FIGURE 5.2
A counselor-in-training (CIT) teaching children in an after-school program

In order to have normal social development, children need to have a context in which they can play, as well as acquire and practice the skills that will allow them to gain mastery and feel competent in the accomplishment of various tasks. They need to do this in the company of a group of peers with whom they can identify, form relationships and interact freely. . . . It makes sense, from the point of view of personality development, to ask adolescents in the early teen years to begin to contribute and to function as staff. It also makes sense from the perspective of the children that their role models be young people with whom they can identify in terms of their cultural, ethnic, and community background. Therefore, the school-age childcare program is staffed by young adults and older teens in the community who work part-time, and by younger volunteers. In this context their training and development as staff are viewed as part of age appropriate activities. A community center organized in this way supports the passages from childhood to adolescence and from adolescence to adulthood and makes them highly visible to the whole community. (Kixmiller and Onserud 1995:13–15)

Use of Performing Arts

A third distinguishing characteristic of the community school programs is the extensive use of performing arts as a means of encouraging individual self-expression and meaningful group action. Julie Stein Brockway, director of the Life Lines community arts project at Middle School 136 noted: "My vision . . . has always been the use of arts to create community." The other program directors and the staff frequently cite her leadership in developing a service model that emphasizes the use of group performing arts activities to build cooperation and self-esteem, teach new ways of learning, and provide fun for the youth participants. Group public performances at each of the schools also serve to engage large segments of the community. According to John Kixmiller,

> Performing arts is the integrative program activity because everybody does it. And when we do large events, there's always a performing arts component that everybody's involved in, so it ends up being one of the things that pulls everybody else in with it. . . . Events are the greatest organizing tools that we have.

RESEARCH FOCUS AND METHODOLOGY

We focused our research primarily on the community school program at P.S. 314. Although the other two programs are equally successful and interesting, we concluded that given the study's resource limitations, we would probably learn more by focusing in-depth on one of the three community school programs. The selection of P.S. 314 as the primary study site was made in collaboration with the center's directors. This site was selected primarily because the center had been awarded a Beacon School grant by the New York City Department of Youth and Community Services and selected to serve as lead agency in collaboration with other community agencies in developing a year-round program of day and evening activities at P.S. 314. Thus we anticipated that focus on this community school program would give us greater insight into the center's processes of program development than we might have gained at the other school sites. That we studied the Project Youth (now Youth to Work, as previously noted) program in both the P.S. 1 and P.S. 314 school sites is the one exception to this plan. Some program activities for these youth are conducted jointly, and inclusion of the participants at both sites gave us a larger sample on which to base our conclusions.

As discussed in appendix A, we used several qualitative approaches (in-depth focused interviews, focus group meetings, participant observation, and content analysis of letters written by program participants) to learn about the community school project and to capture the dynamics of its various components. In addition, we conducted a telephone survey of a random sample of parents with children in the after-school program (n = 139). This study was conducted in English, Spanish, and Cantonese. Finally, we employed a multimethod approach to examine the impact of Project Youth on the psychosocial functioning of the program participants that included in-depth interviews with staff and participants, focus group meetings with parents and youth, analysis of intake and outcome records, and administration of two rapid assessment instruments at the end of two school years: 1994 and 1995. Because the benefits of after-school child care have been so well documented in the literature, we did not attempt any evaluation of the outcomes of this program. (See, for example, Posner and Vandell 1994; Miller 1995; U.S. Department of Education and U.S. Department of Justice 1998). Instead, we focused on what is somewhat different about the center's program and parental and youth perceptions of the community school services.

OVERVIEW OF COMMUNITY SCHOOL PROGRAM AT P.S. 314

This community school program has five distinct service components: after-school child care for school-aged children, preventive and parent support services, teen center, counselors-in-training (CIT)/Project Youth Program, and summer day camp. Three times a year the program also publishes a community magazine. This magazine is distributed to staff, students, and families of the children, interested community members, and patrons, yielding a total circulation of about eight hundred. It contains pictures of recent events, drawings and articles by children and youth, announcements, and notes from each unit of children participating in the after-school program.

P.S. 314 is housed in a large modern building with extensive indoor facilities appropriate for after-school and weekend programming. These include a large cafeteria, gymnasium, and auditorium. There is very limited outdoor space for recreation. The building is well maintained and conveys an atmosphere of order and cleanliness.

The total enrollment of the school was 1,699 in 1997, which was slightly above capacity. Like other schools in the Sunset Park community, P.S. 314 serves a large proportion of children from low-income Latina/o families and increasing numbers from low-income Chinese immigrant families. In 1996–1997 77 percent of the students were Latina/o, 15.7 percent Asian. 4.5 percent black, and 2.8 percent white. Nine out of 10 (90.7 percent) students were eligible for free lunch, 36.2 percent had limited English proficiency, and 11.4 percent had immigrated to the United States within the past three years. Not surprisingly, many of the children demonstrate a range of academic and learning difficulties as well as many social, emotional, and economic problems.

Given these factors, it is impressive to note that the children at P.S. 314 generally perform close to the New York City mean on standardized tests of language arts and math skills and above the mean on measures of movement toward or attainment of English language proficiency. P.S. 314 is also well above the mean on citywide tests to determine percent of students performing at or above grade level in math and reading in comparison to "similar schools," defined as those with a similar percentage eligible for free lunch and a similar percentage with limited English proficiency (Center for Family Life 1998:54–55).

As indicated earlier, in 1993 the city designated P.S. 314 one of the new Beacon Schools, and the Center for Family Life was named lead agency for this project. The Beacon Schools are school-based community centers established in each of the city's community school districts. Each Beacon center is expected to be open after-school and evenings, six days a week, and offer a range of social service, recreational, educational, and vocational activities designed to meet the needs of the community's children, youth, and adults as identified by the Community School Board and the Beacon School's Community Advisory Council. The lead agency is responsible for working closely with the Community Advisory Council to plan and assess programming and to manage space in nonschool hours, making it available to diverse community groups for meetings and activities.

As a result, in addition to administering its own programs, the center's community school program at P.S. 314 is now responsible for working with a range of agencies to create a six-day-a-week calendar of activities for Sunset Park residents. Other agencies now offering services at the school include the Chinese-American Planning Council, the Discipleship Educational Center, Brooklyn College, the New York City Board of Education, the Boy Scouts, and Lutheran Medical Center. Programs sponsored by these groups include ESL classes, GED classes, teacher training, a men's basketball league, health career and civil service career workshops, weekend sports and performing arts, and tutoring programs. In addition, the center publishes the *Beacon Quarterly*, a newsletter that includes articles about the programs of other agencies at P.S. 314, a calendar of upcoming events, and letters from community leaders. In this chapter we will focus only on the programs at P.S. 314 administered directly by the center.

Population Served

During the 1999–2000 school year a total of 1,943 youth and parents were recorded as participating in the CFL program at P.S. 314. This is most likely an undercount because some of the recreational programs do not maintain regular attendance records. The numbers of participants in different program components and activities during this year were as follows: School-Age Child Care, 476; Summer Day Camp, 397; Summer Youth Employment, 130; Project Youth, 144; CIT Program, 95; Teen Evening Center, 297; Youth Council, 24; Tutoring, 24; Sports Activities (basketball, football, softball, cheerleading), 588; Teen Computer Class, 18; Teen Dance Company, 20; Learning Academy, 38; Parent Advisory Council, 22; and Adult Computer Class, 10. These numbers do not include participation in activities sponsored by other organizations at the Beacon School site.

The demographic composition of the service population is presented in table 5.1. There is, of course, some overlap in the participation in several of these programs. For example, most of the children in the after-school program also enroll in summer camp, many CITs and participants in Project Youth/Youth to Work also attend teen center, and many teen center participants belong to one or more of the sports groups.

It should be emphasized these figures represent annual, not daily, attendance. To illustrate, the after-school program can only handle about 300 children a day, but they allow a total registration of about 350 at any given time because of anticipated daily absences. Also, there is always some turnover in registration during the course of the year because of family moves and changes in parental employment status. The teen center is open to all youth in the neighborhood and has unlimited enrollment. However, there are waiting lists for some of the other programs because of staff and space limitations.

The significant difference in the number of males and females participating in the community school program is due almost entirely to differential participation in teen center and other adolescent activities. Many Latina/o parents have said they prefer to keep their daughters home in the evenings, often expecting them to help with child care and household

TABLE 5.1

Demographic Characteristics of Participants Enrolled in CFL Programs at P.S. 314, 1999–2000 (N = 1,943)

Age Range	Number	Percent
5–9 years	429	22.1
10–13 years	464	23.9
14–16 years	395	20.3
17–20 years	298	15.4
21+ years	352	17.9
	GENDER	
Female	666	34.3
Male	1,277	65.7
	RACE/ETHNICITY	
Asian	158	8.1
Black	196	10.1
Latina/o	1,441	74.2
White	56	2.9
Other	92	4.7

chores. Moreover, there is an interesting difference in the higher proportion of Asian children attending the programs for younger children versus the proportion attending the teenage programs. Many older Chinese youth are expected to work part-time. Otherwise the picture of the program's participants closely resembles the demographic composition of the child and adolescent population of the Sunset Park community.

Service Access and Integration

Since the community school programs are considered "open enrollment" programs, they are open on a first-come, first-served basis to all community residents who meet the age requirements. Although participants may be referred by social workers in other center programs, most families become involved on a word-of-mouth basis. Parents and youth typically hear about the community school services from relatives, neighbors, friends, teachers, or representatives of other community agencies and simply walk in or call to see if they can participate. Similarly, there is no formal case termination process. Youngsters simply discontinue their involvement in program activities when they grow too old, become bored, move, or find other interests.

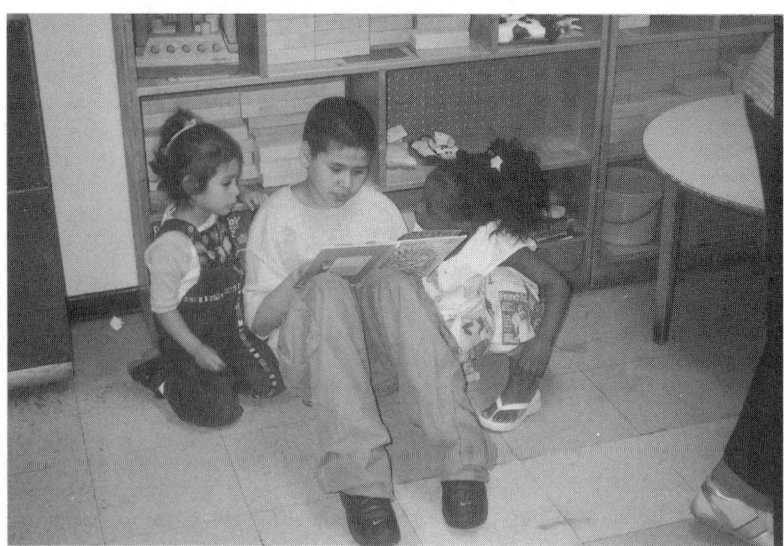

FIGURE 5.3
A volunteer CIT reading to a child in an after-school program

Unfortunately, because of budgetary, staff, and space limitations, the P.S. 314 community school program is now forced to maintain waiting lists for several service components. Potential participants must register almost immediately once applications become available to obtain space in the school-age child care and summer day camp programs. The after-school program has a waiting list of approximately two hundred children at any one time. Youths interested in SYEP are also required to apply almost immediately to obtain one of these slots, and those who want to participate in Youth to Work must often wait until an individual staff mentor becomes available.

Many of the families whose members are engaged in the community school program also receive services either sequentially or simultaneously from other components of the agency. Table 5.2 presents the proportion of all families enrolled in any of the activities at P.S. 314 in the 1994 and/or 1995 calendar years who were identified as receiving services in specific Center for Family Life programs either prior to, concurrent with, or subsequent to receiving services at P.S. 314. It is important to note that these numbers represent total family units. A family is identified as participating if one or

TABLE 5.2

Additional Center Service Use by Families Enrolled in P.S. 314 Activities in 1994 and/or 1995 (N = 702 Families)

Service Program	Percent of Families Active at P.S. 314
School-age child care	42.7%
Summer camp	47.0
Youth recreation/teen center	46.4
CIT program/Project Youth	26.9
Summer youth employment	13.7
Parent program	41.2
ESL Class	2.0
Preventive services	11.7
Advocacy clinic	0.6
Emergency services/Thrift Shop	5.7
Foster care program	0.6
Employment program	2.8

Mean number of services used per family = 2.4, S.D. = 1.6.

more family members were enrolled. If individual family members were counted, the numbers would be much higher because several siblings are often active at the same time.

Organization and Staffing

The community school program at P.S. 314 has a total adult staff of eighteen who carry responsibility in its major service components (School-Age Child Care, Preventive and Parent Support Services, Teen Center, CIT/Project Youth Program, and Summer Day Camp), and assist with publications. The director, a professional social worker trained as a group worker, has been an agency employee since 1983. He initiated this program and continues to play a central leadership role. He is assisted by two social workers, one of whom directs Project Youth and one of whom who coordinates parent programming, three specialists in art, performing arts, and language arts, a Cantonese-speaking assistant in preventive and parent support services, an office manager, and ten unit leaders in the after-school program, several of whom assume other roles, such as part-time security guards and aides in the teen center. In addition, there are fifteen paid youth assistants who assist the unit leaders and the arts and performing arts specialists, and approximately seventy volunteer CITs who help with child care and the organization of children's activities during the course of the year (forty to fifty CITs at any one time). Many staff members are community residents, a sizable number of whom are bilingual Latina/os. Most of the center's paraprofessional staff grew up in the neighborhood; many were former participants in the center's youth programs. The majority of unit leaders, as well as some of the assistant leaders, are college students who work part-time.

As this brief description suggests, this program employs a complex staffing pattern that emphasizes utilization of individuals' various talents and interests. Concerted efforts are made to accommodate the individual needs and school schedules of the youth staff. Perhaps as a consequence, there is relatively low staff turnover and high levels of expressed work satisfaction, loyalty, and pride in the program's accomplishments.

Although the office manager was able to draw a relatively clear organizational chart when we asked her to do so, the program director expressed strong concern about publishing this because he works hard to develop a sense of teamwork and mutual responsibility among all participants. No hierarchical chart, he believes, can convey the flexibility of roles, sharing, and networking that characterizes the flow of work and authority in this program.

Participants' Perceptions of the Community School Program

Perhaps the best overall view of consumers' perceptions of the community school program is conveyed in some data we obtained serendipitously. Late in 1994 approximately 265 residents of Sunset Park wrote letters to Mayor Giuliani in response to his proposed budget for the 1995 fiscal year threatening drastic cuts in funding for the Department of Youth and Community Services. The letters were precipitated by a letter to participants' families from the center's directors explaining the threatened cutbacks and asking for letters of support.

We conducted a content analysis of the letters to identify the reasons the authors offered for continuing support of the community school programs. Table 5.3 presents in rank order the arguments given by parents and other concerned citizens and youth for sustaining funding for these programs. The numbers in the column on the right indicates the frequency with which each reason was mentioned.

TABLE 5.3

Arguments Made by Parents, Children, and Concerned Citizens As to Why the Center for Family Life's After-School Program Should Not Be Closed

In the Words of Concerned Citizens and Parents		
A	The center keeps kids from becoming "latchkey kids" whose working parents can often not afford babysitters.	45
B	The center keeps kids "off the streets."	22
C	Kids are our "future" (therefore the center is an investment).	18
D	"Do it for the kids because they love it."	18
E	The center's program is "educational."	17
F	The center "helps with homework."	14
G	Kids are "safe" at the center.	13
H	The center offers opportunities for kids to participate in recreational activities (sports, theater, art, etc.).	12
I	The center's activities "help reduce the risk of drug use, crime, and violence."	10
J	"It is wrong," "unjust," and "abusive" to cut funding.	7
K	"Parents need the help raising the kids correctly" (that the center provides).	5
L	Kids learn to "respect" one another and themselves at the center.	5
M	The center is one of the few programs for youth in the community of Sunset Park.	4
N	"Parents like what the center does with kids" (parents see improved behavior in the home).	3
O	Kids are learning in a "multicultural" environment at the center.	3
P	Children make new friends at the center.	2
Q	Children should not be punished for the financial dilemmas of adults.	2
R	The center "enhances and provides positive alternatives."	2
S	"For the best of the children"—do not cut funding for the center.	2
T	The center teaches "cooperation."	2
U	The center enhances the academic performances of children.	2
V	The center is especially important for "minority families."	1
W	The center replaces television with education.	1
X	"Tolerance" is taught at the center.	1
Y	The center provides jobs to young people in the community.	1
Z	The center allows parents to meet other parents.	1
A(2)	The center gives parents an opportunity to become more involved.	1

TABLE 5.3 (*continued on next page*)

TABLE 5.3 (*continued from previous page*)

	In the Words of the Children	
A	The center helps with homework/school.	56
B	The center keeps kids "off the streets."	53
C	The center is "fun."	45
D	The center keeps "me"/"us" "out of trouble."	40
E	Kids make a lot of new friends at the center.	28
F	There is nowhere else to "hang out" besides the center.	28
G	The center teaches "us" how to "work with children."	24
H	The center enhances and encourages performing activities (dance, art, drama, sports, etc.).	22
I	Cutting the center's resources would be like destroying an institution or a "tradition": children identify their childhood with the center.	22
J	The elimination of the center's activities would be like "taking down a part of my life": "it's like a second home" or "family."	18
K	Kids can not play safely without the center.	15
L	The center helps "prepare me for the future."	15
M	The center provides child care to parents who often can not afford babysitters while they work or go to school.	14
N	The center teaches "us how to perform on the job."	14
O	The center helps kids develop "confidence."	11
P	"We love the center."	11
Q	The center teaches "cooperation."	10
R	"My parents are proud of me" and "I like the center."	10
S	Kids find people to "trust" at the center.	6
T	The center gives "us"/"me" "role models."	5
U	"Don't take (the center) away from the neighborhood."	4
V	The center keeps "me from watching TV" and "playing Nintendo."	2
W	"People are poor and don't have much—don't take away one thing they enjoy and have."	1

Both adults and teens identified a number of factors that they value about the community school programs. This is not surprising given the wide range of needs the community school programs address. Overall, the adults tended to emphasize the center's child care function, capacity to keep children safe and off the streets, and developmental opportunities. Although the teens also stressed the importance of the center keeping them "off the streets" and the developmental opportunities and educational supports it offers, a number emphasized its socialization functions and the ways in which the center has become a neighborhood institution, a "tradition," "a part of my life," "a second home," "like a family."

The School-Age Child Care and Parent Programs

As discussed by Kixmiller and Onserud (1995:11), the community school program "uses school-age child care as its integrative component and includes several other programs that overlap at various points; this allows for intense participation during the school year on the part of children (15 hours a week), but potentially even more for teenagers (up to 21 hours a week)." Engaging teenagers in volunteer and paid work with the children in the after-school child care program serves several important economic and socializing functions. First, the provision of free after-school care enables many low-income parents to be able to attend school and/or work, which they would not be able to do if they had to pay the full costs of child care. Second, the positions that teens and young adults hold in the after-school program give them a sense of the value of meaningful work and some modest income without interfering with their own education. And, third, the leadership activities performed by the older youth provide role modeling for the school-age children while educating the adolescents about the developmental needs of children and child care skills.

The program provides free child care for elementary school-age youngsters from 3:00–6:00 P.M. during the school year. About 80 percent of the participants are enrolled at P.S. 314 and the remainder attends other elementary schools in Sunset Park. The program is designed primarily for children of parents who are working or attending school or job training during the school day. However, some children are referred by preventive service workers at the center because of an assessed need for child socialization and/or parental relief time.

The after-school program is open during the public school year, closing for most school vacation days and holidays. Summer camp, which is also held at P.S. 314, is open from 8:00 A.M. to 3:00 P.M. daily for six weeks during the summer. There is no child care program for about four weeks from mid-August to mid-September to allow time for staff vacations and training of the youth staff for the coming school year. As a consequence, parents must make alternative arrangements for their children when the program is closed.

At the beginning of the school year, each child is assigned to one of ten units organized by school grade and gender (when age appropriate). The average unit size is about twenty-five, but the units for young children are smaller than those for the older children. Each unit has a leader who stays with the group throughout the school year as well as one or more assistant unit leaders and/or CITs who assist with the supervision of the children.

Each day's activities begin at 3:00 P.M. when children are brought to the cafeteria and greeted by their unit leaders. They know to go immediately to their assigned seating areas where they have light, nutritious snacks. After the children have settled in and finished their snacks, the first of two hour-long activity periods begins (approximately 3:30 P.M.). The children rotate in their assigned units through these activity periods and are picked up by their families between 5:30–6:00 P.M.

The primary program activities are

1. performing arts (preparing and rehearsing for a stage performance involving singing and dancing),
2. language arts (designed to enhance writing and reading skills through use of imagination, arts and crafts, and games),
3. creative arts (preparing sets for stage performances, as well as other arts and crafts projects),
4. homework supervision, and
5. reading (depending on age, children are read to or read by themselves).

The children may also be scheduled for an informal activity period in which they are supervised while they visit quietly, read, color, etc. Each program activity is supervised by an activity specialist who is assisted by youth staff and CITs. All these activities require that the supervising staff attends to the various physical, social, educational, and developmental needs of the children.

The program year is organized in part around preparation for two annual musical performances in which all children participate. These are held in

FIGURE 5.4
Mother and son at the center's storefront center signing youngsters up for summer camp

the school auditorium on a weekend prior to Christmas and on a weekend at the end of the school year. Each production is usually an adaptation of a musical or book (e.g., Aladdin, the Wizard of Oz) and is written, designed, and produced entirely by the children and staff.

The performances are attended by the children's families as well as by other students, local residents, civic leaders, and school officials. The two performances that the researchers attended had packed houses with wildly enthusiastic audiences of four to five hundred children, adults, and elderly relatives. It was interesting to observe the high level of energy, excitement, and interaction among members of the audience, which was primarily Latina/o but also included significant representation from the Chinese community. The performances clearly demonstrated the children's sense of pride in their achievements and strong sense of communal participation. In conjunction with these programs, the community school program also sponsors an annual fair at the school on the Saturday of the Christmas performance and a weekend street fair on the weekend of the spring performance.

These performances not only provide valuable experience for the children and youth participants in working together in a disciplined, collaborative manner toward shared goals, but also help to create a sense of community and give staff meaningful feedback about the value of their work. As Jennifer Zanger, the social worker who directed Project Youth at P.S. 314, commented:

> My favorite time is show time, when the whole community comes together. It just so fills you to see parents and teenagers and kids together. I think the center brings out the most positive things about people. There are so many institutions and bureaucracies that bring out the most negative. It feels really good to be a part of that.

Parent Support Services

Two parent program coordinators work to engage parents and coordinate their activities. Parent participation is viewed by staff as critical to the success of all three community school programs. Since the child care program is free, all parents are expected to donate one hour of time a month. Their contributions vary widely and include making costumes for a show, monitoring activities, assisting behind the scenes at a performance, running an activity at the street fair, helping prepare a post-performance communal meal, selling raffle tickets, and raising money for the Reading Is Fundamental (RIF) program in which books are purchased at very low price and distributed free to the children. As might be expected, a core group of parents participates more actively than others. Some resentment is expressed by this group about the parents who do not contribute regularly. As part of the parent support program, a Parent Council is open to all parents. The council meets monthly to provide input to the staff about how the program is running and allow the program director to discuss new developments with parents. The entire group of parents typically meets first for announcements and is then divided into three subgroups for discussion in English, Spanish, and Cantonese.

A volunteer Parents' Executive Committee defines objectives for parent involvement and support and deliberates ways to ensure this. For example, to encourage increased parental participation, the committee sponsored a contest between the different children's units related to hours of parental participation. The secretary of the executive committee reported to us that they were considering starting some mother-daughter and father-son sports activity nights to encourage greater parental involvement.

In addition to activities designed to increase parent support for youth services, this program component sponsors a series of monthly workshops for parents aimed at enhancing parenting skills and helping with some of the common problems faced by parents in this community, e.g., raising a child in two cultures. The workshops (usually given in English, Spanish, and Cantonese) are led by center staff, school personnel, and outside speakers.

Particular efforts have been made to extend the center's services to the increased number of Chinese immigrant families through cosponsorship with the Chinese-American Planning Council of various social, recreational, educational, and parenting programs at the school and the presence of Cantonese-speaking workers in the parent support program. These workers are available to provide individual and family counseling services to Chinese families as needed.

Parents' Views of the School-Age Child Care and Parent Support Programs

Data collected through focus groups. We convened two focus group meetings (one in English and one in Spanish) with parents of children in the after-school program in the spring and summer of 1994. Although we had planned a series of such meetings, it was difficult for the staff to get a sufficient number of parents to attend them as a result of parents' work and family schedules. Therefore, after two meetings we moved directly to conduct the telephone survey reported below.

The fourteen parents who did attend the group meetings had extensive experience with the program and were uniformly positive. They spoke most enthusiastically about the benefits for their children of participation in the program. Some of the particular advantages they cited were as follows:

- safe, secure child care
- range of activities available to children—plays, art, language skills, sports, etc.
- help with homework and building of academic skills
- development of social skills, including learning how to get along better with other children and adults
- opportunities provided to talk out problems with other adults
- linkages formed between younger and older children

- development of self-esteem through the competencies acquired and frequent praise and support given by staff
- opportunities for developing new friendships, becoming known in community

The parents also spoke quite readily about the benefits they themselves derived from the program. Most important is the help they receive in caring for their children. As a single parent noted:

I'm raising my daughter alone, and when I come here to pick her up, her homework is already done. When we get home . . . I cook something. By 8:00 she's in bed. So then it's my time from 8:00–10:00 P.M. If it weren't for this program, a lot of us would find ourselves in a jam. I think that what helps most is the homework business. Can you imagine us coming here at 6:00, taking them home, and starting to do homework with them at that time?

Equally important to a number of parents is the security they feel about knowing their children are in a safe setting where everyone knows all the youngsters by name. One parent commented, "Any of the counselors, you come in and give the kid's name, and they'll say, 'The big one or the little one?' They know the kids. It's great." Similarly, several parents noted that they had heard bad things about a number of after-school programs in which the children are essentially warehoused. They feel it's different at P.S. 314. "There's a flier when you come in, and it tells you what room your kid's in. You have a right to walk in at any time and see who's taking care of your kid and what they're doing. So it's not like they're hiding or anything like that." In relation to the issue of security, parents also mentioned the importance of knowing that if an emergency arises and they cannot get to the school to pick their children up on time, the children will be taken to the main office of the Center for Family Life at 7:00 P.M.

Although several of the working parents said that they would be willing to pay for this service if necessary, they all commented on the wonder of receiving this help for free. They mentioned that in the summer they pay for baby-sitters after 3:00 P.M., and in the few weeks before and after summer camp the cost ranges from $40 biweekly to $50-$75 a week. The parents also commented on the fact that any fees that are charged for children's costumes or equipment are very low, e.g., $5.00 for a costume.

The parents who attended focus group meetings also spoke at some length about the importance of the work they do for the program and how much they enjoy this. They noted that it was difficult to find the time to volunteer, but felt that the program really tried to accommodate different parents' working schedules and to utilize different parents' skills. "They recognize everybody. . . . And that's what I appreciate. It makes me want to do more." Also, parents find that participation in the program gives them a way to meet other parents and to get to know the staff better.

Another theme identified in the parents' comments was the sense of community derived from participation in the program. Several reported noticing that, since participating in the program, when they walk down the street with their children they find that other children and young adults often seem to be saying hello. One, pointing around the circle, commented: "You know why it's good? It's good because my kids can get to know her kids, and her kids can get to know his kids. . . . They know me. It all becomes a whole family. We're there for everybody."

Finally, several parents highlighted the value of the parenting workshops they had attended and the individual help the program director had given them with specific parenting problems. For example:

> I'm a single father and the program has helped me so much. There are a lot of subjects that us as parents, especially in the Latin community, are afraid to touch upon. We were taught that way, that there are taboo subjects you don't speak about. Here at the center, they prepare the children, and the children come home and make it so much easier for us to deal with. For instance, the other day my daughter was watching an animal show, and there were two chipmunks mating. She asked me what they were doing. My jaw hit the floor. So I went and asked a kindergarten teacher I know. She said that any question my daughter asked, I should answer exactly what she asked and nothing more. Any information she wants, you give her, but nothing more. I came here and spoke with John [the program director]. It was close to the Aladdin show, so he was really busy. He came and sat in the lunchroom and spent a good hour with me having a long talk. I feel funny, a twenty-five year old sitting and talking to a therapist, but I can come here and see John as a therapist. He will listen and listen and in no way put you down. He'll respect you and respect you. He's like that with the children. And the children bring that back home.

The only drawbacks the parents could identify in the program were 1. the 3:00 P.M. closure during summer months, 2. the lack of special resources for children who want to be more challenged academically or physically, and 3. the lack of resources for children who are in special education. These concerns were voiced only after extensive prodding and were stated more as wishes than complaints. Overall, it was clear to us that the parents in the focus groups were very satisfied with the program's operations.

Data collected through telephone survey. In 1995 we also conducted a survey by telephone of a random sample of 139 parents of children who had attended the after-school program. This sample represented 39.7 percent of the 350 parents identified as having children who attended the after-school program that year. While no parent refused to be interviewed, incorrect telephone numbers were listed for 17 percent of the original random sample. Although correct numbers were eventually identified for most of these, other, randomly selected parents were contacted to substitute for those who could not be located. We have no reason to assume this record-keeping difficulty affected the responses we received but were concerned that the program did not give more attention to maintaining current parent contact data. Forty percent of the interviews were conducted in English, 32 percent in Spanish, and 27 percent in Cantonese. Most parents (86 percent) had either one or two children who participated regularly in the after-school program. Almost two-thirds (63 percent) had one or more children who also attended the summer camp program. Although almost one-third (32 percent) reported they had adolescent children, just fewer than 14 percent reported having teenagers who participated in any of the teen programs at P.S. 314.

The majority (71 percent) of these parents were employed, most full-time (thirty-five to forty hours per week), although less than half the Spanish-speaking parents were employed outside the home. Fifteen percent worked over fifty hours per week, and approximately 14 percent of the total sample worked part-time. Chinese parents were overrepresented in the group working the longest hours, accounting for two-thirds of those working fifty to seventy hours per week.

The survey findings confirm the comments of participants in the focus groups regarding the importance of the after-school program as a resource for working parents. They also highlight the important economic and socializing functions served by engaging teenagers in volunteer and paid work with children in the after-school program. The provision of free after-school care enables many low-income parents to be able to attend school and/or work, which they would not be able to do if they had to pay the full costs of child care. Moreover, the positions held by teens and young adults in the after-school program give them a sense of the value of meaningful work.

Survey findings also indicate that parental perceptions of program value are heavily influenced by their cultural backgrounds. To illustrate, parental responses to a question about how the program benefits their children tended to fall into five general categories: assistance with homework, 70 percent; trips and recreation, 65 percent; development of social skills, 58 percent; "good" environment where children can make new friends, build character, and have adult role models, 44 percent; safe, secure environment, 36 percent. Help with homework, the most frequent response, seemed to be of equal importance to all three groups, as were the trips and recreation. However, over half the parents who cited safety as a program benefit were Cantonese speaking and 43 percent of those who emphasized the development of new skills were Spanish speaking. The parents who commented on the beneficial environment created by the program were predominately English speaking (66 percent).

Responses to a question about how the program benefits parents clustered in six general categories. Not surprisingly, the most frequent responses dealt with issues of parental work and security for the children. Seventy percent said that by providing after-school child care the program enabled them to work. This response was more common among the English- and Cantonese-speaking parents than among the Spanish-speaking respondents. Almost two-thirds (63 percent) also commented that the availability of the program made them feel more secure about being away from home. This response was fairly equally distributed among the three ethnic groups.

Four other program benefits were not cited as universally but were very important to some parents. For example, 37 percent, mostly English-speaking parents, emphasized the concept of time, clearly a precious commodity for many parents. They noted that the program gives them time for themselves and their homes, and extra time to spend with their children on activities other than homework. Just over one-quarter (26 percent) said the program helped their children to learn in ways that they themselves could not assist them by providing help with homework and improving English language skills. The majority of parents who cited this benefit were Spanish speaking. One-fourth, primarily Cantonese speaking, emphasized the value of parenting advice they received from staff in the program. A somewhat smaller number (18 percent), mostly English speaking, spoke of the importance of the parental involvement encouraged by the program staff. They emphasized that they enjoyed participating in the children's activities and meeting other parents.

Slightly over half the parents in the sample (56 percent) said they had attended at least one parent program at the school, and many reported attending more frequently. Approximately 21 percent of the Spanish- and English-speaking parents had participated in a formal parenting activity such as ESL classes, parenting workshops, or the Parent Council. A somewhat higher proportion of the total (30 percent) had attended informal activities, such as the shows or street fairs. The Spanish-speaking parents were most likely to report having assisted with these events, whereas the Chinese parents were more likely to have restricted their involvement to attendance at parent meetings. The most common reasons parents gave for not participating in any activities at the school were lack of time, scheduling problems, and responsibility for caring for very young children or children with disabilities at home. When asked what they would do if there were no after-school program, most parents indicated that this would create serious problems for them. The initial response was frequently, "I don't know," followed by some discussion of the specific family problems this would cause, such as the difficulty of finding safe, reliable child care and the financial hardship they would experience. The most common response among Cantonese-speaking parents was that they would have to leave work early to be at home with the children, and this would mean a loss of family income. The Spanish-speaking parents were more likely to say that they would look for a baby-sitter or rely on relatives or friends for child care. A number of parents said they would have to look for another after-school program. Fewer than 10 percent said they would either quit their jobs or leave their children home alone, which indicates that neither of these options were viewed as acceptable by the respondents.

Almost half (47 percent) of the parents reported that they would have to pay for an alternative form of child care if the after-school program were not available. Estimates of what this would cost ranged wildly from a low of $20 per week to a high of $400 per week. Approximately half the sample estimated the cost would be $55 per week or less, 30 percent thought between $55 and $100 per week, and 15 percent guessed more than $100 per week. Most (72 percent) of those who estimated the cost at $50–$100 per week—probably the most realistic figures—were English-speaking. The Spanish-speaking parents were more likely to estimate the cost as less than $50 per week, which may reflect a tendency to rely on relatives or friends for child care. The Cantonese-speaking parents were more likely to estimate over $100 per week, which suggests they may have been thinking of loss of income as part of the cost, as many had said they would have to stay home and reduce their work hours. Unfortunately, the survey did not ask how these cost estimates were made.

Overall, the survey respondents expressed strong satisfaction with the after-school program. Almost half (49 percent) said they would make no changes in the program. Those who made any suggestions for change were interested only in strengthening what is currently available by increasing resources, expanding existing programs, and requiring children to spend more time on homework. The respondents' general comments, like those of the focus group members, tended to be very positive, praising the program as a whole, or specific program activities or staff members, or citing specific benefits to their own children. Criticism was rare and seemed to revolve around security concerns. A few parents commented that they felt the training and supervision of the teenage participants was inadequate. A total of 18 of the 139 parents surveyed (13 percent) had children who had withdrawn from the after-care program, usually because the child did not like the program or there was a specific family problem. Four of these parents, all Cantonese-speaking, withdrew their children because they were not satisfied with the amount of time spent on homework.

In summary, the data from the telephone survey as well as from the focus groups indicate that the after-school program fills an important need in the diverse community that it serves. It not only allows parents to work or attend school but also allows them to feel secure about their children's safety. Further, it provides the academic support and developmental opportunities they want to ensure for their children.

Teen Center

The teen center is a drop-in program at P.S. 314 for adolescents in the community who want a place to socialize and/or engage in activities in the early evening hours. The guiding principle behind teen center, which was viewed as an integral part of the community school program when it was founded, is that youth in the community need free safe public space in which to gather and play. The program was originally open two nights a week from 6:30–9:30 P.M., but expanded to five nights a week when P.S. 314 became a Beacon School. It attracts an average of 80–120 youths a night. The primary activities offered are sports, particularly basketball, and board games, art, dancing, a computer center, and informal rap. The key operating rule is that any youth who drops in must engage in an activity of his or her choosing. No one is allowed just to wander around the building. The adult staff of the after-school program also runs teen center, but many of the CITs attend as participants in the evening program.

A few years ago a troubling incident occurred that was instructive in relation to the way the community school programs operate and evolve over time. A youth who was in the performing arts program at the P.S. 314 teen center was badly beaten up by a group of youth who followed him as he started to walk home. It was later established that the fight had started earlier in a Manhattan club where members of a rap group were performing and felt they had been disrespected by some members of the audience from Brooklyn. Members of this group happened to be at teen center and recognized the youth they beat up as one of those who had been "dissing" them at the concert. Although none of these youth were regular participants of teen center, as a consequence of this incident and a couple of other minor ones, the staff decided to close teen center for a week and to reorganize it on the basis of discussions held first with staff alone, then with CITs, and finally with a wider range of teens.

As a result of these deliberations, a number of programmatic changes were initiated that were supported by the youth members. Participants in the teen center are now required to show an ID card before entering, and staff and teens are encouraged to work closely together and engage in early intervention in order to prevent similar incidents. Special staff training was offered on the topic of teen violence, and the CIT meetings were reorganized so that there would be more staff involvement and focus on topics such as violence. A Youth Council was established parallel to the Parents' Council, and youth and staff organized a joint early intervention effort to prevent future incidents. Also, one issue of *MIX*, the center's youth magazine, was devoted to articles written by youth about this problem.

Unfortunately, the staff and Youth Council members were relatively unsuccessful in getting parents of adolescents to attend meetings on the topic of youth violence or to volunteer as chaperons for a teen dance they wanted to sponsor. However, the youth agreed to help with a family night requested by parents of preadolescent children. The program continues to struggle with the problem of gaining increased parental involvement for adolescents. The program director's interesting observation on this experience is very reflective of his conviction about the importance of providing services that link youth to the larger social community. John Kixmiller, program director, observed:

Of course, parents are very busy, have too much to do and all that. But there are motivations and circumstances beyond the usual necessary to explain this [the difficulty in increasing the involvement of teens' parents]. I think that, to some extent, as frightening as teens find their world, parents find it [equally] frightening to approach . . . and experience it as embarrassing or inappropriate to discuss it publicly. There we find some of the emotional components that go with the current isolation of teenagers in a subculture, the current divisions in social life between adults and teens, and the current social problems of crime, teen pregnancy, etc., that affect this population of marginalized youth.

This view has guided many of the developments in the community school program. The director argues that for healthy development children need a community setting in which to socialize with older youths and adults of all different backgrounds. Yet the public school system has created a series of age-segregated institutions in which youths are essentially forced to create their own subculture. Since this subculture can be destructive and is often frightening, there is a tendency for adults to avoid it rather than seeking ways to influence it. In contrast, the director believes the primary mission of the community school project is to essentially "infiltrate" this subculture and offer youth the range of role models and alternative developmental experiences needed to prevent the social problems common to many communities today.

The Counseling-in-Training (CIT) Program and Project Youth

The counselor-in-training (CIT) program. The initial vision for the community school programs was a combination of after-school child care, teen center, and parent support services. However, the program administrators gradually recognized that they were offering little to early adolescents who were too old for the after-school program but too young to be hired as staff or to take full advantage of teen center. The concept of the counselor-in-training program evolved from this recognition of an unmet need. The program was initially very small, but has expanded rapidly at both P.S. 1 and P.S. 314.

Although most of the current CITs are youth who participated as children in the after-school program, this is not a requirement. To participate as a counselor-in-training, a youth must be twelve to nineteen years old, willing to volunteer at least two afternoons a week, and be sponsored by one of the senior staff or unit leaders who is willing to supervise the CIT on an ongoing basis. Although it is common for leaders to sponsor several CITs who will help them in their work, there is still a waiting list of youths who want to become CITs. Some CITs later become unit leaders or assistants. There is, however, no guarantee that this will happen because those hired in staff roles must be selected on a merit basis.

The CITs' principal responsibilities are to help supervise the children and to assist their sponsors in their primary tasks. For example, a CIT sponsored by the art director might help make props for an upcoming play. One working with the language arts director might help students write a short story. A CIT working with a unit leader might help a child rehearse for the play or read a story to a group of younger children. Often the CITs help to settle arguments or talk with youngsters who are upset about some incident. They thus serve both as apprentices to the older staff and role models for the younger children.

The CITs are all required to attend regular meetings in which they discuss work issues as well as problems of daily living. They are also invited to attend two weekend retreats held at an upstate camp. The retreats, held once in early fall and once in the late spring, are designed to provide training for the youth and emphasize teamwork, leadership, responsibility, and bonding. Since many CITs have never had an opportunity to stay in the country, they experience the overnight retreats as a major benefit of the program.

A key advantage that this program offers participants in addition to socialization and training opportunities is that those who are income-eligible are guaranteed work through the Summer Youth Employment Program in the summer camp program. In addition, each youth who attends the after-school program at least two days a week, has regular school attendance, and earns passing grades receives $40 a semester and a certificate at an awards ceremony held twice each year.

Perhaps the primary benefit this program offers, however, is ongoing contact with and role modeling from the adult staff. The CITs are bombarded daily with opportunities to succeed, guidance, praise, and unconditional regard. They socialize frequently with staff members, whom they respect, as well, and are made to feel they are part of a community that cares about what happens to them. One young adult staff member, a former CIT, described having participated in center activities since she was six, beginning with the after-school program. She reflected upon the staff and CITs being

like big brothers and big sisters to me. I depended on them to help me if something was difficult and I depended on them if I had a problem with the other kids. So they were like the referees, or something, if we had a fight. I depended on them to get me through it. [Participating in the center] shows me how much responsibility I can handle. I shows me that I can do much more things than just being a doctor if I wanted to, and it shows me that people enjoy each others' company, and it shows me that children have a hard time in their lives, and I'd like to do something to help them.

Another former CIT's sense of possibility is reflected in a description of the single most important thing that participation in the counselor-in-training program did:

Kept me in school. I wasn't going to drop out, but I was cutting a lot and I stopped. [If I hadn't been in the CIT program] I would have done bad at home, at school. . . . The social workers, the people who work here . . . I learned from them, I learned from their mistakes. They got some wise people in the center . . . I plan on finishing college.

Project Youth. In the early 1990s the program administrators noted that although the vast majority of CITs handled their responsibilities in the program well, a number were not doing as well as they could academically. Consequently, the center sought foundation funding to support more intensive services for these youths. This led to the establishment of Project Youth, a program that provides mentoring, tutoring, and family life and sex education to the CITs and other youth who want to participate. The program was initiated in 1992 at P.S. 314, and in 1993 at P.S. 1.

Although the original plan was to involve all CITs in Project Youth, a few resisted. Currently, it is estimated that about 98 percent of the CITs participate as well as a few teens who have not been CITs. The goal is to have a total active enrollment of fifty at each site at all times.

To enter Project Youth (now Youth to Work), an applicant must have an individual intake interview with a program coordinator focused on individual and family history, school performance, contacts at home and at school, weekly schedule, and plans for the year. The youngsters at each school are then assigned to one of four small working groups that meet one hour weekly for group discussion focused on family life education and sexuality, school issues, relationships with parents, careers, and other issues. Topics for discussion come from the group and cover such issues as cultural differences, homosexuality, AIDS, youth violence, and death in the family.

The participants are also assigned to mentors, usually staff members who are a little older and have some college education. The mentors are expected to develop relationships and meet individually with each of their assigned youths at least twice a month to discuss their progress, review report cards, and talk about any family or school problems they may be experiencing. The mentors are also asked to refer any youngsters who are having difficulty in school for tutoring. Although the mentor role is viewed as key to program success, the project coordinators who run the discussion groups and conduct the intakes are also available to help the teens with personal or family problems. Since the program coordinators are professional social workers, they often become involved with clinical issues that are too complex for the mentors to address. In addition, referrals are sometimes made to the center's preventive program for family counseling.

The initial response to Project Youth/Youth to Work by both the participants and the staff has been very positive. Self-referrals to the program have increased, and there is a waiting list for enrollment at the beginning of each year. However, it is still a relatively new program and has had to address some expectable start-up problems. For example, some of the older, more experienced CITs were initially quite resistant about participating because they feared the program might violate their privacy and/or remove their cherished status as program volunteers. Also, some who were very successful in their child care roles were uncomfortable about exposing the parts of their lives in which they are more vulnerable, e.g., low school achievement.

Another issue that is still being addressed is the increased demand the mentoring role places on program staff, many of whom are already overextended. Although most mentors find this role very rewarding, some were initially skeptical and hesitant to volunteer for what they viewed as additional work. Also, because all staff members assume many roles in the community school program, it has been difficult for the coordinators to schedule needed group meetings for the mentors. Despite these struggles, the program coordinators report that Project Youth has enabled them to get to know the CITs much better, to learn more about their needs, and to provide more support and guidance to them than was possible in earlier years. Therefore, they believe that the program will ultimately contribute to better outcomes for these teens.

Available data regarding the progress of participants in this program confirm staff observations. To illustrate, two rapid assessment instruments (Hare Self-Esteem Scale and Nowicki-Strickland Locus of Control Scale) were administered to teens in Project Youth in 1994 and 1995, and difference scores were calculated by subtracting the 1994 scores from the 1995 scores. The Hare Self-Esteem Scale is a thirty-item instrument that measures self-esteem of children ten years old and above in relation to peers, parents, and teachers. The sum of these three ten-item subscales provides a general self-esteem measure (Hare 1987). The Nowicki-Strickland Locus of Control Scale is a forty-item instrument that measures "whether or not a child believes that reinforcement comes to him or her by chance or fate (external locus of control) or because of his or her own behavior (internal locus of control)" (Nowicki and Strickland 1987:402–403). To assess program efficacy, the mean scores that 50 of the Project Youth participants obtained on these tests were compared to the mean scores of an age and gender matched sample of junior high school students who participated in an alternative intervention and to the mean scores of an age and gender matched sample of children who did not receive any intervention. Both matched samples were drawn from a pool of children that were followed during the same time period by two of the researchers on this project for a New York State funded assessment of a drop out prevention program in located in Manhattan. The total number for analysis equaled 150.

Table 5.4 presents the mean scores and standard deviations obtained on the psychometric tests by the members of the three groups in 1994 and 1995. This table also includes mean difference scores. Higher difference scores on the self-esteem scales indicate improvement in psychosocial functioning. Lower difference scores in the locus-of-control scale indicate that participants felt more in control of their lives. Superscripts within the table cells denote significant observed differences ($p < .05$) within the test year across the three groups using Scheffe's post hoc testing procedures.

Project Youth participants obtained significantly lower self-esteem scores than did the alternative intervention and control groups on the 1994 administration of the scale. By the second year of testing, however, the teens in Project Youth had equaled or exceeded the self-esteem mean scores of the alternative intervention and control groups. In fact, the grand self-esteem mean scores of the Project Youth participants increased by over ten points while

TABLE 5.4

Mean and Standard Deviations of Psychometrics by Matched Group Membership (N = 150)

Psychometric Test	CFL	Dropout	Control	Total
PEER SELF-ESTEEM				
1994	24.9 (3.0)[a]	27.5 (3.5)[b]	28.3 (4.2)[b]	26.9 (3.8)
1995	27.7 (3.6)	27.7 (3.4)	27.7 (4.2)	27.7 (3.7)
difference	2.8 (4.7)[a]	0.2 (1.7)[b]	-0.6 (2.0)[b]	0.8 (3.4)
PARENT SELF-ESTEEM				
1994	26.1 (4.4)[a]	30.8 (5.0)[b]	28.8 (5.7)[b]	28.6 (4.4)
1995	30.5 (5.4)[a]	29.2 (4.2)	27.7 (4.3)[b]	29.1 (4.8)
difference	4.4 (7.1)[a]	-1.6 (1.6)[b]	-1.1 (1.9)[b]	0.6 (5.1)
TEACHER SELF-ESTEEM				
1994	25.0 (2.9)[a]	27.7 (2.9)[b]	27.4 (1.9)[b]	26.7 (2.5)
1995	27.7 (3.3)	28.2 (3.3)	26.4 (4.5)	27.5 (4.1)
difference	2.8 (4.6)[a]	0.6 (3.1)[b]	-0.9 (4.2)[b]	0.8 (4.2)
GRAND SELF-ESTEEM				
1994	76.0 (8.0)[a]	86.0 (8.0)[b]	84.5 (10.3)[b]	82.1 (9.9)
1995	86.0 (8.6)	85.1 (8.6)	81.9 (9.9)	84.3 (9.3)
difference	10.0 (11.4)[a]	-0.9 (3.7)[b]	-2.6 (5.2)[b]	2.2 (9.4)
LOCUS OF CONTROL				
1994	14.2 (4.1)[a]	21.2 (6.2)[b]	21.2 (6.7)[b]	18.9 (6.6)
1995	14.1 (4.9)[a]	16.4 (4.5)	16.8 (4.4)[b]	15.8 (4.7)
difference	0.1 (5.5)[a]	-4.8 (2.7)[b]	-4.4 (3.2)[b]	-3.1 (4.5)

both the alternative intervention and control group lost points over time as can been seen in the grand self-esteem difference score comparison.

Project Youth participants obtained significantly more internalized locus-of-control scores than did either the alternative intervention or control group on the 1994 test as indicated by the lower mean score obtained on the N-SLCS in Table 5.4. While both the alternative intervention and control group moved toward a more internalized locus-of-control in the second year, the Project Youth scores remained almost the same.

Additional outcome data collected on participants in Project Youth consists of reports made by the project directors on the known status of youths

TABLE 5.5
Profile of Project Youth Participants at P.S. 314, 1993–1996

Gender: N=164		Ethnicity: N = 164	
Female	54.3%	*Latina/o*	83.0%
Male	45.7	*Asian*	9.2
		Black	1.2
		White	0.6
		Other	5.5

Marital Status: N = 139	
Single	99.3%
Married	0.7

Current School Status: N = 121		Parental Status: N = 142	
In High School	81.0%	*Had no child before age 20*	96.5%
In College	9.9	*Had child before age 20*	3.5
Dropped Out	5.8		
In GED Class	3.3		

Current Role at CFL: N = 164	
Participant in teen center	24.4
Continuing in CIT role	22.6
No formal role, but still in contact with CFL staff	18.3
Continuing participant in Project Youth	17.1
Participant in Youth Council	8.5
Employed as unit leader or assistant	7.9
Participant in Summer Youth Employment Program	3.7

who were active in the project between 1993 and 1996. Table 5.5 summarizes what was known in the summer of 1996 about Project Youth participants at P.S. 314 from 1993–1996. The numbers provided with each item indicate the total number about which the relevant information is known. Overall, this profile indicates that Project Youth participants are developing along a healthy developmental path in late adolescence and early adulthood. The vast majority were still in school, had avoided teenage parenting, and were maintaining positive relationships with one or more staff members at the Center for Family Life. A number had moved out of the community or simply lost touch with program staff, and two were reported to be in foster care or residential treatment. Given the high rates of school drop out and teen pregnancy in communities such as Sunset Park, the data suggest that in general these youths are doing better than would be expected given their socioeconomic backgrounds.

Because of the success of Project Youth as well as the center's Summer Youth Employment Program, and the program administrators' increasing conviction about the value of work to the youths they serve, they decided to reorganize Project Youth in 1999 into Youth to Work, a year-round program that combines work experiences, support services, sports and recreation, and academic enrichment for teenagers who are placed in a range of work settings. This program builds on Project Youth but extends job opportunities to more youths than are able to work as CITs and gives all participants the opportunity to receive the mentoring, tutoring, work training, and socialization groups formerly available only to CITs.

Views of Counselors-in-Training (CITs) About Their Experiences

We conducted four focus group meetings (two with boys and two with girls) with CITs at P.S. 314 and P.S. 1 in the late spring of 1994. A member of the research team also observed a spring training weekend and had a number of informal conversations with the CITs during the weekend and while making earlier program observations at P.S. 314. Another conducted semistructured interviews with twelve center employees who had formerly been CITs. They discussed the impact of being a CIT on their own development and compared their experiences with those of friends who had not participated in Center for Family Life programs.

The CITs who participated in the focus groups ranged in age from thirteen to fifteen. Most had been CITs for one to three years. A number had previously been enrolled in the after-school child care program and said they essentially "grew up" in the program. Others had no contact with the center prior to becoming CITs; they had all learned about the CIT role informally through contacts in the program and relatives or friends who were CITs. In discussing their entry into the CIT role, a number pointed with some pride to the fact that they had to be "picked" by one of the staff members and there is a waiting list for CIT slots. The youths all spoke readily about their experiences. A common theme was how much they had grown in this program. For example, "When you were in the [after-school] group, you weren't expected to work. Just play activities and do homework. That's it. Now you have to watch out for the kids, help them with their homework, help them with their activities, and so on." Several noted that they found the CIT role very difficult to handle at first because it's so hard to manage the younger children. Over time they learned to ask for help when needed and began to understand how best to handle the children. Several youth's comments illustrate:

It was horrible in the beginning, but I stayed. I just don't let it bother me anymore.

It's really nice now. You communicate. You tell them [the children] to do something and they're listening. They're not giving you a hard time.

At the beginning, it wasn't like that. If you were a CIT, they'd see how far they could get over on you and see how bad they could be without getting in trouble with you. But now, since we've been here so long, they respect us.

My boys, from the beginning, we teach them how to respect. . . . You don't respect them, they won't respect me. That's why you have to show respect for them before they'll give you any respect.

As the years passed by, I learned how to deal with the kids more. I used to curse at them, even at times hit them. Now I know not to do that. Just walk away or talk to them.

When asked to describe their responsibilities, the CITs were very clear about their primary obligations. For example, different teens responded similarly as follows:

Help the kids. Keep them out of trouble.

Work with the kids. Talk to them if they got problems.

Teach them right from wrong. . . . Be a role model.

Basically help them with their homework and assist them in things they can't do, like projects. It's like you're more of a friend than a CIT with them.

When I see kids crying, I'll go up to them and ask them what's wrong, and I'll talk to them, even if they're not in my group.

It's our responsibility to see that the kids have fun, have a good time at the center and finish their work.

The CITs were also very clear about their responsibilities to the larger program. Their comments in this regard indicate that they have been carefully socialized to understand the ways in which inappropriate behavior on their part could damage the program because they represent the program to the external world:

I have to have a lot of self-control. No cursing. You have to come in at a certain time. You have to show them you're capable of this job, taking care of kids. If the parents see you fooling around, they'll go to John.

You represent the program. You have to make a good impression. You can't go out there and say one thing, then do another.

Parents have to go to work and they can't take care of the kids. So they leave them here and they think the kids are safe. We're trying to keep kids safe and that's a big responsibility. Keep them safe, make sure nothing happens to them, that they get their homework done, and do good in school. That's a big responsibility.

In discussing what they like about the program and why they stay involved, the CITs identified a number of factors. One key theme was that the program allows them to go out and get away from the boredom at home while keeping them safe and away from trouble. They noted their own and their parents' fear about violence on the streets, use of drugs, teen pregnancy, and illicit activity and said that the program keeps them safe from these potential problems. To illustrate, two members of one of the boys' focus groups commented as follows:

My friends [who aren't CITs] are selling drugs. My friends who I associate with outside, they steal cars. Sometimes I'm tempted to go, but then I think about if I go, I'm going to get locked up—if I sell drugs and get caught. I don't want to do time. First, I think about my mother, and then I think about other things—and the center tops that too!

For other people, since they got nothing to worry about, they don't care. The difference between them and us is we got responsibilities; we got a whole bunch of responsibilities to do. Before we do something, we have to think about it twice. With them, they don't think twice. Whatever goes in their heads, they do it. That's the way I used to be. A friend of mine came up to me a few weeks ago. He was stealing a car and asked me to get in. I said no because if I went with him, my life would just go down the drain.

And the following dialogue took place among seven girls in response to the question "How would your life be different if you were no longer a CIT?"

Oh, my God.

It would be boring.

My mother wouldn't let me come outside.

I'd start doing bad things.

I'd be goofing off all the time because I live far away and I wouldn't see any of my friends.
I'd be on the streets doing bad things.
Before we started working here, we used to hang out until like three in the morning.
We used to hang out on the corners, in the park, in front of the school, starting trouble.
We used to be like that, but now we hang out here. And we go home or we meet on the outside.
When I was younger, I ain't got a friend, so I used to hang out with older people. . . . We used to smoke and drink. Stupid things to do.
The girls we hung out with, they got kids. I see them all the time.

Another central theme was the satisfaction the youths derive from the respect given them by the children and parents. A number noted that they enjoyed being role models and having the little ones look up to them, even if they don't know them individually. For example:

One of the good things is that the kids look up to us—so do the parents. Kids go home and brag about their CITs and counselors. It gives their parents a lot of trust in us.
The little kids respect all the CITs and the group leader. That's what I like about it. You're role models. You feel big.
It's like you walk in the street and you see them, [the children] say hello to you. They have a smile on their faces. It's like you're doing something good. You feel part of something.

Most of the teens who had been CITs for an extended period talked at length about the sense of loyalty they feel to the program. For example, one noted, "It's like I'm attached to the center. . . . I feel like I'm a staff member. But really I'm only a CIT. I feel like I have to come. I feel like I'm getting paid. But really I'm not." Another said, "I feel loyal. Some of the kids respect me. I feel like I'm one of the big guys now and part of the staff."

Similarly, some of the older staff and graduates interviewed in other contexts talked extensively about what a difference the program had made in their lives and how important they feel it is to go back for reunions with staff, observance of performances, and so forth.

One graduate who is now a New York City policeman commented that he goes back frequently to "get energized."

In contrast, those who were relatively new to the center and the CIT role said that, although they liked it, they did not feel any loyalty yet. Some said they were not used to working with kids and found that difficult. A couple of others noted that they did not get along with some of the senior staff. And one said, "I think I have to work here a couple of more years to feel that [loyalty]. I like coming. I like coming, [but] I think if I weren't to come, things would be running the same."

Asked to identify the good and the bad things about the program, the CITs focused primarily on the positives. In particular, they noted the value of the activities in the teen center, the trips, and the opportunity to make new friends and "hang out" together. The only negatives identified were that they sometimes got hot and tired in the after-school program and that some of the unit leaders were difficult to work with initially, prompting them to change to different units. They also talked—with some enjoyment—at length about some of the traditional rivalries between the groups at P.S. 1 and P.S. 314 and the tensions many experienced around the incidents of violence in the teen center the preceeding year.

Senior Staff Members' Perceptions of the Community School Programs

In-depth taped interviews were conducted with the senior staff members of all of the community school programs as well as a series of interviews with the director of the program at P.S. 314. These interviews focused on the respondents' views of the variables contributing to the programs' success, concerns about the programs, the programmatic changes that have occurred over time, and their own roles in these programs.

There are striking similarities in the ways the different staff members described the theoretical rationale for community school programs and the value of these programs to participants. All spoke of their belief that parents need assistance with child care and children need opportunities for socialization in a safe community context where they experience supportive relationships, a sense of adult authority, and a sense of continuity and connectedness over time. They also emphasized the importance of helping youth to develop attachments to adults and peers of different ages, of giving youngsters a sense of hope and future purpose, and of academic learning and skill building activities that build a sense of competency and self-esteem.

The senior staff members' views on the contributions of the programs to the CITs were also very similar. They each spoke about the importance of connecting adolescents to the larger community, getting them embedded in a system where they have responsibilities and are doing something they value, and giving them an experience of working. Thus it seems clear that a consensus exists among the senior staff about the service mission and functions of their different programs.

In addition, several stressed the economic development functions their programs serve for the community by freeing low-income parents to go to work, giving teenagers paid work, and developing career ladders for some of the older youths who enroll in college (with some scholarship assistance from the center) and assume more responsible positions in the community school programs.

The senior staff members also voiced similar concerns regarding the programs they have developed. The primary concerns they identified are the instability and cutbacks in funding for youth services, the lack of adequate resources to accomplish all that they would like, and the current devaluing of programs such as theirs by many public officials.

Other concerns identified by one or more respondents relate to the difficulties inherent in sharing space with school personnel, who are reluctant to give them storage space and become very upset if anything is out of order, the limited success they have experienced in engaging parents of adolescents, the fact that although they are succeeding with the adolescents with whom they are connected, they know there are large numbers of gang members and drug-involved youths in Sunset Park they have not been able to engage, and the overenrollment and waiting lists in some programs.

Several also mentioned their general tendency to become so overextended that they are stretched thin, must engage in crisis management, and often lack the time required to do adequate record keeping, convene needed meetings of staff subgroups, or do sufficient long-term planning. As one program supervisor commented:

> It's functional for it to be so chaotic, in a way, but it can also be frustrating when it comes down to nitty-gritty accounting for what you've done and making sure the work is getting done in a way that you'd like it to get done. I'm fairly sure that it always does get done because people have those relationships and they want to sit down and eventually they do. But for me to know about it and for me to have some record of it . . .

There is very low turnover among the senior staff, a factor that undoubtedly contributes to the success of this program. Therefore, another question we pursued at length with senior staff members was what draws them to this work and sustains them. Several laughed, indicating that it was certainly not the salary or the working hours. Their salaries are relatively low for people with their training, experience, and responsibilities, and they work long hours, including several evenings a week. The key variables mentioned by all respondents are the strong relationships they have with other program staff, the support they receive from the center's directors, and the value they place on this work. The latter was described in various terms. For example, one said, "It's a calling, not a job." Another stressed, "It's a shared sense of mission." And a third described it as an obsession: "The sisters are obsessed, they hire people who become obsessed, and, in fact, over time the kids and the families become obsessed with the importance of the work."

Several noted the struggle experienced in trying to balance their own needs and those of their clients, especially when they have families of their own. But they all clearly get enormous satisfaction out of the work they are doing. Some of the specific characteristics of the work that they identified as important were the opportunities for creativity, the sense of autonomy, the wide variety of tasks, the room for flexibility and spontaneity, the high standards for performance, the balance between short-term demands and long-term planning, the resiliency of the clients they serve, the sense of productivity and excitement they feel when they help youngsters get connected and get recognition for their accomplishments, being paid for doing work that is fun, the energy and synergy within the program staff administrative group, and the pleasure that comes from being part of a developmental process, a living organism that keeps growing and changing.

As discussed earlier, many key variables that emerged as critical to the success of the community school program were also identified as important characteristics of the preventive services program. These include the holistic nature of services, close coordination, integration, support of staff members from the various program components, continuity and long-term involvement of staff and youngsters in the program, the dynamic leadership provided by the program director, who has been with the program since its inception, the strong common conviction about program mission expressed by all staff members, and the flexibility displayed by the staff in adapting the program to changing individual and community needs.

Other variables were identified as contributing heavily to the success of the community school programs. One is the *heavy emphasis placed on age integration and parental and community involvement as the primary way to address the developmental needs of teenagers.* It was this conviction that led to the establishment of the after-school program as the integrative component of the community school program. And it is this theme, as well as careful attention to the developmental needs of children and adolescents and frequent arts performances at the schools, that leads to the high level of parental satisfaction and the strong sense of group identity and loyalty that youth participants feel about the community school program.

Another important characteristic of this program is the *strong mentoring or quasi-extended family role that the staff members assume for the youth.* Many children and youth who participate in the center's programs also develop close relationships with center staff. As one of the young staff members cited earlier who had participated in the program since she was six years old commented: the staff and CITs were "like big brothers and sisters to me." In most instances the nature of the attachment relationship is typically that of mentor or parent or older sibling surrogate, although the relationship may incorporate therapeutic activities, including discussion of past experiences and exploration of the effects of these on current thoughts, feelings, and behaviors. As discussed earlier, many youth who are selected as counselors-in-training (CITs) have participated in center programs since early childhood. As CITs they may also participate in Youth to Work, which provides them with a mentor (typically a staff member who is older and has some college education), tutoring, and family life and sex education. Their involvement in the community school programs, first as young children, then as counselors-in-training, and, in some instances, as paid young adult staff, provides them access to a range of adults who may for a brief or lengthy period of time serve as mentors or surrogate siblings or parents. Close relationships with center staff function as a secure base for children and youth to explore their own developing identities, interests, and talents as well as their relationships with their families, friends, teachers, and employers.

The continued success of this program also derives from three important organizational characteristics that are often ignored in program development and replication efforts. One is the enormous *time and patience* required to allow a large, dynamic, and cohesive initiative such as this to evolve into an established community institution. As Tom Randall, former director of the program at P.S. 1, commented:

The community school program is something that has been created and built up and evolved over time. When we first started, it was a skeleton of what it is now. And it can only be what it is now because of people being in it as children, and growing up through it, and becoming teenage volunteers, and then moving on to become staff people. It can only be what it is now because of the gradual evolution of a team staff, many of whom, even though they are part-time workers, have been with us more than five years, and some have been with us ten years. The rapport and cohesion and the professional working relationships that have built up between people over that period of time is part of what allows it [community school program] to be what it is now.

Other staff members also emphasized the importance of this *long-time perspective*. For example, John Kixmiller observed, "Everything is a cumulative effort over a long period of time. Things that are done build on a foundation that was laid before. Any community center consists of building blocks." And in another context, he commented:

From the beginning, this was a very open system where people could come in and out of it. They could volunteer for a few months and stop for a while and come back. The whole program was always organized in a way to be available, where people could to an extent come and go from it. It wasn't exactly like school, where you had to come. A parent could take two weeks vacation and take their child out and put him back in. Teens could concentrate on schoolwork for a few months and pass a few exams and return. Somebody could get into karate and be gone for a year and just come by and say hello to people. It wasn't set up in such a way that if you left, you were sort of out beyond the pale. And the result is that over a long period of time, people have tended to come and go, and the thing over the years that's most remarkable is the way people come back.

Although it is rare to find such flexibility and long-term perspective in formal social service programs, these are, of course, common characteristics of extended family and community networks and may indicate, in part, why residents of Sunset Park find the center such a comfortable community setting. Yet this long-term perspective can extract a price from program administrators and staff. As Julie Stein Brockway noted, when she initiated the idea of creating the new program at Dewey Middle School, she had to decide whether she was willing to commit the additional time this would require. She and her husband had just had their second child, and she asked herself,

" 'Am I willing to stay in Brooklyn and do this work for another five to eight years? Is that realistic?' Because I didn't want to start something and not get it to the point where I could leave and others could carry it on. . . . It's still not at that point yet. . . . I'm in my fifth year and I'm just beginning to reap the benefits . . . and that is a very big burden of the job."

The other critical organizational variable that emerged in our study of the community school program is the amount of *time and the resources devoted to staff supervision and networking.* Tom Randall stressed that one of the distinguishing features of the center's community school program is the attention paid to nurturing group supervision.

> I doubt that too many similar programs would build in and pay for supervision at all levels of the program. Our teenage volunteers meet with their immediate group leaders, three or four of them with one group leader. They also have a meeting once every two weeks, just the CITs and the Project Youth coordinating staff. All the paid staff assistants get supervised once a week by their group leader. All those group leaders get supervised once a week by the senior staff. So the system of supervision is keeping our finger on the pulse of what's going on with people. Sister Geraldine's comment is that most of what we do is through relationships.

In a different context Helene Onserud, one of the Project Youth directors, commented that

> another piece of the program that's not talked about very much, that's not officially put down on paper, is all of the networking that goes on between supervisors . . . all of the networking that goes on between myself, the mentors, the supervisors, the tutors. There's countless relationships that are very, very important in the way the program works. And it goes back, I think, to being a community center.

Finally, it is important to note the multiple ways in which the community school program has sought to expand over time by *opening its service boundaries and working collaboratively with other community institutions.* This is very apparent in the close collaboration between program and school administrative personnel, the expansion of the Beacon School program, and the increased involvement of youth and staff participants in community development activities. Without this openness and willingness to adapt to changing expectations, resources, and demands, it is doubtful the community school program could be as successful as it is.

Ultimately, it seems clear that the community school program incorporates all the components that contribute to healthy community and youth development. To illustrate, J. B. Hyman (1999), consultant to Public/Private Ventures, Inc., has proposed a very innovative and meaningful framework for youth development. He argues that, if we are to help secure better futures for low-income, urban, minority youth, there are three spheres of community influence (formal programs and services, informal community supports, and local opportunity structures) that must mesh with the three spheres of youth development (skills, attitudes, and experiences). Pointing out that youth development strategies have traditionally relied primarily on the delivery of formal programs and services to specific target populations, he suggests that this emphasis has led to neglect of the equally important spheres of opportunity structures and communal networks. The latter are sometimes referred to as social capital and reflect the familiar concept that "it takes a village to raise a child" (p. 24.). More specifically, Hyman notes:

> Consequently, this sphere encompasses the cadre of individuals, groups, organizations and institutions that nurture young people and contribute to their socialization. It is here where the break with traditional service strategies must occur. Rather than providing reactive interventions to identified youths or targeted groups, this sphere stresses the need for collective responsibility within the community for proactive supports for all young people. Hence, the focus is on the roles and contributions of individuals and organized groups within communities rather than those of institutions and programs. . . . In this sphere we look across communities for the role models, cultural norms, standards for behavior and discipline, and levels of social organization that form the social organization that form the social context in which children grow and define themselves. (pp. 24–25)

It is not difficult to see how the center's emphasis on community development in the context of youth development fits with Hyman's strategy for youth development. Every effort is made to encourage the development of social capital and opportunity structures for youth within Sunset Park, while the school-based and clinical staff also work directly with youths to enable them to acquire the skills, attitudes, and experiences needed for healthy development.

6

SUPPORTING FAMILY AND COMMUNITY DEVELOPMENT

> The center itself consisted of only about eight people when we started, but how that staff was comprised tells you that we had a lot of the pieces of everything that's since grown into bigger components. . . . Our casework supervisor, our community developer, and I would meet weekly in my office, and we would think about the things that were coming up that we were hearing. The core was always the casework, but we would always review what we were hearing that was presenting issues and conflicts for clients who came in. We would put newsprint up and write all the needs on this side and all the resources that we had on that side. And we'd try to figure how to put the two together. We were being flooded at the front door with people . . . (whose) food stamps didn't arrive or their welfare cases were closed. . . . And we began to think about ways in which we could make sure that everyone who came to the center's door had an opportunity to say what they wanted and (we would) not just push them out.
>
> Sister Geraldine

As Sister Geraldine's explanation for the initiation of the Storefront Center demonstrates, the center's staff members were committed from its earliest days to a comprehensive, holistic, noncategorical service approach. That orientation has demanded that services to meet community residents' basic needs are provided and staff members and administrators alike engage in ongoing advocacy and community development initiatives. In this chapter we describe the services provided at the Center's Storefront Center, Employment Services Program, and community development initiatives, varied programs that are essential components of the center's comprehensive services model. We also examine the way the center integrates these family and community development efforts with its clinical services.

THE STOREFRONT CENTER

As described above, the Storefront Center evolved in a somewhat unplanned way from the early discussions of the director and two key staff members.

Not only were they keenly aware of the specific entitlement and benefit problems confronting many neighborhood residents but, as Sister Geraldine explained,

> Those of us who were founders of the program are scavengers. We are resource developers, and we knew people with resources, and people in situations really needing winter clothes, furniture, whatever. So we started getting people to bring stuff here. I felt uncomfortable about all of us rummaging through boxes, and started saying, "Gee, someday, I'd really love to have some kind of a place (like the Thrift Shop we founded in Park Slope) for a thrift shop here." During this same period, the community developer was collaborating closely with a colleague who was working on a hunger hotline and food emergencies, and she started saying, "I think we have to figure out a way in which we can handle food emergencies."

These three pressures—food emergencies, donated clothing, and advocacy requests—led to the decision to open a storefront center. They had no resources for this at the time, but applied for a VISTA grant to staff the program and located a small low-cost empty storefront. It was in terrible shape, but Sister Geraldine and two of the social workers (one of whom was a former carpenter) engaged a handful of neighborhood fathers and teenagers to work with them in cleaning and repairing the shop and building shelves and counters. The Storefront Center was opened in this space in 1980 and staffed by a VISTA volunteer.

Several years later the rent for that space increased too much, and the program was moved to a storefront in a set of five dilapidated buildings on a busy street a block and a half way from the Center for Family Life's main offices. This move made the Storefront Center part of a management corporation of tenants and small business operators who worked to rid the block of drug dealers and renovate buildings. Since the center took the risk of opening the first storefront, the move gave a boost to others who were thinking of developing storefronts on this street. The Storefront Center is still in this building, which is now on an attractive block of well-maintained storefront shops and apartments.

The Storefront Center colocates three main program components: an emergency food program, a thrift shop, and an advocacy clinic. The food pantry is cosponsored by a number of other community organizations. The shop has a window showcasing some of its wares and a narrow glass door. Upon entering, one is struck by the long, narrow room with clothing hanging on rails that cover the side walls. Toward the rear are a desk and two chairs, which serve as the site of the advocacy clinic. There is a second small desk used by the coordinator of the emergency food program. Behind these desks is another room, the food pantry, with shelves filled with nonperishable foods and large plastic bins holding packets of rice and cereal.

The program director, Magda Santiago, is a Latina woman who has lived in the community for many years. She started at the agency as a VISTA volunteer about fifteen years ago. She works full-time in the storefront, where she is primarily responsible for staffing the advocacy clinic. Magda also manages the thrift shop, supervising the collection and distribution of donations, and has administrative responsibility for the emergency food program. The food program is coordinated by a Sister of St. Joseph who volunteers full-time. A retired school principal who was one of the founders of the program, she lives in a local parish. The program director is supervised by a professional social worker who is the community developer for the center and also carries a small caseload of families receiving services in the preventive program.

The program administrators are assisted by part-time drivers who collect and deliver donations and by four volunteers, elderly Latina women from the community who help customers select items and keep the shop and donations in order. They usually sit in the front of the shop and welcome people requesting clothing, food, or advocacy services. The entire budget for the Storefront Center is about $35,000 annually.

Table 6.1 presents a summary of the sources for all formal referrals to the Storefront Center during the 1996 fiscal year. Over two-thirds (69 percent) of the total (n = 2,975) were referrals for emergency food.

Emergency Food Program

Although this program is housed by the Center for Family Life, it was started as a collaboration of community organizations and is actually titled the Sunset Park emergency food program. The original program design, which is still in place, called for all community groups that wished to join to do at least one of the following: donate food, conduct food drives and provide storage space when the food pantry is full, and/or provide volunteers for pickup and delivery of food supplies. In return, the participating groups

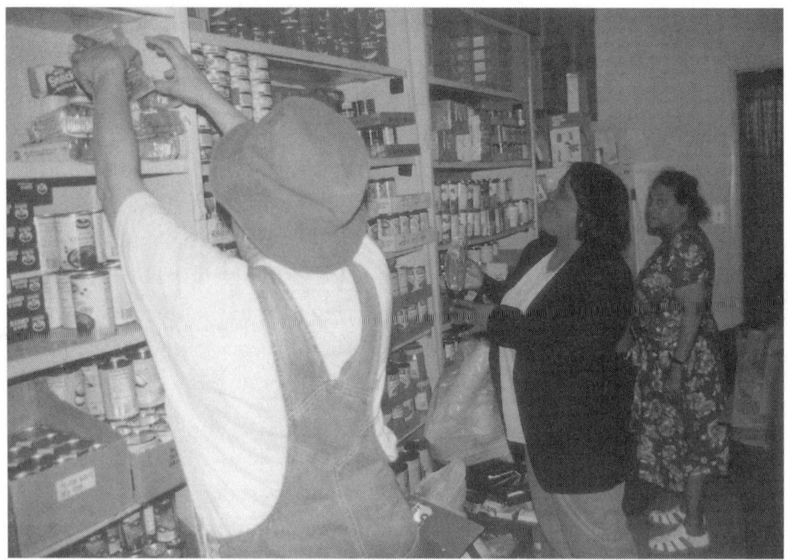

FIGURE 6.1

Volunteers stocking shelves of the emergency food program at the Storefront Center

could provide food vouchers to any of their members or clients in need of emergency food. Limited program funding is provided by two New York City programs: Supplemental Nutrition Assistance Program and the Emergency Food Assistance Program.

Anyone in need of emergency food is provided a three-day supply of the protein, carbohydrates, calcium, and so forth required for an age-appropriate nutritious diet. The actual amount of food supplied is determined by family composition. The program depends as much as possible on donations, but purchases additional low-cost items such as beans, rice, cereal, peanut butter, and tuna fish as needed.

Since the program was designed to meet emergencies, not chronic need, clients were originally restricted to receiving food a maximum of three times in any one year. However, this ceiling was lifted a few years ago when it became apparent that some clients simply could not earn sufficient funds or receive sufficient public assistance to ensure adequate food for all family members. Each participating agency is responsible for assessing need and providing the voucher that entitles a family to food.

TABLE 6.1
Referrals to Storefront Center in Fiscal Year 1996

Source of Referral	Number
Center for Family Life	1,725
Our Lady of Perpetual Help Church	1,278
St. Agatha's Church	542
Ethic Organizations (2)	357
Lutheran Medical Center	104
St. Michael's Church	86
Community Organizations (3)	78
Victim Services Agency	58
Senior Citizen Organization	49
Other Churches (4)	28
Food and Hunger Hotline	23
P.S. 314 & P.S. 169	7
Head Start Centers (2)	5
Total	4,340

In fiscal year 1996 the emergency food program served 4,468 adults and 4,271 children. A total of 2,975 referrals were made for these recipients. Table 6.2 presents a summary of the reasons given by the referral sources for the emergency food requests in 2,692 of these cases. The reasons for referral in the remaining cases were not recorded. It will be noted that the primary reason given for the vast majority of families was simply insufficient funds.

The Advocacy Clinic

Although this program is termed the *advocacy clinic*, its director actually provides extensive information and referral services as well as case advocacy. The clinic is used by a wide range of community residents, some of whom are regulars whereas others are seen only once. Most have learned about the service through word-of-mouth in the community; others are referred for help with specific problems by staff in various center programs and other local agencies. Originally designed to help with public benefits and entitlements, the service has expanded over time as the director has been asked to help with various tasks, such as reading or translating governmental forms and applications, filling out income tax returns, and helping to make funeral arrangements for a woman who lived alone and feared no one would be available when she died. As a consequence of the recent

TABLE 6.2

Reasons for Requests for Emergency Food, Fiscal Year 1996

Reasons	Number
Insufficient funds	2,058
Unemployed	359
Public assistance cut-off	63
New application for PA pending	41
Public assistance reduced	5
Public assistance check not received	4
Application for food stamps pending	38
Food stamps cut-off	29
Food stamps reduced	11
Food stamps not received	4
Food stamps stolen	4
Money lost or stolen	8
Disaster	5
Other	63
Total reasons	2,692
Total referrals	2,975
Total persons served	4,468 (adults) 4,271 (children)

welfare "reform" initiatives, the director is now also spending more time on job and child care referrals.

One of the director's primary tasks is to conduct prescreening for Medicaid, food stamps, and public assistance programs. She is then able to inform people whether or not they are eligible, answer their questions about how to file applications, and help them compile the required documentation. The director also coaches clients about how to handle their contacts with the public assistance personnel and others they will encounter in the bureaucracy. She asks them to call her from the public assistance office if they encounter problems, tells them to get the names of everyone they speak to, and teaches them to keep copies of every document they receive.

Her goal is to prepare clients to act on their own behalf whenever possible. Yet, whenever any problems arise, she gets directly involved. For example, if there is a lack of communication between the client and public assistance caseworker, clients are not receiving the full benefits to which they are entitled, or a client who does not speak English has to reschedule a face-to-face interview, the director is likely to call the public assistance office and speak directly with the caseworker or supervisor to resolve the difficulty. Her strategy ordinarily is to inform the caseworker that she is representing the client, imply that she is familiar with the department's policies and regulations so she is going to make certain that the client is treated fairly, and offer to help if the client is not presenting the right documents. She finds that most difficulties can be resolved on the telephone; therefore she seldom has to accompany a client to an appointment.

According to the director, what gratifies her most about the work is helping clients gain independence: "When I have a client come back and tell me 'I made it. I'm over. I'm out. I'm on my own.' That makes me feel good." Available data indicate that this program meets a wide range of service needs in the course of a year. Table 6.3 presents a summary of the types of requests for help received at the advocacy clinic during the 1996 fiscal year.

TABLE 6.3
Problems/Needs Presented at Advocacy Clinic, Fiscal Year 1996

Type of advocacy request	Number
Income tax preparation	179
Public assistance application	37
Public assistance case closed	37
Public assistance reduced	3
Public assistance recouped	1
Fair hearing for public assistance	21
Public assistance—other	104
Medicaid application	12
Medicaid problem	24
Food stamps application	21
Food stamps reduced	6
Food stamps—Other	57
SSI	85
Social Security	17
Housing problem	67
Landlord-tenant problem	36
HEAP (Heating Emergency Assistance Program)	16
Information re: jobs/employment	5
Need for homemaker/home attendant	1
Other	261
Total	990

The Thrift Shop

Most thrift shops are established to raise funds for specific charities. In contrast, the purpose of the center's Thrift Shop is to provide clothes, household goods, and children's books and toys in good condition at low-cost to families in the community. It is open to anyone who wants to go in and buy a particular item. Free clothing is provided to anyone who has a letter from a community organization specifying need. The total income from purchases at the shop is only about $8,000 a year.

Two principles that are reflected in much of the work of the Center for Family Life have also guided the development of the Thrift Shop. One is that people must have a sense of dignity, not shame, in using the service; the second is that a person who needs help one day is likely to be donating something (or giving help) another day. A policy was established at the time the Thrift Shop was opened that every item in the shop should be something that the staff members would be willing to put on their own children or wear themselves. As a consequence, approximately half the donations are thrown away because they are dirty or worn out. The hope is that customers will find things they can define as a "real buy," not anything that is soiled or ripped or seems like a "hand-me-down." Many of the customers are "regulars," and the volunteers and staff all speak happily of former customers whose situations have improved and now arrive to donate bags of food, clothing, or children's toys.

The cost of various items is low and somewhat flexible. To illustrate, while a member of the research team was observing, two women bought winter coats for $7 each, a man bought two pairs of pants and a down jacket for $10, and a woman bought a stereo set that was originally priced by the shop at $30 for $15. The items in the store are not marked with prices. Instead, one of the volunteers who knows all the regular customers assesses what the person can afford and sets the price accordingly. Credit is discouraged, but items will be held briefly for customers who do not have sufficient cash available at the time they see something they want to purchase.

Employment Services Program

Now in a new setting, the Employment Services Program[1] was formerly near the waterfront in the Bush Terminal "Industry City" area of Sunset

[1]Some of the material presented in this section was previously reported in Brenda G. McGowan (1994), *Asking New Questions: Introducing a Family Needs Assessment Into an Employment Program* (New York: Foundation for Child Development).

Park, where it shared space with the Southwest Brooklyn Industrial Development Corporation. It is unusual for a family service agency to sponsor an employment program, but in 1981, after three years' experience in the community, the center directors decided to move in this direction because they had repeatedly noted the negative, dispiriting effect that unemployment and underemployment has on the heads of families. These problems are particularly acute in Sunset Park because of the high proportion of households headed by immigrants. This population is commonly intent on finding immediate employment rather than job training, but faces formidable barriers because of limitations in language skills, education, and work experience. The Employment Services Program is designed to reach the diverse adult population of the community by providing preemployment counseling, job readiness activities, and job search and job placement assistance.

The Employment Services Program was initially funded by a state CETA (Comprehensive Employment Training Act) grant and later received modest foundation support and funding from the Private Industry Council and the City's Human Resources Administration. It was supported primarily by the City's Department of Employment (DOE) from 1988–1995. However, in 1995 it lost this funding base because the city, in accord with the policy direction taken by the federal Jobs Training Partnership Act (JTPA), had started to emphasize occupational skills training and decided to fund only those programs that offered specific occupational skills training. The center was unwilling to redesign its services to meet this new mandate for two reasons. First, its objective is to serve the full range of community residents, not simply those who want to acquire a particular set of job skills. And second, experience in the program suggests that a job is often the best preparation for job advancement for residents in this community because they gain needed self-esteem and competency by working, not by experiencing prolonged periods of welfare dependency and schooling/training. Since they were unwilling to shift the program's focus, the center has had to raise the funds privately for this service for the past five years. The annual budget for fiscal year 2000–01 was $378,822.

Influenced by the family service orientation of the larger center, the administrators and counselors in this program consistently define their mission as not only helping people achieve economic self-sufficiency but also as "empowering an ethnically, socially, economically, and psychologically diverse population," "enhancing clients' sense of competency and self-worth," and "allowing clients to gain dignity, self-respect, and self-esteem."

The current and former program coordinators are both bilingual professional social workers who have always encouraged the staff to conduct individualized, holistic assessments of applicants' employment needs, to make referrals as needed for emergency needs and other services, and to provide ongoing support with job search and retention in order to help clients through the lengthy trial and error process often essential to ultimate employment success. Although success in employment programs is commonly measured in terms of job placement and job retention rates, the employment counselors at the center are proud of the fact that they will work with anyone who wants to work, no matter how many barriers to employment she or he faces. As one counselor commented:

> We are people-oriented. We believe that everybody deserves a chance. We believe that everybody has the potential to achieve something, whatever that may be. If somebody's not reading at the eighth grade level, that doesn't mean that they cannot work someplace. . . . We hear over and over from people that go to other programs that when they talk about an issue that might become an obstacle for them to be placed [in a job], they say, "No. We cannot work with you." We look at it in a different way. If you're willing to put yourself through the process, if you allow us to work with you, then we'll work with you and hope that the end result is going to be a job. But if it is not, and you got something else out of it that is going to help you with your family, that's fine.

Despite this acceptance of clients' limitations, the program is clearly directed toward helping clients secure jobs. It has a staff of eight, including the program coordinator and a full-time job developer. Although the service is targeted primarily to residents of Sunset Park, it is open to all residents of Brooklyn. Many clients call or drop in simply on the basis of word-of-mouth referrals from community residents and former Employment Service clients, while others are referred more formally by community agencies or staff in other programs at the center. Moreover, the city's Human Resources Administration does regular mass mailings to welfare recipients in different neighborhoods informing them of available employment programs. A number of the employment program's clients are recruited through these mailings.

The intake specialist screens all requests for assistance, checking for age eligibility, motivation, and interests. (When the program was funded by JTPA, it also had to follow fairly strict income eligibility guidelines, but now that the service is funded by private grants, it is able to be more flexible about income guidelines). The primary objective of the intake screening is to determine whether the potential client is looking for the types of services the program can provide. If so, the client is scheduled to attend a group orientation and testing session. If not, he or she is referred to another program able to provide the type of assistance requested, such as specialized skill training.

At the group orientation and skill testing sessions, clients are also asked to present documentation regarding age, address, prior employment, and eligibility for employment in the U.S. Since undocumented immigrants and those without green cards cannot be referred for jobs, they are not enrolled in the program. Instead, they are referred to an organization that can help them with their immigration status.

During the two-week orientation phase, which includes a series of workshops on job seeking, communication skills, and so forth, each client is assigned to an employment counselor. The counselor conducts a very individualized assessment regarding education, work history, work skills, English language skills, family situation, interests, aptitudes, attitudes toward employment, and potential obstacles to work. Sometimes clients are sent out on a job interview during this period if an opening arises that seems appropriate, but most require more individualized service planning. The counselors meet almost daily with the clients during these first two weeks and then encourage them to attend for about six more weeks for ESL classes and/or computer literacy training and individual work.

In addition to seeking to match clients with available jobs, the employment counselors often spend extensive time helping clients work out family difficulties that are likely to interfere with employment. They may refer them to the center's preventive program for family counseling, or to another community agency if they are not residents of Sunset Park, assist in working out child care arrangements, refer for substance abuse counseling, help with children's special education needs, and/or provide information about potential health care plans and benefits. Many clients can be placed in appropriate jobs within this initial two-month period, but some take three to four months, and a few may take as long as a year. Also, clients frequently return for help if the initial job placement did not work out because it was a temporary job, or the client experienced travel or child care problems, or the client was fired.

The three issues the employment service staff find most challenging are

1. recruiting sufficient jobs in the community that are permanent, pay adequately, and are suitable for clients that may have limited work and/or English language skills,
2. helping dislocated workers who have been laid off after working in the same position for many years, are losing unemployment benefits, may be in danger of losing their housing, and lack the skills necessary to conduct a job search or move into a new area of work, and
3. helping clients who have been on public assistance deal with the potential loss of health care benefits they face if they go to work.

Two recent efforts made by the employment program to address issues related to the limited availability of appropriate jobs for this population were 1. the creation of an advisory committee for the program composed of potential employers and people with strong connections to the work world and 2. cosponsorship of a community job fair with the local state senator. The Employment Services Program enrolls about 20–25 new clients a month, serving a total of 792 in fiscal years 1997, 1998, and 1999, an average of 264 a year. Typically, just over two-thirds of these clients are women. Over three-quarters are Latina/o, 10–15 percent black, about 5 percent white, under 2 percent Asian, and the remainder other. The clients in this program range in age from eighteen to sixty-five, but the vast majority, as might be expected, are ages twenty-six to forty-five (Center For Family Life 2000).

It is difficult to calculate the Employment Services Program's actual success rate in a single year because of open enrollment throughout the year, help extended to clients who may have enrolled in a prior year, the difficulty of obtaining data regarding job retention, and the length of time it takes to secure an appropriate, permanent job placement. However, data gathered by Metis Associates indicate that by June 30, 1999, 556 (70.3 percent) of the 792 clients served in fiscal years 1997–1999 had obtained employment, 132 (16.7 percent) had left the program for other reasons, and 104 (13.1 percent) were still in the program. The mean hourly starting wage for those who obtained employment was $8.15 per hour, and the mean wage for those still employed who could be contacted a year later was $9.21 an hour (Metis Associates 1999).

These achievements are impressive, especially when one considers the limited reading and math skills of the clients enrolled in the program. A total of 62.8 percent of the enrollees in fiscal years 1997–1999 received TABE

Math Scores of 1–7.9, and 55.2 percent received TABE Readings scores of 1–7.9, which defines them as a "difficult to serve" population (ibid.).

Limited data regarding the families' use of other center services in addition to the Employment Services Program are available through FACTORS. During the 1994 and 1995 calendar years, one or more persons in 614 families used the Employment Program. For two-thirds (n = 405) of these families, the Employment Services Program was the only center program used by the family. The percentages of the other 209 families known to have used other center services either prior to, concurrent with, or subsequent to use of the Employment Program's services were as follows: youth recreation, 11.6 percent; youth development, 11.6 percent; the preventive program, 11.6 percent; school-related parent programs, 9.4 percent; after-school child care, 8.3 percent; summer youth employment program, 8.1 percent; summer day camp, 8.1 percent; emergency services, 7.5 percent; the advocacy clinic, 3.9 percent; ESL, 2.4 percent; parent recreation, 0.3 percent, and foster care, 0.3 percent. These findings demonstrate the value of providing employment services in the context of a comprehensive family services program.

Advocacy and Community Development Initiatives

Since advocacy and community development efforts permeate the work of the center, it is impossible to describe these as a single or separate program initiative. Instead, in this section we shall simply try to convey the flavor and range of multiple advocacy and community development activities in which administrators and staff are engaged.

Despite the existence of the advocacy clinic, social workers at the center clearly define ongoing advocacy on behalf of their individual clients as an integral component of their professional role. They are quick to go to the assistance of individual clients who may be having difficulty obtaining appropriate special education plans for their children, securing public assistance benefits to which they are entitled, or having their progress and needs adequately represented in family court proceedings. In addition, the program directors identify and respond to new policies or procedures that may pose a threat to client rights or well-being and attempt to mobilize their staff members to take action around these issues. To illustrate, at a staff meeting that the researchers happened to attend, the casework staff discussed several recent developments that could negatively impact clients and agreed to work in teams on these advocacy issues, each person selecting one problem area in which he or she would work.

The center's primary strategy has been a collaborative one in which the administrators and staff attempt to inform or educate public officials about the potentially harmful effects of proposed changes in public policy. This is usually accomplished through letters or meetings in which frequent use is made of case examples from the center. In fact, Sister Mary Paul has acquired some notoriety in the child welfare community for her multiple, charming, but speedy and forceful letters challenging practices that may be harmful to families and children. (See figure 6.2 for an illustration).

One of the primary issues the center has pursued is the right of preventive service clients to privacy and confidentiality. When the city decided some years ago to ensure accountability by requiring all voluntary preventive service providers to submit detailed, computerized records to a centralized city and state management information system, the center spearheaded a lawsuit challenging this procedure on the grounds of client confidentiality. This case, which was filed in U.S. Supreme Court, resulted in a settlement decree, *Advocates for Children v. Barbara Blum*, in which it was agreed that the city would send accountability workers to read case records on site rather than requiring the storage of records in a centralized system. Since that time the center has worked assiduously to ensure that this agreement is not violated by other attempts to centralize individual case records.

Most recently, Sister Mary Paul has been engaged in correspondence with numerous officials including the commissioner of the Administration of Children's Services (ACS), the secretary of the U.S. Department of Health and Human Services, administrators of the Child Welfare League of America, and the New York Council on Family and Child Caring Agencies to raise questions about ways in which implementation of the Statewide Automated Child Welfare Information System (SACWIS), commonly known as Connections, and the New York State Risk Assessment and Services Planning Model may threaten client confidentiality. Despite these concerns about information systems that provide case-specific data regarding individual clients, the center has argued equally strongly for the development of research studies and aggregate databases that could provide the information required to ensure program accountability.

Other recent examples of advocacy efforts in the child welfare system include the center's decision to send written case reports to family court judges after ACS took the position that voluntary foster care agencies could

comprehensive,
family-centered services
on behalf of children and youth

May 6, 1997

Honorable Charles J. Hynes
District Attorney, Kings County
Municipal Building, Room 400
Brooklyn, New York 11201

Dear District Attorney Hynes:

We read with special interest the account in the May 3rd issue of the New York Times of the bureau you have established "to deal exclusively with prosecuting crimes against children".

We have long known of your concerns about children, and we recognize the signals which you and the Mayor want to give, to outlaw violent behavior toward children at the hands of those who are responsible for their caretaking. Yet there are new practices which we find very alarming and counterproductive -- a growing criminalization of parents who may mistakenly or in isolated instances inflict a punishment which is excessive or ill-advised but not a crime or at all serious enough to warrant such a designation. In a very recent instance, a mother was arrested, incarcerated overnight and her three children placed in foster care (ages 6, 4 and 2) when her crime consisted in hitting her child's hand with a fly swatter when she resisted doing homework. We don't condone that punishment, but terrorizing the parents and three young children by that kind of penalty seems way out of proportion to the wrong committed. The hardworking immigrant parents thought they were being caring and responsible. The three children were placed in a non-Chinese speaking foster home, and the foster care agency does not have a social worker able to commumunicate in that language. As we write, we are trying to advocate for the children's return home and allowing them to use the Center's support services in their own neighborhood.

We believe that arest and incarceration should be a consequence of investigation that shows abuse that rises to the level of a crime -- not before investigation. We believe that sufficient, clear information needs to be given to parents and caretakers that are being investigated by your office and/or ACS so they understand what rights and protections they can call on. In the above instance, where the father's earnings are so meagre that the family receives supplementary public assistance, the very frightened parents hunted to pay $1,100 to a Chinese-speaking lawyer who went through the first adjournment dates without being able to represent them at the actual court hearing for fact-finding, because the fees for the first three dates were exhausted and they could pay no more.

345 - 43rd Street
Brooklyn, New York 11232

(718) 788-3500
Fax: (718) 788-2275

sponsored by St. Christopher - Ottilie

FIGURE 6.2

(FIGURE 6.2 *continued on next page*)

Honorable Charles J. Hynes
District Attorney, Kings County

May 6, 1997
page 2

It seems to us that the use of deterrents may be a part of the consideration for a very conspicuous use of out-of-home placements, arrests and other very intimidating measures among ACS, the police, and your own staff at times, but our experience over many years is that people need to find it safe to ask for help. In New York city, as in most parts of the country, the public agency is not only feared; it is hated, and therefore people evade and hide instead of seeking help.

We also do regret that a backlash against "family preservation" as it was proposed in the form of a cheaper form of "quick fix" behavioral change of parents, has obliterated the importance of "family work" as a critically important prevention as well a solution for the kinds of cases that reach the indication of child abuse or neglect.

It is our sincere hope that in your own continuing work with the Mayor and ACS Commissioner, a much better balance will be struck between that "family work" and criminalizing.

Respectfully,

Sr. Mary Paul

Sister Mary Paul, DSW
Director of Clinical Services

cc Hon. Nicholas Scoppetta

not testify at court hearings regarding children in their care, a letter to the commissioner challenging a memo by the agency's general counsel restricting workers from presenting written reports to the court or discussing their views with foster children's law guardians, a letter to the Brooklyn district attorney objecting to the establishment of a new bureau devoted exclusively to prosecuting alleged parental abuses against children prior to a full case investigation by Child Protective Services, and a letter to the commissioner of ACS raising question about his proposed plan of action that emphasizes protection of children without adequate attention to preventive work with families.

It would not be an overstatement to say that the many staff members and administrators at the center are constantly engaged in various community development activities. The supervisor of the Storefront Center, Valerie Segal, has the title of community developer and devotes extensive attention to her work with the Sunset Park emergency food program and the Human Services Cabinet for Community Board 7, of which the center was a founding member. To illustrate, when she received information about threatened cutbacks in emergency food programs under Mayor Giuliani, she drafted letters to the mayor, the president of the City Council, and two local council members pointing out the continuing need for emergency food programs and the potential harms that would accrue from these cutbacks. These letters were duplicated and distributed to parishioners at a local church who were encouraged to send their own letters to local politicians.

The community developer's activities have also included participating in the Sweatshop Task Force of the Human Services Cabinet, which was established to organize around workers' rights, safety issues, and fair pay for community residents employed in the garment industry, sending regular mailings to community agencies to inform them about the program, distribute food vouchers, and solicit donations, participating in the Children's Corner, an advocacy group that meets monthly at the local welfare center to address welfare issues experienced by different clients, and conducting parent workshops at P.S. 1 and P.S. 314 around issues related to parenting, child education, immigration, and citizenship.

The staff members in the community school programs also engage in frequent community development activities related to parent and youth education and organizing. The advocacy effort described in chapters 1 and 5 related to educating and mobilizing the community about threatened cutbacks in youth services provides a good illustration of their work in this arena, as does a more recent effort at P.S. 314 related to threatened cutbacks in the Summer Youth Employment Program. The director is strongly committed to this program because it provides a way of accomplishing his objective of integrating youth into the community. Therefore, when this funding was threatened a couple of years ago, he initiated a series of meetings with Beacon directors from different parts of the city. Although they thought initially of organizing a march, they decided this would be futile because a march would imply a protest against the city, and the problem really was a lack of federal support for this program. Instead, they planned a daylong conference for teenagers from around the city in order to educate them politically, introduce them to some leading politicians, and mobilize them to participate in whatever protest actions were taking place. About six hundred teenagers attended the meeting held during a school vacation week, participated in workshops on topics such as voter registration and accessing the Internet, watched a performance by the center's performing arts company, listened to speeches by the local congressman and City Council member, and wrote letters to their representatives in Congress.

The community school programs contribute to community development by providing numerous workshops for parents and by collaborating closely with the PTAs and the school administrators and teachers on issues of mutual concern. For example, the Youth Council at P.S. 314 volunteered to provide security at the exits of the school for a parent-teachers night at which there may be as many as 1,800 participants. More recently, the Beacon Advisory Council sponsored a communitywide fair with paid amusements designed to raise funds for an industrial-strength copier machine and maintenance contract needed by the school. This carnival gave parents and youth experience in planning a large community event, recruiting participants, staffing various activities, and fund-raising.

A key strategy that seems to guide most of the center's community development activities is to focus on issues that may affect the whole community and will encourage people to work together rather than getting caught up in issues that divide. For example, Sister Mary Paul worked extensively with a community coalition organized to seek federal "enterprise community" funding for Sunset Park. Under a U.S. Department of Housing and Urban Development initiative, Urban Enterprise Communities receive opportunities and resources to overcome seemingly insurmountable problems. The director of the community arts program at Middle School 136 worked closely with the principal of the school in a successful effort to secure Annenberg Foundation funding for arts education in the school. The center is currently sponsoring and recruiting participants for a program of free legal services for immigrants provided by New York Association for New Americans. And Sister Geraldine and the staff at P.S. 314 were heavily involved in efforts to protest the reconstruction of the Gowanus Expressway, a superhighway that divides the community geographically, poses a serious environmental threat, and hampers the quality of life in its immediate vicinity. The testimony presented by Sister Geraldine before the New York State Department of Transportation about the proposed reconstruction (see figure 6.3) provides a clear illustration of the careful research and collaboration that guide the center's advocacy and community development initiatives.

The efficacy of the center's full range of family and community development initiatives cannot be measured in traditional ways because most of the staff's community work is carried out in collaboration with others and the results frequently depend on economic and political forces outside the purview of any community-based agency. The varied programs and activities described in this chapter are essential components of the center's comprehensive services model. Recently, a center staff member observed the increasing number of community residents for whom "precariousness is a chronic condition." The services provided at the Storefront Center and Employment Services Program and the staff's advocacy and community development initiatives are designed to address the needs of these community residents.

The processes of social action, like the center's other programs and interventions, are carefully designed and implemented, and the results are persistently monitored. It is clear that the center's collaborators and clients are generally very satisfied with the quality of the center's work and the staff's high level of commitment to a common agenda. The letter of appreciation presented in figure 6.4 typifies the way the center's advocacy initiatives are usually perceived by the intended beneficiaries of these activities. The letter also provides an excellent illustration of the range of community action efforts in which the center engages. Few traditional child and family service agencies would define support of Chinese garment workers in a pay dispute as integral to their agency mission. Yet the administrators and staff of the center are quick to engage in any effort to enhance the quality of life for residents of Sunset Park.

comprehensive, family-centered services on behalf of children and youth

Testimony
before
NYS Department of Transportation (DOT)

Scoping Meeting for the Environmental Impact Statement (EIS) on the Proposed Gowanus Expressway Project

January 22, 1997

My name is Sister Mary Geraldine and I am presenting this testimony as the Director of Center for Family Life, a community based program in Sunset Park. There are two serious issues at stake regarding the Gowanus Expressway Project. First: the detrimental, longstanding negative effects of the very existence of the Expressway for people who live under or near it; as well as the increased harmful effects that will occur for these families during a reconstruction period. Second: the importance, at this opportune moment, to consider an alternative to the Gowanus.

Sunset Park is a community of over 100,000 people with about a third of the population under the age of 18. As a just and humane society, we are impelled to make decisions that over the long term will do no harm to children. As a caring society, we are encouraged to do what is best for children. The children of Sunset Park deserve a safe, healthy environment where they are offered a quality of life. **There should have never been a Gowanus Expressway over a predominantly residential community.** We know that Sunset Park has the highest rate of respiratory illnesses and asthma than any other neighborhood in Brooklyn and one of the highest in all of New York City. We attribute a significant degree of our problem to the pollution of our air from the Gowanus. **The period of reconstruction will increase contamination of our air quality and leave us, after all the hardship and cost of reconstruction, with the same harmful effects of the Gowanus for years to come.**

An additional note regarding air quality: the Clean Air Act that was passed in Washington this year has a stipulation (inserted by Congresswoman Nydia Velasquez) that the surrounding community of the Gowanus Expressway receive protection regarding decisions about repair as they apply to air quality. Advocates in Sunset Park **will be conscious of any infractions of this Act in our community.**

345 - 43rd Street
Brooklyn, New York 11232

(718) 788-3500
Fax: (718) 788-2275

sponsored by St. Christopher - Ottilie

FIGURE 6.3

(FIGURE 6.3 *continued on next page*)

Testimony on Gowanus Project page 2
January 22, 1997

We have always been concerned about the wide roadways (such as Third Avenue under the Gowanus) where cars and trucks speed through our community. We expect this problem will be magnified during the reconstruction period. Who will cross children and our elderly who want to attend churches along Third Avenue on Sundays. Also, Center for Family Life has afterschool programs for over 700 children a day in three public elementary schools Monday through Friday from afterschool hours until as late as 9:00 P.M. Who will cross children who leave our afterschool programs at P.S. 1, P.S. 314 and Dewey Middle School 136 (all exit on to Third Avenue) at various hours of the day while repair work is taking place? We worry now about safety; we expect our safety concerns will be totally unmanageable during reconstruction.

The issues about quality of life in Sunset Park are extremely important for the future of our families and children. Hard working class families deserve to have their homes protected; we know homes under the Gowanus are constantly affected by the vibrations of traffic on the Gowanus. The roadway has been a pall over Sunset Park for too long. We had a thriving commercial strip before it was built; later we got garbage, prostitution, and crime. The people of Sunset Park are fighting for a renewal; we want parks, shopping, businesses. Now the Gowanus is an obstacle for this growth and development; the reconstruction period would certainly destroy renewal.

As can be deemed from these comments thus far, **the removal of the Gowanus instead of reconstruction** is critical, in our opinion, for the life and continued development of Sunset Park.

The second consideration of this testimony is concerned with viable alternatives to reconstruction. We would be satisfied with any alternative that protects and takes into account the issues presented above regarding the life of Sunset Park. To our knowledge, options that have been presented have included a tunnel, improved transit system, a tunnel and improved transit, and a ground highway along the waterfront.

The last option, a ground highway along the waterfront, we believe deserves full exploration. This option was not given any consideration in the State's environmental assessment. Such a plan would certainly remove the highway from the residential section of Sunset Park, eliminating most, if not all of the problems listed above. Manhattan benefitted from the removal of Westway and has reaped untold economic advantages from the ground highway.

While we cannot be aware of all the objections to a ground highway, we are aware of a few. Lutheran Medical Center is located in this area and there is concern about pollution, noise and safety for patients if a highway is close to the hospital. Safe access to the

(FIGURE 6.3 *continued on next page*)

hospital could be explored through bus routes and overpasses that have successfully been utilized in many highway areas around the country. Likewise, walls have been built along certain sections of highways in order to eliminate negative effects of traffic. Unquestionably, the protection of our local hospital is of primary importance to the wellbeing of the community. However, modern engineering technology should be examined for solutions to any problematic effects of a ground highway to Lutheran Medical Center before this option is eliminated.

The development of the waterfront is of primary importance to the economic and social development of neighborhoods such as Sunset Park, Gowanus, and Red Hook. It has been left to deteriorate for too many years. The outcome has left the community **without jobs and with crime.** Mixed economic, social and recreational development of the waterfront could be tied to a ground highway. It happened in Manhattan with the development of the West Side Highway, it could happen here too.

Finally, the advances in modern engineering technology are extensive and it is not within the capacity of most of our community to understand and know all aspects of our options. For this reason, we strongly request an Independent Community Engineer be assigned to the Gowanus Project. According to the ***Tri-State Transportation Campaign***, the Gowanus Expressway is a mammoth project that is not cost-effective or comprehensively planned.

We cannot afford a boondoggle. We should not be short-sighted. We have to plan well for the next century. This project has so much to do with the growth and development, safety and health of several highly populated neighborhoods and surrounding communities in Brooklyn that have much to offer for the future of New York City. We have an obligation to give it our best.

The center programs and activities described in this chapter demonstrate the center's comprehensive, integrated, holistic service approach. As Carol Heiney-Gonzales, quoted earlier in chapter 1, noted, as she reflected on the orientation of the center's founders: "We deeply believed . . . that attuned clinical interventions went hand-in-hand with the best of community work. . . . The center was a place to try things out—not clinical things, not community things, but human things."

UNITE! A MERGER OF THE AMALGAMATED CLOTHING & TEXTILE WORKERS UNION & THE INTERNATIONAL LADIES' GARMENT WORKERS' UNION

August 11, 1997

Sister Mary Geraldine
Project Director
Sister Mary Paul
Director of Clinical Services
Center for Family Life
345 43rd Street,
Brooklyn, N.Y. 11232

Dear Sister Mary Geraldine and Sister Mary Paul,

Thank you for your support in our campaign to get our back wages. Without your help and the support from the rest of the community, we would not have been able to win our pay from A-1 Garment Factory and Cool-Wear.

It is important to us that the Sunset Park community is behind us in our fight to recover our back wages at A-1 Garment Factory and also in our fight to change sweatshop conditions in Sunset Park.

In solidarity,

CHI WAI
YEE HEUNG
Lai Chen
xiang yu
JIAN RONG
MU XIAN
DE ZONG
BING ZHEN
juan
XING
Jie

The workers of A-1 Garment Factory

GARMENT WORKERS' JUSTICE CENTER
UNION OF NEEDLETRADES, INDUSTRIAL AND TEXTILE EMPLOYEES, AFL-CIO, CLC
218 WEST 40TH STREET NEW YORK, NY 10018-1509
PHONE: 212 819-0959 • FAX 212 819-0885

FIGURE 6.4

7

LESSONS LEARNED FROM THE CENTER FOR FAMILY LIFE IN SUNSET PARK

■

The well-elaborated practice model that has been developed at the Center for Family Life in Sunset Park brings family and community practice together in ways that build on the strengths and contributions of each. In this chapter we identify the core components of the center's model, practice principles that inform the center's service design and delivery, and organizational principles that inform the center's leadership and management (see figure 7.1). Many of the principles that underlie the center's model do not reflect new concepts. Rather, they embody ideas that have been promulgated in the social work and the management literature for years. To illustrate, based on a study of programs that have been successful in promoting positive outcomes for children living in adverse circumstances, Schorr with Schorr (1988) concluded that the common elements are "comprehensiveness, intensiveness, family and community orientation, and staff with time and skills to develop relationships of respect and collaboration" (p. 294). These are all components of practice at the Center for Family Life, which was one of the programs included in Schorr's research. It is important to emphasize, however, that what is important is that the center is *actually implementing* all the core components and principles identified in figure 7.1, creating a dynamic synergy between them and illustrating that doing so *is feasible* and can make a difference in practice.

Moreover, our research suggests that it is the *combination* and the ongoing complex interplay of practice and organizational principles in the center's day-to-day operation that is critical to the center's effectiveness. Thus, no single practice or management principle alone is likely to have a significant or sufficient impact; rather it is the consistent and balanced adherence

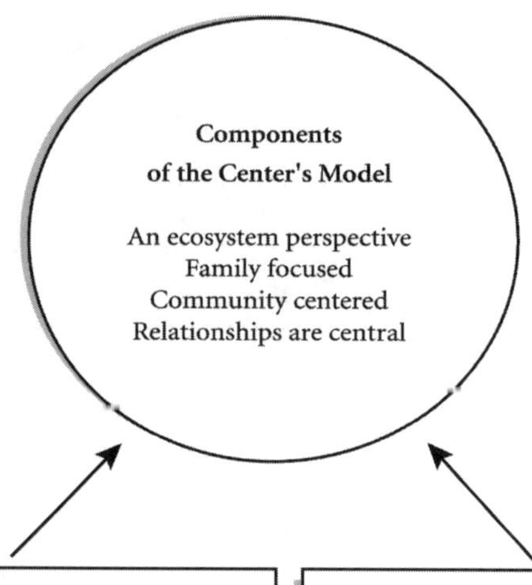
Components
of the Center's Model
An ecosystem perspective
Family focused
Community centered
Relationships are central

Practice Principles that Inform Service Design and Delivery	Principles that Inform the Organization's Leadership and Management
Holistic, integrated, comprehensive	A clear sense of mission
Nonstigmatizing	Dedicated and creative leadership
Addressing a continuum of needs	A learning organization
Integrating clinical and community services	Long-range planning and investment
Developmental perspective	Funding strategies follow philosophy
Continuous and accessible services	Stretching boundaries while containing costs
Empowering families and practitioners	Priority to staff recruitment and development
Culturally sensitive	Sense of community within agency
	Efficient institutional alignments

FIGURE 7.1

to multiple principles over time that has built the center's mission, philosophy, programs, and organizational culture.

In the section that follows we present the core components of the center's model. Following that discussion, we examine the ways in which the practice and organizational principles that have guided the center's directors, program directors, supervisors, and staff might be applicable in other settings. Finally, we discuss the implications or lessons for professional practice, education, and research and for child welfare policy that can be gained from studying the center's experience.

SERVING FAMILIES IN COMMUNITIES: CORE COMPONENTS OF THE CENTER'S COMMUNITY-CENTERED, FAMILY-FOCUSED PRACTICE MODEL

The four central components that framed the center's model when it was established over twenty-two years ago continue to powerfully shape its services and activities. These include an approach to services that reflects an ecosystems perspective, is children, youth, and family focused, is community centered, and in which relationships are central.

An Ecosystems Perspective

The ecosystems perspective on practice has been proposed by many leading scholars over the past generation. (See, for example, Bronfenbrenner 1979; Hartman 1970; Germain 1973; Germain and Gitterman 1980; Lindblad-Goldberg, Dore, and Stern 1998; Meyer 1976, 1983; Schorr with Schorr 1988). Sister Mary Paul was among the first social work scholars to argue the value of this perspective (Janchill 1969), and this orientation clearly guides all services and activities at the center. Nothing is done on a case or program level that does not reflect careful assessment of the interaction between multiple individual, familial, community, and broader environmental factors and the ways that these may affect or be affected by the proposed action. This approach pervades the thinking of all staff members.

Perhaps the clearest indicator of the center's commitment to the ecosystems perspective is the way in which it extends to community residents multiple points of entry to service. This flexibility is based on the systems concept of equifinality, which suggests that many different starting points can lead to the same end. As noted earlier, Sister Geraldine once commented,

> I can't emphasize enough how much all of Mary Paul's deep embeddedness in systems theory has been the life of the center. . . . We couldn't help any one individual child without being part of the process of stimulating the school's interest in the social life of children, the family life of the children, the community life of the children.

The ecosystemic perspective is also apparent in more subtle ways. To illustrate, the Storefront Center provides a very simple and low-cost mechanism for ensuring that adequate attention is given to the very basic economic and advocacy needs of the families in Sunset Park. And Madga Santiago, who directs this program, reflected her keen understanding of the center's ecosystemic perspective in her description of the principles that have guided the development of the thrift shop: "People must be given a sense of dignity, not shame, in using the service; a person who needs help one day is likely to be donating something—or giving help—another day."

Family Focused

Since establishing the Center for Family Life in Sunset Park, its cofounders have unequivocally emphasized that the primary investment of the center's leadership and staff is in Sunset Park's families. The core center services were designed with a blueprint that included a range of family services: emergency services, counseling and employment services, and community school services, with family life education, socialization, and learning to be provided at the schools. The center's mission, as stated in its first progress report (Center for Family Life 1979:1), emphasizes its focus on promoting the integrity and well-being of families with children:

> The Center for Family Life has as its purposes the provision of an integrated and full range of personal and social services to sustain children and families in their own homes, to counter the forces of marginalization and disequilibrium which impact on families, to prevent delinquency, and to prevent inappropriate uses of foster care and institutionalization.

Our observations of program activities and our interactions with center directors, program directors, supervisors, and staff have been rich with comments about the center's family focus, such as, "The key is that we work with the family, with everybody"; "What's good for the families of Sunset Park is good for the community of Sunset Park, since families anchor the community"; "Every family that you meet . . . has something to get from the center and something to give."

Community Centered: A Long-Term Commitment

It was also striking for us to note the frequency with which different staff members at the center referred to Sunset Park and discussed the many ways that the center's location in this community has influenced their practice.

Some have chosen to live in this community. Others live at a distance but still a convey a sense of belonging. And all worry about the ways in which their activities may help or hinder community-building efforts.

To outsiders there is nothing especially different or intriguing about Sunset Park. It is similar in many ways to a number of other low-income immigrant communities in other big cities. But the staff and clients of the center view Sunset Park as a very special place, and this sentiment undergirds the staff members' professional activities. There are numerous ways in which the center's commitment to the community is demonstrated. Most simply, its official name, the Center for Family Life in Sunset Park, conveys an important message, as does its primary intake criteria, which require only that the family have at least one member aged eighteen or younger *and* live in Sunset Park. The center has consistently approached the Sunset Park community and its families as interdependent. Other ways in which the center's commitment to the community are demonstrated include the provision of services based upon community needs, the inclusion of community development and advocacy as core services from the center's inception, the incorporation of a broad range of community-building activities, the commitment to "be there" for community residents for the long-term, and the establishment of partnerships with other community institutions, agencies, and community groups.

Center services reflect community needs. As noted in the introduction, Sister Geraldine conducted a thorough needs assessment of Sunset Park before the directors initiated services in this community. Although both cofounders had experimented with a similar model of practice in Park Slope before undertaking the development of the services at the center, they remained flexible and have opened new services as needs emerge in the community. To illustrate, the center's establishment of the Employment Services Program and the Storefront Center reflects its commitment to the Sunset Park community. These programs lay outside the center's original mandate to serve families in which children are at risk of maltreatment and/or foster placement. They were initiated only because the directors recognized the community's need for such services and sought additional resources to support them.

Community development and advocacy are central. The fact that the center has consistently employed a staff person who serves as community developer also testifies to its commitment to enhancing the Sunset Park community. Since the center's establishment in 1978, the social workers in this position have always been quick to engage in activities designed to benefit the larger community, such as organizing the Sunset Park Human Services Cabinet, working with the Sweatshop Task Force, and advocating against cutbacks in funding for welfare, housing, and food programs.

In addition, the other staff members have always been encouraged to engage in advocacy activities related not only to their own clients but also to other neighborhood families that may be in similar circumstances. In this sense staff members embody the "case to cause" framework that has long been heralded but seldom implemented in family service agencies (Sunley 1970).

The center focuses on a range of community-building activities. The community school program illustrates in a particular way the agency's commitment to community and community building. As discussed in chapter 5, this program is premised on the idea that the school should be the hub of the community. The program's staff members have found many different ways to build community through their various activities. For example, its focus on intergenerational activities, expectations for community service from parents and youth participants, and cosponsorship of programs with the schools and other community agencies all help to create a sense of community. Similarly, the performing arts classes and public performances that attract large segments of the community are emphasized not only as opportunities for skill building for the community's children and youth but also as community-building activities. Family members, friends, and other community residents gather and share the experience created by center program staff and participants. The performances create a sense of pride both among the children and youth performing as well as the family, friends, and other community residents who attend.

The center's commitment to community building is very consistent with extensive recent research demonstrating that poverty is the largest single risk factor for children and families (National Research Council Panel on High-Risk Youth 1993) and that neither child welfare services nor clinical family services alone are sufficient to reverse the threats to child and family well-being posed by residence in impoverished communities suffering the effects of widespread violence, substance abuse, unemployment, and beleaguered public schools (Lindsey 1994). Instead many experts in the field are now experimenting with programs such as the Empowerment Zone Initiative, which focuses primarily on building community economic resources, while others are calling for programs that enhance social capital in low-income communities (Hyman 1999). For example, Wynn, Costello, Halpern, and Richmond (1994) at the Chapin Hall Center have proposed three key principles for the reorganization of services: 1. there must be a large expansion in what they term primary services, which are conceptualized as a network of resources designed to enhance child development and family life, e.g., toddler day care and play groups, after-school programs, mentoring programs, sports teams, recreational and arts programs, and drop-in and support programs for parents; 2. these primary services should play a much larger role in the organization of traditional problem-oriented child and family services; and 3. the linkages that can lead to such a service reorganization can best be sustained at the community level because neighborhood jurisdictions can be made most responsive to the needs of local families and children (p. 5). In many ways these recommendations mirror the center's efforts to link a continuum of mutually reinforcing clinical services, community-based family support services, and community-building activities in ways that enhance youth and family development.

The center's commitment to Sunset Park is long-term. Since the establishment of the Center for Family Life the message given to the Sunset Park community has consistently been that the center is there for the long-term. This has helped to build trust between clients, community leaders, and colleagues in other service systems. Sister Mary Paul stressed that "the center's attachment to the community and the community's attachment to the center has deepened and evolved over time." The fact that the sisters chose to live on-site certainly helped to build confidence in the center's long-term commitment to the community, as has the long-time employment of many of the staff. However, the sense of longevity has been conveyed in other ways as well. For example, as noted in chapter 1, Julie Stein Brockway decided that she could not start a new junior high school arts program unless she was prepared to stay at the agency for another four to five years because it would take that long to ensure that the program was fully operational.

Productive community partnerships are nurtured by center staff. A number of community partnerships are essential to the center's programs. As noted earlier, when the center enters a partnership with another agency or institution, neither the center nor the partner gives up its identity, mission, or structure. Examples of productive partnerships include those with the Sunset Park community schools, the member organizations of the Sunset Park Human Services Cabinet, the community and New York City agencies participating in the Beacon School project, other community organizations that share in cosponsoring the Sunset Park Emergency Food Program (food pantry), the Sunset Park families that provide foster family care, businesses that provide internships and summer employment for youth, and many other formal and informal groups that join with the center in providing community services as well as in community development and community-building activities.

Relationships Are Central

The center's organizational sanction and unequivocal support of the staff's development of close ongoing relationships with community residents is central to its community-centered, family-focused practice model. Throughout this volume we have described the center staff members' willingness and sophisticated ability to develop and maintain purposely close and meaningful relationships with Sunset Park's families. These relationships have become a safe, nurturing resource to children, youth, parents, and grandparents in their exploration of individual interests, talents, and goals, of family and social relationships, and of the world beyond the neighborhood, including the worlds of higher education and of employment.

Close relationships with center counseling staff provide a secure base for children and youth to explore their own developing identities as well as their relationships with their families, friends, teachers, and employers. Social workers in the center's preventive program serve what might best be described as an extended family member function for parents who are overwhelmed with parenting responsibilities and environmental demands.

Youth participants in the community school programs also often develop close attachments to individual social workers, to activity counselors, and to the center as a whole. The involvement of youth over many years, first as young children, then as volunteer counselors-in-training, and, in some instances, as paid young adult staff, provides them access to a range of adults who may for a brief or lengthy period of time serve as mentors or parent or older sibling surrogates. In many instances former community school program participants return regularly to the center from the worlds they have explored to share their successes and disappointments with center staff, to problem solve, to receive encouragement, and to contribute to the center's programs and activities.

Staff members in all center programs repeatedly articulate the importance of relationships to the ongoing development of individuals, families, and the community. Perhaps more important, it is evident that staff members understand and make the investment necessary to develop close relationships, particularly with parents and children who have difficulty in trusting others. As described earlier, program participants include many immigrants who worry about disclosing information to strangers as well as persons who have been abused or neglected, who experience severe and persistent mental illness, or who have experienced professionals as less than fully helpful. Thus, it is not unusual for community residents to voluntarily seek the center's services or to follow through on a referral to the center while at the same time conveying ambivalence about trusting and working with center staff. Consistent with center staff members' experiences, Halpern (1997) emphasizes that

> multiply vulnerable young parents often have difficulty with relationships, and may recreate hurtful patterns from earlier (and other contemporary) relationships with those who offer formal help. They have learned, repeatedly and painfully, that expectations of positive responses from others lead to disappointment.

He further notes that "a provider's commitment to a parent may be tested, sometimes repeatedly; likewise the boundaries of the relationship" (p. 258). Yet, according to family members and to staff, when close, often long-term, personal relationships are established, they greatly support program participants' efforts to make changes in the ways they express themselves and relate to others in a range of roles.

A secure base. As discussed in chapter 1, the center's strong commitment to being continuously accessible over time to community residents and to the development of relationships with program participants often contributes to the experience of the center as "like home" or "an anchor." We believe that conceptualizing the center as "a secure base" to which Sunset Park's family members may turn and return as needs arise is useful. It is most likely that community residents' relationships with the continuously accessible, responsive, sensitive, and trustworthy staff in all programs makes possible the perception of the center as "like home," and that this perception greatly facilitates families' willingness and ability to seek services as soon as they identity their needs, and thus prevent crises, rather than seeking services only when a crisis arises.

CORE PRACTICE PRINCIPLES THAT UNDERLIE THE CENTER'S MODEL

As outlined in figure 7.1, we have identified a number of principles that have powerfully shaped practice at the Center for Family Life in Sunset Park. As indicated above, it appears that it is the consistent adherence over time to *all* these practice principles across center programs that contributes to the effectiveness of its services.

Services Are Comprehensive, Holistic, Integrated, and Nonstigmatizing

Center directors and staff have designed and provided comprehensive services that address a broad continuum of family members' concrete, social, therapeutic, educational, economic, and expressive needs, and have provided these services in an integrated, individualized and mutually reinforcing way. Holistic services are defined by the center staff as services that address the whole individual and the whole family and approach families and communities as interdependent entities. Moreover, to center directors and staff holistic practice integrates clinical and community services seamlessly, avoiding dichotomies in goals, processes, and method. The center's approach is consistent with the recommendations of Halpern (1990), who stresses that "the model that increasingly seems necessary for young families is one that provides a flexible mix of concrete, clinical, and supportive services in a nonbureaucratic, family-like context. It has to be a model that can work simultaneously and comfortably at multiple levels" (p. 15).

Despite its constant struggle to secure sufficient funding for the comprehensive services it provides, the center has always prided itself on its refusal to accept any funding that would require labeling clients as belonging to specific problem categories. Moreover, despite frequent requests from graduate social work students and new staff members to start targeted counseling groups for participants with special needs such as battered women, adolescent substance abusers, or children who have been sexually abused, the administrators have not permitted such problem-focused groups. This orientation is consistent with the recommendations of the authors cited above who argue for programs aimed at entire populations of youth, suggesting that treatment for specific targeted groups often undercuts the whole concept of youth, family, and community development.

Families as well as staff members have repeatedly emphasized the importance of the center's adherence to these interrelated commitments—that services be comprehensive, holistic, integrated, and nonstigmatizing. Our research suggests the center's consistent application of these interrelated principles is important because doing so ensures that participants are treated as whole people, not in a fragmented way as problem categories, and removes any stigma from parents and youth who chose to participate in the center's activities.

Unfortunately, most public and private funding sources prefer to award grants for specific problem groups. Few funders are willing to accept available evidence (Dryfoos 1990) that youth at risk of different negative outcomes, such as school drop out, teen pregnancy, delinquency, or substance abuse, share common risk characteristics and can best be helped by services aimed at eliminating these risk factors, not by specialized interventions aimed at preventing specific problems. Thus, the center's commitment to accept only noncategorical funding has extracted a high price from the center's administrators. Extensive time has been required for fund-raising, and the stress related to periodic threats to funding has affected both program staff and participants.

A Developmental Perspective Guides Activities in All Program Components

Throughout its program activities the center maintains a developmental perspective on the potential for change and growth in individuals, families, and the community at large. This perspective encourages the flexible use of time by casework staff in setting objectives for work with individuals and families and in encouraging program participants to use particular services, such as therapeutic groups or the summer camp programs, when they are ready, to leave when their needs have been met, and to return at a later date for more assistance if new needs emerge or when they are ready to address other long-standing problems.

This developmental perspective is particularly apparent in the activities planned by the community school staff members. They encourage youths, based upon their developmental needs and their interests, to choose to participate in one or more of a variety of different programs, to move on to other activities when they are ready, and then to become engaged in other center programs later, often in roles with increased responsibility, consistent with their changing developmental needs and interests. Groups, such as focused activity groups, are extensively integrated into ongoing programming for children and youth to enhance development and social functioning through specific types of group experiences and to establish peer relationships.

Perhaps the most important component of the community school program from the perspective of youth and community development is its structured effort to have children move from being participants in the after-school program to assuming roles in the program as volunteer counselors-in-training and to later being hired as paid youth staff. As discussed in chapter 5, this trajectory gives high-risk youth an enormous sense of belonging, increased competence, and importance, and prepares them for roles with greater responsibilities within and outside the Sunset Park community.

To illustrate, a few years ago, the young policemen who was a former CIT, and has said he goes to visit the program to get "refreshed," asked if he could make a brief announcement before the start of one of the large community school performances. He then asked one of the youth staff members who also had grown up in the program and was working on the performance to come out on the stage. He got down on his knees and asked her to marry him, and she accepted. He explained that he wanted to do this publicly and to share his joy with the audience because he regarded this community as his family. The young couple later asked community and staff members to join them at their wedding.

Services Are Continuous and Accessible

Many have observed that recently emergent family support programs have built upon the settlement house movement of the early 1900s (Halpern 1988, 1991; Weissbourd and Kagen 1989; Lightburn and Kemp 1994). Through their emphasis on the accessibility of comprehensive, developmentally oriented services to all families in a community, such programs inevitably are characterized as continuously available over time. Since the establishment of the center, its programs have been continuously available at no cost to any Sunset Park family with a child younger than eighteen. As a consequence, over the past twenty-two years, children, youth, and parents have met no bureaucratic obstacles in accessing services in accordance with their needs, thus encouraging participation in center programs *before* their difficulties result in family breakdown, and participation for *as long as needed* and in *as many programs as are needed.*

As we have emphasized, however, the center's inclusion of intensive clinical services designed to prevent the unnecessary placement of children in out-of-home care (the preventive services program) as one of its continuously available and accessible core programs differentiates it from other family support programs as well as from current family preservation programs (Hess, McGowan, and Botsko, 2000). The center's definition of *all* its services as continuously accessible to all children and families in Sunset Park empowers families and the center practitioners who serve them.

Empowering by Providing Choices and Creating a Sense of Possibility for Families and Practitioners

Choice is central to empowerment. The location of a continuum of services in the neighborhood facilitates residents' awareness of services and ease of access. Equally important is the families' control of, or participation in, decisions regarding their need for different services at different points in time. These principles are key to providing early preventive intervention. At the center clients are invited to invent futures toward which they can strive rather than becoming victims of their current life circumstances.

In her history of the empowerment tradition in social work, Simon (1994:26) has suggested eight principles that guide practice truly committed to client empowerment, all of which reflect the attitudes and behavior of social workers at the center:

1. All oppression is destructive of life and should be challenged by social workers and clients.
2. The social worker should maintain a holistic vision in situations of uncertainty.
3. People empower themselves; social workers should assist.
4. People who share common ground need each other to attain empowerment.

5. Social workers should establish an "I and I" relationship with clients.
6. Social workers should encourage the client to say her own word.
7. The social worker should maintain a focus on the person as victor, not victim.
8. Social workers should maintain a social change focus.

Although implicit in our discussion in earlier chapters, it is also important to stress that center staff members are encouraged by the organization's leaders to openly identify the challenges they face in their work and to engage in problem solving in their team and program meetings, with center directors and supervisors, and within the Monday morning center staff meetings. This not only further reinforces the sense of shared responsibility for the accomplishment of the organization's mission, it also provides mutual support and parallels the empowering, collaborative partnering process staff members engage in with children and families. This ongoing open problem solving also makes possible the continuing relevance and evolution of the center's programs.

We were very interested to learn what draws the staff members to the center and what retains them. Clearly the sense of belonging to a committed community of professionals in which they feel empowered is a significant part of the answer.

Cultural Sensitivity Pervades the Center's Activities

As Jenkins (1981) has suggested, because child welfare agencies assume some primary group functions, "to practice family and child welfare without regard for ethnic variables is to truncate the potential for service" (p. 7). The style of practice at the center reflects sensitivity to the desire of many Latino immigrant families to receive help on an informal, flexible basis from people with whom they share a mutual sense of trust and respect. "The relationships between staff and clients give the center a quasi-extended family aura because the relationships tend to be diffuse, mutual, personal yet respectful, non-hierarchical, and convey a sense of endurance" (McGowan 1988:58).

It is also possible to identify cultural sensitivity in the center's use of what Germain (1976, 1978b) has described as two significant but frequently neglected variables in social work practice: time and space. Rather than maintaining the future-oriented, carefully delimited use of time customary in many modern American service agencies, the center maintains a present-time orientation that prohibits any waiting list except in the school-age child care program, encourages workers to see clients on a drop-in basis whenever necessary, and stresses the provision of open-ended services.

The center's use of space reflects a similar sensitivity to cultural norms. The physical arrangements of the center, as well as the presence of the codirectors' apartment on the top floor of the main building, create a homelike atmosphere in the agency. The use of public schools for much of the youth-age programming further helps to minimize social distance between clients and workers (McGowan 1988).

One criticism raised occasionally about the center by outsiders is that few of the senior staff members are Latina/o. As discussed earlier, the primary reason for this is that, although Latinos/as now constitute 64 percent of the total staff, the majority of social workers in supervisory and administrative posts are white and have been at the center for many years, so there has been almost no turnover in these positions. Currently (2002), Latina staff members head up the employment and storefront programs and codirect one of the community school projects. What may be as important as staff composition in demonstrating cultural sensitivity within an agency is the way in which different service programs are implemented.

ORGANIZATIONAL PRINCIPLES THAT GUIDE THE CENTER'S LEADERSHIP AND MANAGEMENT

Several organizational principles that are consistently applied by the center's leadership, management, and supervisory staff also emerged in our study. These principles, outlined in figure 7.1, have been central to the development of the center's organizational climate, its high staff morale and remarkable staff retention, its fiscal stability, and its reputation within the community and nationally as a successful program. Adherence to many of these has been advocated by experts in the worlds of business and of human services. Center directors and supervisors are committed to these principles because they are consistent with their professional and personal values and because doing so "makes sense" to them.

Because of the uniqueness of the center's leadership, questions have been raised repeatedly about the potential replicability of its programs. In response to such questions, the center's directors have stated clearly that they would not want their program to be replicated because such an effort would violate one of their primary beliefs, which is the importance of making every child and family service agency responsive to the unique strengths and needs of the community in which it is located, and no other community is exactly like Sunset Park. Yet, it would be foolish for anyone to conclude, as has often been done, that because the center was founded and directed by two Sisters of the Good Shepherd who lived on-site and devoted most of their waking hours to the work of the center, the core components of the center's model and the interrelated principles that shape its services and its leadership and management cannot be replicated.

It would clearly cost more to have an agency similar to the center administered by lay people. The sisters have traditionally carried a small salary that would not be sufficient to hire high-caliber lay directors. Also, they have happily lived on-site and made themselves available to clients in person from early morning until almost midnight and for emergencies twenty-four hours a day. This would not be a realistic expectation of most administrators. Yet it is perfectly feasible to ask program directors and supervisors in an agency to rotate emergency coverage by telephone, and it might be possible to locate a couple or a family who would be willing to live on-site, as is often done in residential treatment settings.

What seems to us much more important than the idiosyncratic features of the center's leadership is the complex interplay of replicable practice and organizational principles that have guided the center over the years. The principles that have contributed to its success can definitely be implemented in other child and family service settings. This is illustrated by the comments of a state-level administrator of an initiative funded by the Annie E. Casey Foundation to develop community-level foster care and other family support services. Having visited the center many times to learn about the center's community-based foster care program, he commented, "We never honestly believed that we could replicate what they do. There's an intangible element which you cannot duplicate. It has to do with the two sisters . . . 'It's the singers, not the song.' Actually, it's a bit of both!" He continued:

> You have two women who have a strong belief in values and goals. The program has enormous credibility because it has a sound practice base. We have used the center as our model—the process of the community being

used in family support. Ours has not been an exact replication. . . . That would be the antithesis of what we are trying to do, which is to meet the specific needs of our communities.

A Clear, Consistent Sense of Mission

A critical task in developing an effective service is locating administrators who possess the needed leadership skills, either singly or in combination. One reason that the team of Sister Geraldine and Sister Mary Paul worked so well is that they brought very different strengths to their partnership. Sister Geraldine was a community organizer par excellence with an enormous love for life, boundless enthusiasm, and keen programming and administrative skills. Sister Mary Paul is a gifted clinician who approaches challenges in a careful, scholarly way, designs services creatively and comprehensively, and charms community members, public officials, and potential benefactors alike when she describes family and program needs and resources in her quiet, intense manner.

Together they shared a clear sense of mission, an unwavering commitment to the importance of their work, a strong social work identity, and a readiness to lead in the ways that Northouse (2001:258–264) suggests demonstrate the principles of *ethical leadership*. Although the center has expanded in multiple ways to meet the needs of the community, it has never wavered in its definition of agency mission. A recent progress report (2000) states: "The mission of the center takes form in a variety of services and activities that are designed to enrich personal and family functions, while also engaging in community building processes." This same statement could easily have been written in 1978, when the center was founded, and it has guided the center's development over the years.

Unlike many agencies that shift target populations and/or service strategies in order to meet the requests of funding sources and/or public officials and assure agency survival, the center's cofounders and staff have consistently refused to shift its central purpose. This steadfastness and clarity of mission have contributed significantly to client and community trust in the integrity of the center. The importance of clarity regarding organizational mission has been highlighted by Peters and Waterman (1982) in their analysis of the variables that contribute to organizational success. In the words of these authors, excellent, innovative companies always "stick to the knitting" (p. 15).

Creative and Dedicated Leadership

Since establishing the center, the sisters have demonstrated creativity and strong conceptual skills, delineating clearly how the different components of the center fit together, where the center was, and what needed to be accomplished to achieve long-range objectives. For example, although Sisters Geraldine and Mary Paul were committed to hiring professional social workers in counseling and supervisory roles, they have also been creative in making excellent use of paraprofessionals, youth staff, and volunteers to implement many of the tasks that could not be carried out by professional staff. Moreover, they have always struggled to ensure that their conceptual framework is fully understood by everyone working at the center so that there is a consensus among supervisors and staff members about the center's objectives and an understanding of the ways in which each person's efforts fit into the work of the whole.

The cofounders and current codirectors actively participate daily in a range of activities within the center and the Sunset Park community. Further, the center's codirectors have always networked actively with public officials, child welfare administrators, advocates, foundation staff, and researchers at the local, state, and national levels. This involvement has helped to build the center's reputation amd to keep center leadership and staff members informed about potential changes in public policy and potential resources and constraints that might impact on the center.

Overall, the leadership style that Sisters Mary Paul and Geraldine maintained—and that is sustained by the current codirector—is what Peters and Waterman (1982) have termed a "hands-on, value-driven" approach that keeps administrators informed about what is happening while helping to create an exciting work environment through "personal attention, persistence, and direct intervention—far down the line" (p. 279).

A Learning Organization

The concept of organizational learning, first promulgated by Agris and Schon (1978), clearly describes one of the variables that has contributed to the center's success. Although the center's codirectors and lead administrative staff are very committed to the center's mission and the values on which it is based, they have consistently encouraged open discussion and examination of their service strategies and programs. For example, they were enthusiastic about participating in the Annie E. Casey Foundation Evaluation Grants Program, reported here. Sister Mary Paul and Sister Geraldine created many forums for input from program participants as well as from other community residents and leaders, and the center publishes extensive annual reports that provide abundant information about the center's activities, ensure accountability, and encourage feedback. Consequently, there have been frequent modifications in different program components over time. This commitment to organizational learning has definitely contributed to the enthusiasm that staff members and outside observers feel about the center and its capacity to respond to shifting community needs.

A Long-range Planning Perspective and Investment

From its earliest days, the center's leadership has maintained a focus on the organization's and the community's future and has engaged in extensive long-range planning with its many community constituencies. Although the directors and staff members have initiated many new services and programs, they have consistently considered the future implications of any program initiative before moving ahead. Although every social service agency administrator is aware of the need for long-term planning, few recognize the importance of conveying to the client population and to potential funding sources the sense that they have a long-term commitment to the work they are doing and to the community within which this work occurs.

Funding Strategies Follow Mission and Philosophy

It is very tempting for agencies to respond to every request for proposals (RFP) that is issued in order to stay financially viable. However, such an orientation compromises a clear sense of agency mission and creates doubts in the client community as to whether an agency is really there for the community or whether it is more concerned about its own survival. This undercuts the trust that is required for other community institutions and agencies to share resources, information, and power. In contrast, the center has always been very clear about what it can and cannot do and the types of funds it will and will not accept. It therefore enjoys a strong level of trust among community agencies and client groups.

Since the center has had no endowment, its cofounders quickly sought out diverse sources of public and voluntary funding to protect the center's ability to carry out its mission in the Sunset Park community. Sisters Mary Paul and Geraldine have struggled over the years to raise private funds that would enable them to enrich the services supported by public contracts and to build a small reserve fund. This has ensured that the center would not become excessively dependent on any one funding source.

Stretching Boundaries While Containing Costs

Unfortunately, many agencies today consistently limit the services they provide to those for which they can receive public funding. In contrast, although the center maintains its primary focus on child and family services, the codirectors and staff have not hesitated to offer other types of social services that are needed by Sunset Park's families. An excellent illustration of this is the Employment Services Program. Although this program was funded initially by a government contract, when the regulations governing such contracts changed in ways that would prohibit the center from offering the type of employment services the codirectors had determined were required in Sunset Park, they decided to seek private funding for this program.

In contrast, the Storefront Center was started without external funding. When staff members identified the need for such a program, the codirectors found a way to operate it at very low cost. They first obtained a paraprofessional VISTA worker and, when the VISTA contract expired, retained her through use of private funds. They asked staff members to volunteer on weekends to renovate the space they were able to acquire and then recruited volunteers from the community to help in staffing the thrift shop. As a consequence, the center can operate this very valuable service that benefits clients and the larger community with little financial stress.

Perhaps the most striking example of this capacity to move beyond traditional boundaries while containing costs is the center's community school program. Although the center's primary public funding has consistently been for preventive services, which must be directed to families at risk of child maltreatment and foster placement, the sisters were determined to find a way to serve a wide range of families in Sunset Park, not simply those "at imminent risk." Therefore, they obtained initial funding for youth development services through the New York City Youth Board. However, rather than focusing solely on the traditional recreational and group services for adolescents characteristic of most programs that have received Division of Youth Services funding, Sisters Mary Paul and Geraldine designed the after-school child care program to assist families with elementary school-age children and developed the idea of using older youth volunteers to help staff the after-school services. As discussed in chapter 5, this effort to engage youth in providing care for others rather than simply receiving services for themselves has had enormous positive results. Moreover, this program has enabled the center to serve a large number of children at a relatively low cost while providing a valuable youth development service for teenagers and giving them an opportunity to envision high school, college, or employment possibilities for themselves.

Such a program could certainly be replicated in many schools, settlement houses, and family service agencies *if* agency administrators were willing to invest in highly skilled professional program directors who can monitor the quality of care and the amount of stimulation provided to young children, engage parents and youth as volunteers, and offer needed mentoring and supervision to the volunteer counselors-in-training and youth staff.

High Priority Is Given to Staff Recruitment, Support, and Development

Another important principle applied at the center that could well be imitated is the enormous investment in and respect for staff members. Discussing staff qualifications and expertise, Sister Mary Paul stated: "We came from the outset with a commitment that we would have people [on the center's staff] who had a knowledge they could account for and that they could utilize. . . . I can't imagine doing this work with untrained people."

Careful attention is given to staff hiring and development. The center codirectors and program directors are naturally concerned about the professional training and experience of all job applicants, including those of activity specialists, and are eager to hire bilingual workers, but they also interview applicants carefully to ensure that their values are compatible with those of the center and that they have the flexibility, tolerance for ambiguity, and tenacity required to practice effectively in this setting. Thus staff are recruited who understand and identify personally with the center's mission, philosophy, and program model. This is described in various terms by staff. One stressed,

> I just like the whole philosophy of the center—that it's for the community, that people can come in and not worry about all sorts of red tape. . . . The clients accept the atmosphere here, that they're really treated like people . . . They're not treated like patients or clients.

Another noted, "The center is what I am about and what I have always been about . . . even before I got to the center. I found [here] something compatible with me and what I firmly believed . . . the work and the philosophy which I hold to. Workers here really believe in that." Consistent with the observations of the staff, we found a coherence and integrity between the philosophy and structure of the center and the personal and professional philosophies and commitments of the new and experienced staff who implement the center's programs. This greatly contributes to a synergy that both reflects and further enhances the sense of commitment and community.

Of critical importance in recruitment is the potential staff member's natural predilection to look for the strengths and for the potential—the "possibilities"—within the children and families with whom they will work. Staff must demonstrate a hopeful attitude and, as one worker explained, "be constantly willing to learn about a variety of things . . . and be willing to want to try to understand." In their discussions with us staff members voiced a strong belief in the capacity of Sunset Park's children and families, a deep respect for their struggles, a willingness to join daily with children and their families in their struggles, and, in doing so, to permit families to come to trust them.

Once people are hired, extensive attention is given to their supervision and ongoing professional development. Every staff member, including the program directors, receives individual or group supervision weekly. This practice not only provides for quality control but also ensures that staff members at every level receive the support they need to cope with the many challenges and demands placed upon their personal energy and time. As described in chapter 1, the center also provides an ongoing seminar on social group work to supplement staff skills in this practice method, which is extensively used in many center programs.

Staff support is highly individualized and varies dependent upon staff needs and experience. Staff members, like Sunset Park and its families, are viewed by the center directors, program directors, and supervisors as in the process of "becoming." To illustrate, newer staff members emphasized the multiple benefits derived from supervision. Experienced staff members emphasized the experience of a comfortable degree of staff autonomy. A strong commitment to mutual support characterizes staff relationships between the center directors, supervisors, and program staff. From both supervisors and colleagues, staff members receive ideas and encouragement.

It should also be noted that the center maintains flexible policies regarding workers' use of time. For example, although staff members in the preventive program are expected to be available to clients two evenings a week, they are free to start at different times in the morning and to take time off when needed to handle personal emergencies. This flexible attitude regarding time reflects the autonomy given to professional staff members to decide how best they can meet the needs of their clients. It is simply assumed that each person will put in whatever time is needed to work effectively and that client interests will always be placed first. This, of course, is very different from the personnel policies in many large service bureaucracies where professionals often experience little autonomy and feel they are constantly being monitored. In contrast, we found that the codirectors' enthusiasm about the work of the center draws forth an exceptional level of energy and commitment from staff that obviates the need for routine close monitoring or regulation. In a parallel way, the enthusiasm of the directors of each of the community school programs mobilizes a strong sense of responsibility and commitment among the CITs, activity specialists, and youth staff in these programs.

Sense of Community Within the Agency

In our conversations with staff members over several years we were struck by the frequent references to "a community of colleagues," "a sense of professional community," "a shared sense of mission," and "camaraderie" among staff members. This strong collective sense of commitment and community is clearly not accidental. The center's codirectors, program directors, supervisors, and experienced staff have purposefully nurtured a sense of community within the organization that parallels the experiences described by families—including the experience of feeling respected, being involved in important work, and being supported as they grow and change. Thus the center has developed a model that meets not only the needs of clients but also the professional needs of the staff who serves them.

A number of factors appear to contribute to and support this strong collective sense of professional commitment and community. These include

1. the recognition of the value of professional education in a range of disciplines in preparing staff to competently perform their specific roles;

2. the structural enactment of an inclusive definition of center staff (i.e., as discussed in chapter 1, staff in the various center programs are all identified as *center staff*);
3. the establishment of an organizational climate that encourages open discussion of challenges and collective problem solving as described above;
4. the recruitment and retention of staff with a) the inclination and ability to discern families' strengths and potential and to respect, join with, and support families in their day-to-day struggles; and b) personal and professional values congruent with the center's mission and philosophy;
5. the active expression of respect for staff members' professional expertise as well as for their needs for consultation and supervision, resources, and continued professional development.

Many of these factors are present or easily replicable in other human service settings. What appears to be worth consideration is the way in which these factors mutually reinforce each other when *all* are present consistently over time. Despite the multiple demands and severe stresses identified by staff as inherent in daily providing a range of services to impoverished and high-risk families, center staff members emphasize that the synergy created by their shared sense of professional commitment and community enables them to stay. And many staff members stay and stay and stay.

Institutional Supports and Alignments Are Cost- and Time-efficient

Sisters Geraldine and Mary Paul were enormously aided in their efforts by the center's unique organizational arrangement with St. Christopher-Ottalie and its executive director, Robert McMahon. As a satellite of this large agency, the center is able to draw on St. Christopher-Ottalie's resources for many administrative functions such as budgeting, personnel, and computer programming. This cuts their administrative costs and gives the center's directors more time for staff training and supervision, quality control, fund-raising, public relations, and community education and advocacy. In other words, the directors have always been able to stay directly involved with front-line service provision, which permits them to control the quality of services offered, inspire front-line staff with their sense of mission and purpose, and stay actively engaged in Sunset Park and the larger New York City human service community. Similar organizational arrangements could be utilized by other community-based agencies in which the professional staff and administrators know best how to provide effective, culturally sensitive services to clients, but lack some of the administrative skills or time required to manage a large programmatic operation.

THE IMPLICATIONS OF THE CENTER'S MODEL FOR PROFESSIONAL PRACTICE AND EDUCATION

In a fascinating book analyzing the lessons of the International Movement ATD Fourth World for overcoming social exclusion through the formation of alliances between ordinary people, families in extreme poverty, and social institutions (Rosenfeld and Tardieu 2000), Rosenfeld comments:

> In a process that stretched over several years, I realized, first, that there is indeed such a thing as social invention; second, that social work's role is to work with those whom nobody else wants to or knows how to work with; third, that the knowledge needed which today . . . I would define as "actionable" (Schon 1983), *can* be developed on the basis of "success stories," (i.e., actions that have had a satisfactory impact on people's lives); and fourth, that in the tension between theory and practice, theory is not master but equal: that in the field of change, theory more easily contributes descriptive rather than prescriptive knowledge. Theory is derived from what *is* but practice indicates what *is to be done.* (p. 192)

In the spirit of Rosenfeld's suggestion, we would like to highlight a few core themes that emerged from our analysis of the practice model at the center that have clear implications for social work practice and education, as do many of the practice and organizational principles presented above. As we have emphasized earlier, these are not new ideas. They have been underscored by other experts in the family and children's service field.

Flexible use of time and relationship. One important lesson for professional practitioners and educators is the value of social workers using time and relationship *differentially* in their ongoing work with program participants and clients. Unfortunately, due to the recent emphasis on managed care, practitioners are currently more often taught the importance of brief intervention guided by early contracting regarding service objectives and means. This is, of course, appropriate for many client populations. However, our research suggests that this service model may be dysfunctional for many high-risk families who require long-term, open-ended services in order to address their multiple personal and environmental problems and acquire needed skills in family living. Continuous access to services is essential for clients who need ongoing support and episodic emergency assistance provided by agency representatives with whom they have developed a relationship characterized by real trust. As Halpern stresses, "Change [with vulnerable families] takes time because it occurs partly—perhaps primarily—through the relationships that develop with helpers" (1997:265). Practitioners in family and child welfare should be trained and supported to provide this type of "extended family" help as well as planned short-term treatment.

Recognizing strengths and needs from a culturally aware perspective. Another important lesson for practitioners and educators is the need for cultural sensitivity and competence in dealing with different populations. For example, immigrant parents have demonstrated strength and courage in moving to a new country and have great hopes for the futures and possibilities for their children. It is essential that students be taught to recognize these strengths at the same time that they learn to help such parents learn the customs and norms of this country and to acquire the skills that will enable them to secure needed material resources and social supports. Unfortunately, students and beginning professionals too often tend to view low-income families from ethnic and national backgrounds that are different from their own as victims rather than recognizing their strengths and building on these in a culturally competent manner.

Understanding the benefits of service accessibility to families. Our research strongly suggests that it is essential that practitioners learn to value the provision of noncategorical supportive services to all families. It is only when help-seeking behaviors are normalized that immigrant and other families can learn that it is acceptable to obtain help from strangers and that there does not need to be any stigma associated with such behaviors. This is often a difficult learning task for students because it is easier in many ways to offer help to clients who have clearly defined problems than to reach out to all members of a community in ways that can promote healthy development.

Developing skill in designing individualized services. Another important implication of the practice approach employed at the center is the importance of individualizing client needs and services. As discussed earlier, the center's preventive program workers have neither established categories of service recipients nor rigid protocols of intervention. Their aim is to individualize services for each family and its members based on a careful assessment of needs and tasks. This is a more ambitious and ambiguous mandate than that employed in many agencies that have a relatively fixed theoretical approach and menu of interventions. It is important, however, for students and practitioners to learn to live with the uncertainties that an individualized comprehensive service approach involves. The individualizing of service plans enables clients to experience that the agency and their worker genuinely understand their needs and are really there for them.

Developing group work skills. In addition, the experience of the center suggests that practitioners working with children, youth, and families need to learn the value of developmental and activity groups and of integrating the performing arts in such activities. It is also important that social workers become skilled in work with groups and in interdisciplinary collaboration with activity and performing arts specialists (Kurland and Salmon 1998:109–130). As Smith and Carlson (1997) have concluded, based on their review of relevant research, four types of interventions tend to promote resilience among high-risk youth: enhancing self-esteem, promoting social skills, improving academic performance, and strengthening families and social supports (p. 243). The group services provided in the community school program are geared toward these ends.

Moving flexibly from case to cause. Social workers in community-based settings should also learn to move easily from case to cause so they can address the institutional obstacles that clients often face, work in partnership with clients and colleagues around advocacy issues, and help clients learn how to advocate for themselves. Because of the multiple roles social workers must assume in community-based settings, especially when they live in the community, it is also important that they learn how to manage the necessary movement among roles comfortably and become very skilled in conscious use of self in their practice.

RESEARCH IMPLICATIONS

There have been extensive discussions about using evaluation and research information to improve programs and policies. As discussed by Kubisch, Weiss, Schorr, and Connell (1995) there are research dilemmas inherent in any effort to study true community-based services. As these authors point out, a number of factors make it difficult to evaluate in a traditional manner all comprehensive community initiatives. These include the initiatives' horizontal and vertical complexity, contextual issues, flexible and evolving interventions, broad range of outcomes, and absence of a comparison or control group (pp. 3–5). Similarly, Schorr and Kubisch (1996) have argued that to be rigorously evaluated with traditional methods, interventions must meet conditions that are

> precisely the conditions that have been found to be incompatible with program effectiveness. Effective programs are adapted to respond to particular sites, families, and individuals; they change over time, with continuing mid-course corrections to raise the odds of success; they are comprehensive, complex, interactive, and multifaceted; they include efforts to change community conditions; they recognize their dependence on macro-economic and other large social forces, and they count on being able to make operational decisions locally." (p. A-18)

In other words, there is a mismatch between prevailing evaluation approaches and the characteristics of many community-based initiatives. Although the center is a single organization, not a comprehensive community initiative, we faced these dilemmas in the design of this study, the limitations of which are discussed in appendix A. At the beginning of the study period it was recognized that, because of financial, logistical, and ethical concerns and issues, neither an experimental nor a control group design was possible. Therefore, as Rossi (1992) has suggested, we cannot "establish what would have occurred in the program's absence" (p. 77) and thus argue that we *know* the center's approach "works." However, as described throughout this volume, our evaluation of the center's various programs yielded extensive evidence that program goals are achieved and positive changes occur in the children, youth, and families who participate in center programs. Thus, we can say with confidence that all the signs are promising.

Drawing upon our experiences as well as those of other organization staff and evaluators participating in the Annie E. Casey Foundation Grants Program, Weiss and Horsch (1998) articulated several implications for program evaluations conducted in nontraditional ways. These include the importance of flexibility, of nurturing evaluator-organization relationships, of including both qualitative and quantitative data in the evaluative design, and of engaging staff in the evaluation process. For example, the center's program directors, supervisors, and staff members were intimately involved in the evaluation process from the earliest planning stage to the interpretation of the findings. At first glance our proposed quantitative measurement of activities and outcome seemed to conflict with many of the agency's values, particularly their refusal to label clients. Thus ongoing discussions were critical regarding issues such as the inconsistencies between instrumentation and actual practice, the measurement of client problems by practitioners invested in identifying client's strengths, and concerns regarding the possible effects of in-depth interviews with program participants upon the process and outcomes of their engagement with center staff. Such an evaluative effort cannot succeed without the full cooperation of program staff. We have identified several additional implications for future research on comprehensive, multifaceted, flexible community-based programs, such as the center.

Recognition of the benefits derived from systematically engaging practitioners in articulating and reflecting upon their practice. As we emphasized in the first publication based upon this study (Hess, McGowan, and Meyer 1996), when developing policies and programs for low-income families and children, policy makers often draw on client and community experiences and on academic research, "but neglect to draw on the rich experiences and observations of practitioners who are serving these families and children" (p. 121). We found the practitioners at the Center for Family Life to be quite capable of articulating the conceptual bases of their work. We found a striking consistency between the descriptions of the center's operations, service processes, and outcomes by the center leadership and staff in our in-depth interviews with them and the quantitative data we collected about these program dimensions. People are doing what they say they are doing. This authenticity, in itself, is a significant study finding. An implication of this finding is that program evaluators would do well to view practitioners' observations, reflections, and insights about the needs of children and families, the benefits of alternative service delivery models, the obstacles to be surmounted in serving families, and programmatic changes that would support more effective service delivery as essential to ongoing program development and evaluation. We believe that systematic collection and analysis of practitioners' reflections upon their own practice (Hess 1995) is greatly underutilized in building knowledge for practice.

Attention to the sequencing of capacity building and evaluative efforts. Our research design assumed the phasing in of an information management system at the center by an external consultant. Of particular interest to us was the anticipated capacity of this system to determine the actual intensity of the comprehensive center services provided to families, i.e., the specific number of service episodes in multiple center services and the length of service use. Because of the complexity of the center's data needs, however, implementation of a fully functioning database management system took longer than expected. As a consequence, certain information hoped for was not available for the evaluation. Although evaluative research and program capacity building may at times productively coincide, caution is warranted in initiating an evaluation of a complex agency without ensuring that critical internal databases are fully operational. Thus capacity building initiatives and evaluative efforts should be carefully sequenced.

Attention to the phenomenon of recursion. Research on complex service systems such as the center must take into account the phenomena of recursion, meaning the cyclical interaction between information gathering and intervention. In any service system, knowledge regarding the needs and problems of program participants emerges over time. As the service process unfolds, problem definitions and desired outcomes are refined and redefined. What the worker knows about the case at time 1 is different than what he or she knows at time 2. Further, what is known at time 2 is dependent upon the processes that occur between times 1 and 2. This contributes to measurement problems that are difficult to address, particularly when looking at aggregate change across families over time. Although the collection of qualitative as well as quantitative data can inform the understanding of the service process, most instruments, including the Family Assessment Form used in this study, are intended to capture information at one point in time. Further development and testing of instruments to measure changes in individual, relational, and environmental variables that take into account the phenomena of recursion as well as the further development of appropriate analytic procedures are essential to future evaluative efforts.

Recognition of current limitations in measuring the results of community-centered family-focused practice. Finally, in evaluating complex service systems that define the family as the unit of attention and provide multiple points of service entry, researchers must expect an enormous challenge in attempting to determine which problems of which family members had what impact on overall family functioning and which interventions with which family members had what impact on any changes detected in either individuals or the family as a whole. Although systems theory suggests that an intervention at any point in the family system would affect both individual and collective functioning, the field must recognize the limitations that currently exist in measuring such interventive effects.

IMPLICATIONS FOR CHILD AND FAMILY POLICY

As Halpern (1999) concluded in his impressive history of social services for low-income families in the U.S.: "Not least, we have to work from the premise that there are no shortcuts to strengthening supportive services for poor families" (p .258). There have been multiple attempts to find quick-fix solutions to the problems of high-risk and dysfunctional families unable to provide adequately for their children. The most recent of these was widespread adoption of the Homebuilders short-term model of family preservation services, with little attention to the limits as well as the potential benefits of this approach. New York State, which was the first to provide extensive funding for services designed to prevent placement of children in foster care, essentially undercut the real value of this program by distinguishing between "mandatory" and optional cases and ensuring funding only for mandated cases in which children were at high risk of maltreatment and/or foster placement within ninety days. The success of the center's open-ended, noncategorical approach to preventing foster care placement in our study sample of 423 children in families raises questions about the ultimate usefulness of such a targeted approach to preventive services.

The importance of a continuum of accessible service options. Thus a key policy implication of this study is the importance of casting a broad net and providing early and easily accessible intervention to *all* families and children who may be at risk, not simply offering help to those who are already displaying problematic behaviors. Moreover, these early intervention services should be offered on a flexible, voluntary basis that allows families and youth to seek opportunities for growth in multiple ways at different stages of life. From a policy perspective, if we are concerned about enhancing life opportunities for all low-income children, the concern should be too little take-up, not too much take-up, of services that could make a difference.

Unfortunately, most federal programs for children and youth define services in very narrow terms that require diagnostic, behavioral, or income classifications to determine service eligibility, as do many state programs. Moreover, many publicly funded programs essentially prescribe which services should be offered to whom. As a consequence, there is little room for professional discretion or consumer choice. Yet the experiences of the center suggest that service options are essential. As our study indicates, families and children are likely to do best when they have a choice about which types of service they need and want and when they want to receive them.

Rigidity in service time frames, separation of services, and location of services should be questioned. Our findings also raise serious questions about the wisdom of imposing tight time lines on parents trying to resolve problems that may lead to the placement of the children in foster care, as is currently mandated under the Adoption and Safe Families Act of 1997. The center's success in integrating family support and family preservation services also raises doubts about the traditional separation of these services, which was essentially legitimized by the Family Preservation and Support Services Program of 1993, P.L. 103–66. On a positive note, the center's practice of using community-based foster care services that link prevention and after-care services to foster care is now being replicated in a number of locations. If these initiatives prove successful, we would recommend that Title IV-E, which authorizes federal reimbursement for many state costs for foster care, be amended to require more widespread, systematic use of community-based foster care and other community-based supports.

Salaries must compensate for professional training and expertise. The value of professionally trained social workers emerges clearly from our findings.

Yet salaries at the center are relatively low compared to salaries in other fields of practice such as health care. The center's administrators report a constant struggle in hiring highly skilled and experienced professionals because social work graduates typically owe large amounts in student loans. Center staff members described low salaries and the associated sense of being devalued by society despite the importance and difficulty of the work they are doing as a source of stress. To address this problem it is essential that increased federal training grants be made available to students eager to pursue professional careers in family and children's services and that state and local reimbursement formulas for voluntary agencies be modified to reflect the cost of educational preparation and the value of professional knowledge and skills.

Flexible, open-ended, noncategorical service to youth should be supported. The success of the community school program in providing safe, stimulating, relatively low-cost after-school and summer child care for children and in engaging adolescents and parents in nurturing, communal activities that help to build social capital in Sunset Park suggests that this program model could well be replicated if more federal and state funding were made available for services that emphasize age integration in low-income communities. This program again highlights the value of providing flexible, open-ended, noncategorical services to all youth rather than trying to target specific populations at risk.

Finally, we must emphasize, as Halpern (1999) has noted, "Services may work at the margins of family and community life. The support they provide may be modest. Yet that modest support, in its way, is critical" (p. 261). Clearly, neither the center nor any type of family and child service agency can address all the needs in a low-income immigrant community with a high proportion of single-parent families, limited employment opportunities, deteriorating housing, overcrowded schools, and limited child care resources. The families in Sunset Park, like those in similar communities across the country, need a heavy investment of material resources to help them out of poverty. However, services such as those provided by the center can make a significant difference in the quality of family life and the opportunities and aspirations of youth living in such communities.

APPENDIX A

STUDY DESIGN AND METHODOLOGY

■

As described in the introduction, the Center for Family Life was selected as a grantee by the Annie E. Casey Foundation Evaluation Grants Program. The selection occurred through a competitive process in which leading researchers, policy makers, and practitioners in the field of children's services nominated well-established programs with strong reputations that shared the defining characteristics of the foundation's own service initiatives, i.e., they are preventive, collaborative, comprehensive, flexible, and family focused. After the center received notification of this award, its directors and the foundation sought a research team to undertake an independent comprehensive evaluation. The authors submitted a plan for evaluation to the center's directors and the foundation and were subsequently selected to conduct the study.

STUDY DESIGN

We conceptualized the overall study design as a case study (Orum, Feagin, and Sjoberg 1991; Stake 1994, 1995, 1998; Yin 1994) of the Center for Family Life in the context of the Sunset Park community. Within this design we incorporated interrelated multiphased substudies of specific center programs as well as collected data about the center as a whole. Over the study period we employed multiple methods to collect extensive quantitative and qualitative data from different sources regarding the nature of the center's programs.

Stake has noted that, drawing from naturalistic, holistic, ethnographic, phenomenological, and biographic research methods, "case study is the study of the particularity and complexity of a single case, coming to understand its activity within important circumstances" (1995:xi). Yin (1994:13) stated that "the case study as a research strategy comprises an all-encompassing method—with the logic of design incorporating specific approaches to data collection and to data analysis" and emphasized that the case study method is the preferred strategy when the focus is on a "contemporary phenomenon within its real-life context."

This study had as it overriding purpose to understand what can be learned about and from the Center for Family Life as an exemplary case. This illuminative approach to evaluation (Gordon 1991) uses a "variety of exploratory techniques to develop an overall understanding of the entire practice milieu. . . . And the investigation progressively focuses and refocuses on processes, structures, issues, or questions that emerge as significant during the course of the exploration" (p. 371). As Gordon has outlined, an illuminative approach will "(1) focus on practice milieu, (2) progressively concentrate focus, (3) generate descriptive data, (4) ensure variety in data-gathering media and 'triangulation,' and (5) interpret and explain" (pp. 371–372). This approach has enabled us to address the components of the evaluation outlined by the Annie E. Casey Foundation and to provide extensive detail in response to the research questions that we posed (see below).

Study components and questions. As described in the foundation's request for proposals (1993:3–4), the evaluation included the following interdependent components:

1. why and how the center came into being;
2. the center's service array, service delivery strategies, and activity level, and how the center is organized, managed, and staffed;
3. the process of center operations, focusing on the characteristics of the center's participant populations and the experience of participants, from their initial contact with the program throughout their involvement with the center; and
4. service outcomes, including intermediate outcomes, such as participation and retention in program activities and improved family functioning, and, where possible, long-term outcomes, such as reduction in out-of-home placement and improvement in school achievement.

We outlined a number of research questions to be addressed. Many reflected our recognition that identifying and describing the "content and manner of the service being delivered" is a critical stage in the development and evaluation of a program (Cheetham 1992:276). The questions included the following:

1. How are the center's mission and philosophy defined and perceived by the center's administrators, staff, volunteers, and clients? How are these defined by community residents and leaders familiar with the work of the center? In what ways are the center's mission and philosophy operationalized in different service programs?

2. What are the key service characteristics of the different program components? How are the service needs assessed? What difference, if any, does point of access make in the types of services offered to and used by families? What combinations of service are used by different clients at different times in the family life cycle? On what bases and how are clients referred or channeled from one program component to another?

3. How and by whom are different services delivered? What are the key programmatic strategies and practice interventions?

4. What are the characteristics of the client population served by the center? What are similarities and differences between the clients served by the different program components? How does the center's client population compare to the larger population of Sunset Park?

5. What draws clients and volunteers to the center? How do workers and clients view and evaluate the services offered? Do these perceptions vary by program? Do they change over time?

6. How are program accomplishments and client outcomes evaluated at the center? To what degree do clients achieve their initial service goals? How do their service goals and achievement change over time? How do the functional parenting capacities of adult clients in different programs change over time? How do children and youth benefit from their own and parental involvement at the center? What changes can be observed in the youth who participate in the center's various leadership activities? What sustains and discourages client involvement over time?

7. How do different client outcomes relate to different service inputs? What are the service processes that facilitate different types of growth and change for various groups of clients? Which service inputs and processes have little apparent impact?

8. How does the center contribute to the process of community development in Sunset Park? How is its role perceived by public officials, representatives of other established institutions, community leaders, and residents?

What are its achievements as a catalyst for change in this community? What are the obstacles confronted? In what ways do its youth leadership and training programs contribute to the community development process?

9. What are the obstacles the center encounters in attempting to offer comprehensive, developmental, family-focused services at a time when public policies and funding streams generally encourage provision of highly targeted, problem-focused, remedial services to individuals at risk? What are the perceived organizational and client benefits and strains of this approach?

10. How are organizational integration and staff morale sustained? What are the personnel, structural, and community variables that permit the center to pursue its mission and tasks?

Our study approach. We were committed to designing a study that would capture the spirit, dynamism, and complexity of this organization. To that end, we collected detailed data from multiple perspectives, including those of administrators and of professional and volunteer program staff, family members participating in a broad range of center programs and activities, and community leaders. To explore the interrelationships of the center's various services while examining the interventive processes and outcomes of each program component, we conducted multiphased substudies. For example, in the community school programs we initially conducted participant observations and key informant interviews to develop descriptions of the program's goals, design, and activities and to identify issues and themes related to program implementation and experiences of program participants. Questions, issues, and findings emerging from the analysis of these data formed the basis for the semistructured questions used in focus groups with parents of children in the after-school programs and with youth who both served as CITs in these programs and received mentoring and other center services. Based upon the analysis of the transcripts of the focus groups, a telephone survey of a random sample of parents of children enrolled in the after-school program was designed and implemented as described later in this appendix. In each center program multiphased substudies and ongoing data collection and analysis permitted identification and analysis of the specific characteristics and details of each service as well as assessment of the contributions of each to the center's overall functioning.

The authors, the center's codirectors, and the study's funding source agreed that due to financial, logistical, and ethical concerns neither an experimental nor a control group design was possible. Relationships between the services provided through the various programs and perceived changes in family members or families are thus assessed by the self-report of program participants, reports by center practitioners, and study instruments. The study findings establish the nature of the center's services, families' service use patterns, the specific services received by a sample of families served by the preventive program during a thirty-month period, changes in children and families as identified through study instruments, and the process and impact of the services as perceived and reported by center administrators and staff, parents, youth, and other family members, and community leaders.

The study design greatly enhanced the trustworthiness of our data, findings, and interpretations. The length of time spent over the study period at the research site, developing relationships with respondents, interviewing respondents, and collecting data by other methods increased the degree of openness between the agency administrators, staff, and program participants and the research team (Glesne 1999:151). Incorporation of multiple substudies over time permitted extensive triangulation of data and findings, further contributing to their credibility. Frequent, ongoing member/informant checking (Glesne 1999; Spradley 1980) with center administrators, supervisors, and practitioners verified that we were accurately reflecting their perspectives, their rationale for program design and activities, and the issues and concerns that shaped the center's ongoing development and commitments.

DATA SOURCES, METHODS OF DATA COLLECTION, AND DATA ANALYSIS

Data collection began in October 1993 and continued through July 1997. Selected follow-up data were collected during the summer of 1999. The systematic collection of data from multiple sources over time enhanced the comprehensiveness of the data collection and the robustness of analysis (Drisko 1997; Glesne 1999). As depicted at the end of this appendix, data sources and methods of collection included in-depth semistructured interviews with center administrators and staff, families participating in center programs, and community leaders; review of center documents, records, and correspondence; the center's management information system (FACTORS) regarding services to 4,630 families during a twenty-four-month period;

standardized case data collected on a prospective sample of 189 families served in the center's preventive program using the Family Assessment Form (McCroskey, Nishimoto, and Subramanian 1991; McCroskey and Meezan 1997), Intake Recording Form, Monthly Progress Report, Service Needs/Service Utilization Report, and Case Closing Recording Form; participant observation in multiple programs; a telephone survey of 139 families participating in one community school program and focus groups of participants in a community school program as well as staff in the employment program; logs completed by staff in multiple programs; and other standardized instruments completed by program participants and staff. Instruments modified or created for this study are presented in appendix B.

Data were collected, entered, and analyzed by the authors, by Dr. Barbara Simon, and by ten students—eight Columbia School of Social Work (CUSSW) doctoral students, a CUSSW masters student, and an undergraduate student majoring in psychology. All students were fully trained in methods of data collection, data entry, and/or data analysis.

In-depth semistructured interviews. To capture complex interactions among variables expected to account for each program's process and outcomes, the members of the research team conducted in-depth, semistructured interviews from the initiation of the study to its conclusion. Focused interviews were used to identify critical program variables and their relative influence from the perspective of center administration, staff, family members participating in center programs and activities, and community leaders. (Interview guides are included in appendix B.) Thus we were able to examine the detail and nuances of program design and operation and of practitioners' and family members' experiences. Conducting interviews that explored both practitioners' and families' perspectives (Hess and Folaron 1993; Taylor and Bogdan 1984; Wells and Freer 1994) using a series of questions that were asked of each respondent permitted data, investigator, and methodological triangulation (i.e., the use of a variety of data sources, several different researchers, and multiple methods to study a problem; Denzin 1978; Stake 1995). Moreover, extensive interviewing over time permitted us to reach a point of saturation "where further informants repeat data already provided and add no more to the development of codes, interpretation or theory" (Drisko 1997:192).

Interviews were tape-recorded, transcribed, and analyzed using the constant comparative method of qualitative analysis (Glaser and Strauss 1967;

Turner 1981). The ongoing identification of emergent categories, themes, and patterns of responses permitted us to further explore, elaborate, and verify findings prior to the conclusion of the study.

Since one of the authors (McGowan) had studied the center's development in the context of previous research and had published several related reports, we sought to bring a new perspective to the study of the center's mission, history, and relationship with the community of Sunset Park. Therefore, we asked Dr. Barbara Simon, a social welfare historian and practice scholar, to examine the nature and meanings of the relationship between the community and the center since its founding. Dr. Simon conducted in-depth interviews ranging from 40 to 120 minutes in length with 20 informants, including community leaders, principals in the public schools in which the center provides programs, present and former staff leaders, the center's Advisory Board chair, the head of a foundation that has provided center support, and a child welfare advocate. Following interviews with community leaders in relevant positions, Dr. Simon expanded the group of informants through snowball sampling. Her methodology and findings were provided to the research team in an unpublished report (Simon 1995).

Center documents, records, and correspondence. We reviewed program budgets, proposals, and reports, all annual progress reports, the codirectors' correspondence, preventive program case records, newsletters, and other administrative records for data regarding center services and operations and characteristics of program participants. Additional historical and current data regarding the demographics of the Sunset Park community were collected by Barbara Simon (1995), Yvonne Johnson (1997), and Ernst Van-Bergeijk.

Management Information System. Our analysis of program operations drew upon data produced through FACTORS, a Management Information System (MIS) introduced at the time the study was initiated. Peter Martin Associates and Metis Associates collaborated with the center in the development of this system. With the assistance of Metis Associates we were able to extract a file containing a record of approximately 48,000 person-service episodes from FACTORS. This file included the CFL service type, the date of service initiation, and, when applicable, the date of service termination. Botsko analyzed these data to determine which center programs were used by 4,630 families during the 1994 and 1995 calendar years.

We had hoped that the FACTORS MIS would have permitted the tracking of cases prospectively through the center service system from service entry to exit, thereby generating a map of the clients' service pathways as well as identifying the intensity of comprehensive services received by individual families. However, because of the complexity of the center's data needs, implementation of a fully functional FACTORS database management system took longer than expected. Therefore, as noted in various points in this volume, we were unable to obtain the information needed to fully address a few of the research questions. In some instances we were able to substitute data from other sources. For example, in the preventive program, to determine the frequency of worker-family contact, we substituted practitioner reports that are submitted to the public child welfare agency regarding contacts with families. However, with regard to the overall intensity services to families with family members receiving multiple concurrent center services, we could find no adequate substitute for the data expected from FACTORS.

Standardized case data. Because the preventive program is viewed by the agency as the "core" of its work, we emphasized this program in the study design. In addition to data collected through in-depth semistructured interviews, review of records, and from MIS data as described above, we collected extensive case-specific data on the services provided to a prospective sample of 189 families opened for service in the preventive program between November 15, 1993, and May 15, 1995, and served through May 15, 1996, the end of the study's data collection phase. This sampling strategy allowed us to follow all cases for at least one year and up to thirty months subsequent to case initiation. Workers reported case data using a modified version of the Family Assessment Form (FAF), an instrument developed by the Children's Bureau of Los Angeles (McCroskey, Nishimoto, and Subramanian 1991; McCroskey and Meezan 1997). The FAF incorporates an ecological approach to assessing family functioning and requires the family's worker to provide referral and case history, characteristics of caregivers, children, and others in the household, sources of income and housing, assessment of family members and of family interactions on numerous dimensions, and case objectives. The unmodified FAF measures six dimensions of family functioning/family environment using thirty-six Likert-type items: parent-child interactions, caregiver interactions, parental social support, family living conditions, family financial conditions, and developmental stimulation of children. As reported by Meezan (1995), tests of the internal consistency of the FAF subscales using Cronbach's alpha range from a low of .68 (developmental stimulation of children) to a high of .93 (parent-child interactions). Interrater reliability on the nine-point items (plus or minus one full step) is 89.2 percent.

As described in appendix B, we modified the FAF to include two additional questions. The first concerns the caregivers' history of engaging in physical violence; the second concerns the caregivers' attitude toward their parenting roles. A factor analysis performed by Botsko on the modified FAF revealed a ten-dimensional factors structure: home environment, family finances, community environment, social support, parent-child interactions, caregiver responsibility, caregiver emotional control, factors undermining parenting, caregiver victimhood, and self-esteem/stability. Tests of internal consistency of the modified FAF subscales using Cronbach's alpha ranged from a low of .72 (caregiver victimhood) to a high of .96 (parent-child interactions). The underlying factor structure was quite similar to that found by Meezan (1995). We employed the new factor structure to create the subscales used in this study to assess outcome.

In addition to the six measures of family functioning, the FAF contains a behavior checklist that measures a child's school-related problems, health and developmental status, and inner-directed disturbances. The checklist was modified by imposing a Likert-type response frame on each item so that problem intensity could be measured. Previous research by McGowan and Botsko in a school-based drop-out prevention program indicated that this modification improves the checklist's utility as a measure of problem definition and outcome. Factor analysis was performed on the modified version of the behavior checklist. This analysis revealed an eight-dimensional factor structure: positive child behaviors, difficulties in developmental well-being, emotional disturbance, difficulties in relating, physical health, learning difficulties, serious emotional disturbance, and indicators of maturity. Tests of internal consistency of the modified FAF subscales using Cronbach's alpha ranged from a low of .76 (serious emotional disturbance) to a high of .93 (positive child behavior).

The FAF was completed after the third session with the client-family by each family's assigned worker. In order to assess intermediate outcomes and to detect problems that emerged during the course of intervention, repeated measures regarding each family were administered at six-month intervals through the thirty-month period and when each case was closed. Data were collected regarding 189 families following three sessions: 168 families at 6 months of service, 148 families at 12 months of service; 95 families at 18 months of service; and 16 families at 24 months of service. FAFs were also administered at case closing on all 92 families whose cases were closed prior to the conclusion of data collection.

Case-specific data on the 189 study sample families were also collected through the CFL Intake Recording Form (see appendix B), the Monthly Progress Report (an aggregated report of case activity provided by the center staff to the New York City public child welfare agency), a Service Needs/Service Utilization Report, developed in consultation with program staff (see appendix B), the CFL Case Closing Recording Form, and the FACTORS (MIS) data. Data collected through these multiple sources supplemented information gathered through the FAF as well as provided resources for data verification.

Participant observation. Throughout the three-year study period research team members also directly observed interactions in several programs and activities for extended periods of time. These included observations of the after-school child care program over a period of several weeks, a weekend-long observation of a counselor-in-training (CIT) retreat, frequent lengthy observations of service activities occurring at the Storefront Center (thrift shop, food bank, advocacy clinic), and observation of several musical performances, an evening at the Teen Center, a parent Advisory Council meeting, and a community carnival. Participant observations were conducted primarily by doctoral students, who kept field notes, took pictures, and met regularly with Hess and McGowan to review their observations, questions, and findings. In the community school program the findings derived from participant observation served as the basis for further observation and the development of semistructured interviews and focus groups. Drisko (1997) states "participant observation data allow a check of how the [interview and record] texts correspond to enacted programs, staff member behaviors, and client reactions" (p. 190). Consistent with this observation, in the storefront programs (emergency food bank, thrift shop, and advocacy clinic) participant observation, together with key informant interviews and staff logs, generated the findings reported in chapter 6.

Focus groups and telephone survey. The research team conducted seven focus groups that were audiotaped and transcribed for analysis. Six focused upon one of the center's community school projects and were co-led by McGowan and doctoral students. Four were conducted with a total of twenty-four youth providing and receiving services in the counselor-in-training program. Two were conducted with fourteen parents of children who served in a range of community school programs, including after-school child care. A focus group with staff in the Employment Services Program was also conducted by Hess.

Following the identification of the themes and issues emerging from the parents' and youth's focus groups regarding the after-school child care program, we further accessed parents' perspectives regarding the center's community school programs through a telephone survey. This survey of 139 parents, drawn randomly within each of three language groups (English, Spanish, and Cantonese) from a total sample of 350, was conducted in the parents' primary language by three doctoral students, all of whom were trained and supervised by McGowan. The survey (see appendix B) was administered in these three languages.

Standardized instruments. We administered two rapid assessment instruments (Hare Self-Esteem Scale and the Nowicki-Strickland Locus of Control) at four points in time to fifty youth in the Project Youth program. The Nowicki-Strickland Locus of Control Scale is a forty-item scale "designed to measure whether or not a child believes that reinforcement comes by chance or fate (external locus of control) or because of his or her behavior (internal locus of control)" (Nowicki and Strickland 1987:402). Internal locus of control has long been associated with positive academic achievement. The Hare Self-Esteem Scale is a thirty-item instrument designed to measure the general self-esteem of school-age youngsters aged ten or over, as well as their self-esteem in three distinct domains: peers, parents, and teachers (Hare 1987). Findings were compared with young adolescents in a drop-out prevention program at a junior high school in East Harlem and are reported in chapter 5.

Staff logs. To generate data not routinely recorded by the center, at designated intervals staff in the Storefront Center maintained structured logs regarding the number and nature of services provided. The framework for the logs was generated by McGowan in collaboration with the staff who were to maintain them. Data generated through these logs are primarily reported in chapter 6.

Study limitations. As discussed in chapter 7, the current limitations that exist in measuring the results of community-centered, family-focused practice are acknowledged. Although systems theory suggests that an intervention at any point in the family system would affect both individual and collective functioning, the inadequacy of currently available instruments and methods for measuring such complex interventive effects present a challenge in attempting to determine which problems of which family members had what impact on overall family functioning and which interventions with which family members had what impact on any changes detected in either individuals or the family as a whole. Further, although the Family Assessment Form permitted us to capture information regarding family members' problems and needs at several points in time, this instrument addresses neither the refinement and redefinition of family problems and needs that occurs over time nor the cyclical interaction between information gathering and intervention. Further development and testing of instruments to measure changes in individual, relational, and environmental variables that take into account the phenomena of recursion as well as the further development of appropriate analytic procedures are essential to future study of the outcomes of complex programs and interventions.

TABLE A1

Sources and Samples At a Glance

Data Source	Program Sample	Year: 1: 10/1/93–9/30/94 1	2: 10/1/94–9/30/95 2	3: 10/1/95–9/30/96 3	4: 10/1/96–7/1/97 4
THE CENTER AS A WHOLE					
Interviews with CFL administrators/staff	*entire center*	x	x	x	x
Interviews with CFL program participants	*entire center*	x	x	x	x
Program proposals and reports	*entire center*	x	x	x	x
Historical and demographic documents	*entire center*	x	x	x	x
Interviews with community leaders	*entire center*	x	x		
Interviews with visitors from other states	*entire center*				x
Budgets, fiscal data	*entire center*	x	x	x	x
MIS data/FACTORS	*entire center*		x	x	
Interview with full staff	*entire center*		x		
PREVENTIVE PROGRAM/FOSTER CARE					
Intake forms	189 families	x	x	x	
Family Assessment Forms	*189 families*	x	x	x	
Monthly progress report	*189 families*	x	x	x	
Service needs/ utilization report	*189 families*	x	x	x	
Case closing form	*182 families*	x	x	x	x
Semistructured interviews with 20 staff	*all preventive program staff*	x	x		
Semistructured interviews with 11 staff, 11 family members	*11 preventive cases*	x	x		
MIS data/FACTORS	*preventive subsample and entire center*		x	x	

TABLE A1 Sources and Samples At a Glance (*continued*)

Data Source	Program Sample	Year: 1: 10/1/93– 9/30/94 1	2: 10/1/94– 9/30/95 2	3: 10/1/95– 9/30/96 3	4: 10/1//96– 7/1/97 4
	COMMUNITY DEVELOPMENT				
Codirectors' correspondence	*entire center*	x	x	x	x
Periodic interviews with codirectors	*entire center*	x	x	x	x
Interviews with community leaders	*entire center*		x		
	COMMUNITY SCHOOL PROJECT, P.S. 314				
Focus groups, parents	*2 groups, 14 parents*		x		
Focus groups, CITs	*4 groups, 24 youth*		x		
Telephone survey in Spanish, English, Cantonese	*random sample of 139 parents*		x		
Program observation	*after-school program*		x		
Program observation	*Parent Advisory Council*		x		
Program observation	*CIT training/retreat*		x		
Hare Self-Esteem Scale	*50 youth*		x	x	
Nowicki-Strickland Locus of Control	*50 youth*		x	x	
Staff reports school performance	*Project Youth participants*		x	x	
Retrospective interviews CITs	*12 youth*			x	
Intensive interviews, all full-, selected part-time staff	*community school programs*		x	x	
MIS data/FACTORS	*entire center*		x	x	
	STOREFRONT CENTER				
Activity logs	*advocacy clinic*			x	x
Referral outcome logs	*Storefront Center (thrift shop, food bank, advocacy clinic)*			x	x
Program observation	*Storefront Center*			x	
Administrative records	*Storefront Center*	x	x	x	x
MIS data/FACTORS	*entire center*		x	x	
	EMPLOYMENT CENTER				
Focus group with staff	*employment center*			x	
MIS data/FACTORS	*entire center*		x	x	

APPENDIX B

INSTRUMENTS MODIFIED OR CREATED FOR THIS STUDY

■

B.1. The CFL Intake Coding Form

B.2. The Family Assessment Form

B.3. The Service Needs/Service Utilization Report

B.4. Telephone Survey of Parents of Children Served in the After-School Program

B.5. Outline for Focus Group Meetings: Parents of Children in After-School Program at P.S. 314

B.6. Focus Group CFL P.S. 314/CFL P.S. 1 Program

B.7. Preventive Services Program, Guide for Interviews with Workers

B.8. Case Study Interviews with Preventive Services Workers

B.9. Case Study Interviews with Family Members

APPENDIX B.1

THE CFL INTAKE CODING FORM

All families referred to the preventive program are scheduled for an intake interview. With families who self-refer, an intake appointment is scheduled when a family member calls to request services. When someone who is not a family member calls to refer a family for preventive services, the referral source is asked to have a family member call for an appointment.

Approximately an eighth of the families (twenty-four) in the study sample were scheduled for an intake interview the same day as their referral to the agency. Half of the families met with an intake worker within four days of the referral, and 90 percent of the families met with the intake interviewer within sixteen days of the referral contact. The mean number of days between initial agency contact and the intake interview was 6.4 days.

Intake interviews with English-speaking families were conducted by Sister Mary Paul. Spanish-speaking families were interviewed by Anita Cleary, a supervisor in the preventive program, or by another Spanish-speaking practitioner.

Information from the intake interview is routinely recorded by the interviewer on an Intake Recording Form. Through an iterative process whereby several members of the research team analyzed the content of 30 intake forms, 47 categories of caregiver- and child-centered problems were identified and subsequently used to code the information contained in the intake forms for all 189 families included in the preventive program study sample.

After the intake forms were coded, the identified items were collapsed into six caregiver-related problems at intake—personal health/mental health, parent/child conflict, marital/domestic partner conflict, child maltreatment, substance abuse and service needs—and five child-related problems—parent/child/family conflict, victimization, school behavior problems, substance abuse, and personal health/mental health. These eleven categories were then used in the subsequent analysis.

Instructions for completing the CFL Intake Coding Form, the Coding Form, and the collapsed categories follow.

CFL INTAKE CODING INSTRUMENT INSTRUCTIONS

The purpose of the coding instrument is to extract information from the referral narrative detailing the *presenting* and *historic* problems of the client-family as defined by the referral source, the intake interviewer and the client-family members. The instrument is four pages, printed back-to-back on two sheets of paper. Attached to each instrument is a copy of a CFL Referral Form. The Case Name listed on both the Referral Form and the Instrument should match. If they do not match, do not complete the instrument.

Throughout the instructions I refer to the Referral Form as the *form* and the coding instrument as the *instrument.*

The information contained in the referral forms is confidential. Keep the form and the instrument secure at all times.

PAGE 1 INSTRUCTIONS:

Intake Worker: The intake worker is the person or persons listed as the interviewer on the referral form. If there were two interviewers, list them in order of their appearance on the referral form.

Language: Under Language Spoken on the form.

Referral Source: Under Source of Referral on the form. Note: You may discover, after reading the narrative, that there was more than one referral source. Please indicate the Primary or Initial Source of the referral by using the letter "P" and the Secondary Source by using the letter "S" when completing the checklist.

Family Previously Known to CFL: This item refers only to previous contact with CFL's Preventive Service Program. Do not check "yes" if the family was only known because of their contact with the after-school, employment, advocacy programs, etc. . . . There usually is an additional notation typed on the form indicating the date of the original referral. The item on the instrument—"Date of previous CFL contact"—refers to this date.

PAGE 2 INSTRUCTIONS:

Number days between referral and intake interview: There may have been more than one intake interview. To answer this question, calculate the number of days using the date of the client's initial interview.

Number of days between intake and case assignment: Again, use the initial in-person interview date to calculate the number of days.

FAMILY MEMBER TABLE

There are seven columns in this table labeled: ID; Family Member; Questions A thru E.

ID "A1" refers to Caregiver 1—the first Family Member beneath the Caregiver subheading in the table. "A2" refers to Caregiver 2; and "A3" to Caregiver 3.

ID "C1" refers to the first child beneath the Children subheading in the table, "C2" is child 2, and so on.

If "NONE" is printed in the Family Member column, there is no caregiver or child that corresponds to that ID.

These ID's will be used to complete the Caregiver and Child Problem Tables.

> **DO NOT CHANGE THE ID'S OR FAMILY COMPOSITION BY ADDING OR DELETING FAMILY MEMBERS UNDER THE CAREGIVER OR CHILDREN SUBHEADINGS.**

If any individual not listed under the Caregiver or Children subheadings is in attendance at the intake interview, add their names and family roles under the subheading "Other Persons." Refer to these attendees as OP1, OP2, OP3.

There are five questions in the table. Read the narrative carefully to determine the answers to the questions. You may want to complete the Caregiver Problem Table and the Children's Problem Table on the following pages before completing this grid.

Question A: Who attended intake? Check-off any member who attended *any* intake session.

Question B: Who defined problem? This refers *only* to those family members in attendance at the intake sessions. It does not include the intake worker or referral source (if in attendance), or any caregivers or children not in attendance at the intake session.

Question C: Who did client(s) define as source of problem? The client must specify that he/she believes that the behavior or attitude of a family member is causing a problem that needs to be addressed.

Question D: Who did worker define as source of problem? The intake worker must specify that she believes that the behavior or attitude of a family member is causing a problem that needs to be addressed.

Question E: Who did referral source define as source of problem? The referral source must specify that he/she believes that the behavior or attitude of a family member is causing a problem that needs to be addressed.

CAREGIVER PROBLEM TABLE

The purpose of this table is to extract information from the referral narrative detailing how each of the significant case actors at intake are defining both the current and historic problems of the family system.

A "current" problem can be considered the presenting problem, a problem that the family members and the caseworker should formulate their initial contract around. A "current" problem can also be a problem that the family member feels needs to be addressed in the coming sessions. The intake worker, the referral source, and the family member(s) may have different perceptions about what problems that need to be attended to. Your own clinical judgment may lead you to believe that the problem, as defined, may be ill-conceived or poorly articulated, and that the source of the problem may be misdirected. However, we need to know how each *case actor* is defining the situation that led to the intake, regardless of your perception of the problem's authenticity.

A "historic" problem is a past or concurrent event, situation, or behavior that may or may not be contributing to the "current" problem as viewed by the individual case actors. It is not seen as a presenting problem by the individual case actor(s). It is not the individual case actor's focus for the expected formulation of the contract. It is considered to be "in background" by the case actor(s).

Individual case actors may not define the problem in the same way. The Referral Source may believe that Caregiver 2's drinking is a "current" problem, but Caregiver 1 may believe that the drinking is under control and therefore is a "historic" problem.

CFL INTAKE CODING FORM

CFL ID:

CASE NAME:

Intake Worker:_______________ Intake Date: ________________________

Language: English ______ Spanish:________ Other:______

Referral Source:

Formal External:

_____ .CWA _____Police

_____ Child Guidance counselor_____ Hospital Staff Member

_____ Teacher _____ Non-CFL Daycare

_____ Other School Staff Member_____ Non-CFL After-School Program

_____ Other
(What:____)

Internal CFL:

_____ After-School Program ______ Advocacy Clinic

_____ Employment Project______ Parent Group

_____ Project Youth

_____ Other
(What:____)

Informal:

_____ Self _____ Friend

_____ Relative _____ Other
(What:______________________________)

Family previously known to CFL:

_____ Yes _____ No _____ Not Sure

If yes, date of previous CFL contact:_________________________

CFL ID:

Number of days between referral and intake interview: ______________

Number of days between intake and case assignment: ______________

A = who attended intake?

B = who defined problem?

C = who did client define as source of problem?

D = who did worker define as source of problem?

E = who did referral source define as source of problem?

ID	Family Member	A	B	C	D	E
CAREGIVER						
A1						
A2						
A3						
CHILDREN						
C1						
C2						
C3						
C4						
C5						
OTHER PERSONS: LIST NAME AND FAMILY ROLE (E.G. HUSBAND NOT IN HOUSEHOLD, PARAMOUR)						
OP1						
OP2						
OP3						

Reason for referral:

Code C = client defined problem

W = worker defined problem

R= referral source defined problem

Caregiver Problems	Caregiver 1		Caregiver 2		Caregiver 3	
	Current	Historic	Current	Historic	Current	Historic
drug abuse						
alcohol abuse						
physical abuse of children						
neglect of children						
sexual abuse of children						
criminal behavior						
domestic violence perpetrator						
domestic violence victim						
marital/domestic partner conflict						
separation/divorce						
bereavement						
conflictual relationship with children						
parental role problem/ parenting skills						
parent/child communication						
physical health problem						
mental health problem						
educational need						
employment need						
social isolation						
child care						
child visitation						
immigration problem						
other legal problem						
other:						
other:						
other:						

Code C = client defined problem
W = worker defined problem
R = referral source defined problem

Child Problems	C1		C2		C3		C4		C5	
	cur	his	cur	his	cur	his	cur	his	cur	his
drug abuse										
alcohol abuse										
physical abuse										
physical neglect										
sexual abuse										
criminal behavior										
coping with separation/divorce										
bereavement										
conflictual relationship with parent										
sibling relationship problem										
physical health problem										
mental health problem										
school attendance problem										
academic problem										
peer violence victim										
peer violence perpetrator										
child behavior problem (home)										
school behavior problem										
social isolation										
teenage pregnancy										

Family Problems

	CURRENT	HISTORIC
housing		
income		
neighborhood safety		

CAREGIVER INTAKE PROBLEM CLASSIFICATION SCHEME

Parent/Child

- conflict with children
- parental role problem
- parent/child communication
- child visitation
- lack of supervision

Marital

- marital conflict
- sep/divorce conflictual
- sep/divorce nonconflictual

Perpetrator (criminal type)

- physical abuse perpetrator
- domestic violence perpetrator
- sex abuser
- other criminal behavior

Service Need

- child care
- employment
- other legal
- education need
- immigration

Substance Abuse

- alcohol abuse
- drug use

Victimization

- domestic violence victim
- spouse substance abuse

Personal

- mental health
- physical health
- bereavement
- social isolation

CHILD INTAKE PROBLEM CLASSIFICATION SCHEME

Substance Abuse

- drug abuse
- alcohol abuse

Victimization

- physical abuse
- neglect
- lack of supervision
- sexual abuse

Parent/Child/Home Conflict

- parent/child conflict
- behavioral problem (home)
- sibling relationship problem

School Behavior Problem

- school attendance
- academic problem
- school behavior problem

Personal Problem

- coping separation/divorce
- bereavement
- physical health
- mental health
- peer violence victim
- peer violence perpetrator
- social isolation
- teen pregnancy

APPENDIX B.2

THE FAMILY ASSESSMENT FORM (FAF)

In order to access client characteristics, service processes, and outcomes in the preventive program workers reported case data using the Family Assessment Form (FAF). A prospective sample included all 189 preventive cases opened for service between November 15, 1993, and May 15, 1995, and served through May 15, 1996. This form, developed by the Children's Bureau of Los Angeles (McCroskey, Nishimoto, and Subramanian 1991), incorporates an ecological approach to the assessment of family functioning, including family strengths as well as problems.

As discussed in Appendix A, the FAF was modified by the authors. A new factor analysis performed on the modified FAF revealed a ten-dimensional factor structure: home environment, family finances, community environment, social support, parent-child interactions, caregiver responsibility, caregiver emotional control, factors undermining parenting, caregiver victimhood, and self-esteem/stability. Tests of internal consistency of the modified FAF subscales using Cronbach's alpha ranged from a low of .72 (caregiver victimhood) to a high of .96 (parent-child interactions) (see B21). The underlying factor structures were quite similar to those found by Meezan (1995). The authors employed the new factor structures to create the subscales used in this study to assess outcome (see appendix C).

TABLE B2.1

Modified FAF Factors and Reliability Indicators

FAMILY FACTORS	
Factor 1 - Home Environment	Alpha = .90
Factor 2 - Family Finances	Alpha = .85
Factor 3 - Community Environment	Alpha = .82
Factor 4 - Social Support	Alpha = .82
CAREGIVER FACTOR SCORES	
Factor 1 - Parent-Child Interaction	Alpha = .96
Factor 2 - Caregiver Responsibility	Alpha = .83
Factor 3 - Emotional Control	Alpha = .74
Factor 4 - Factors Undermining Parenting	Alpha = .77
Factor 5 - Parental Victimhood	Alpha = .72
Factor 6 - Self-Esteem/Stability	Alpha = .85
CHILD FACTORS	
Factor 1 - General Positive Child Behavior	Alpha = .93
Factor 2 - Difficulties in Development or Well-Being	Alpha = .92
Factor 3 - Emotional Disturbance	Alpha = .86
Factor 4 - Difficulties in Relating	Alpha = .89
Factor 5 - Physical Health	Alpha = .81
Factor 6 - Learning Difficulties	Alpha = .83
Factor 7 - Serious Emotional Disturbance	Alpha = .76
Factor 8 - Indicators of Maturity	Alpha = .88

APPENDIX B.3

THE SERVICE NEEDS/SERVICE UTILIZATION REPORT

At each FAF follow-up, the center's preventive program workers were asked to determine if a family member needed any of forty-eight services, and, if so, whether they received the service at CFL, received the service elsewhere, or did not receive the service. If they did not receive the service, the workers were asked to indicate the reasons why the service(s) were not provided. The information from the Service Needs/Service Utilization Report, which is reported in chapter 3, was used to supplement information that was available from the center's management information system, FACTORS, and the Monthly Progress Report, information reported by the center to the New York City public child welfare agency.

Initially, and at each subsequent administration of the FAF, workers were asked to indicate a family's service needs, based on their assessment of the family, and the services provided. This instrument was an addition to the FAF, incorporating a format developed by Hess, Folaron, and Jefferson (1992). The service listing was expanded to include services provided by the Center for Family Life.

TABLE B3.1

The Service Needs/Service Utilization Form

The following list includes services that may be needed by a family member. Please indicate whether the family member:

1. Needed the service.
2. If the family member needed the service, was the service provided at CFL, at another agency (Elsewhere), or not provided (No)
3. If the service was needed, but not provided, please indicate why it was not provided in the space provided at the end of the form.

BASIC SERVICES	NEEDED		PROVIDED		
A. Emergency Shelter	Yes	No	At CFL	Elsewhere	No
B. Housing Assistance	Yes	No	At CFL	Elsewhere	No
C. Food Assistance	Yes	No	At CFL	Elsewhere	No
D. Financial Assistance	Yes	No	At CFL	Elsewhere	No
E. Utility Assistance	Yes	No	At CFL	Elsewhere	No
F. Clothing	Yes	No	At CFL	Elsewhere	No
G. Furniture/Appliances/ Household Goods	Yes	No	At CFL	Elsewhere	No

HEALTH/MENTAL HEALTH	NEEDED		PROVIDED		
A. Crisis Counseling	Yes	No	At CFL	Elsewhere	No
B. Individual Counseling	Yes	No	At CFL	Elsewhere	No
C. Marital Counseling	Yes	No	At CFL	Elsewhere	No
D. Family Counseling	Yes	No	At CFL	Elsewhere	No
E. Group Counseling	Yes	No	At CFL	Elsewhere	No
F. Self-Help Group	Yes	No	At CFL	Elsewhere	No
G. Drug/Alcohol Counsel	Yes	No	At CFL	Elsewhere	No
H. Drug/Alcohol Residl	Yes	No	At CFL	Elsewhere	No
I. Domestic Viol. Counsel	Yes	No	At CFL	Elsewhere	No
J. Sex Abuse Counseling	Yes	No	At CFL	Elsewhere	No
K. Psychotropic Drugs	Yes	No	At CFL	Elsewhere	No
L. Infant Stimulation	Yes	No	At CFL	Elsewhere	No
M. Medical Care	Yes	No	At CFL	Elsewhere	No
N. Dental Care	Yes	No	At CFL	Elsewhere	No
O. Family Planning	Yes	No	At CFL	Elsewhere	No
N. Diagnostic Assessment	Yes	No	At CFL	Elsewhere	No

PARENT/TEEN PARENT (ANSWER ONLY FOR ADULT/ TEENAGE CAREGIVERS)	NEEDED		PROVIDED		
A. Parent Education	Yes	No	At CFL	Elsewhere	No
B. Homemaker Services	Yes	No	At CFL	Elsewhere	No
C. Day Care	Yes	No	At CFL	Elsewhere	No

TABLE B 3.1 (*continued*)

PARENT/TEEN PARENT (ANSWER ONLY FOR ADULT/ TEENAGE CAREGIVERS)	NEEDED		PROVIDED		
A. Parent Education	Yes	No	At CFL	Elsewhere	No
B. Homemaker Services	Yes	No	At CFL	Elsewhere	No
C. Day Care	Yes	No	At CFL	Elsewhere	No
D. Temporary Child Care	Yes	No	At CFL	Elsewhere	No
E. After School Care	Yes	No	At CFL	Elsewhere	No
F. Respite Care	Yes	No	At CFL	Elsewhere	No
G. Transportation	Yes	No	At CFL	Elsewhere	No
H. FC Visitation	Yes	No	At CFL	Elsewhere	No
I. Legal Assistance	Yes	No	At CFL	Elsewhere	No
J. Money Management	Yes	No	At CFL	Elsewhere	No
K. Employment Services	Yes	No	At CFL	Elsewhere	No
L. Job Referral	Yes	No	At CFL	Elsewhere	No

CHILDREN/YOUTH SERVICES (ONLY ANSWER FOR FAMILY MEMBERS 18 YRS OR YOUNGER)	NEEDED		PROVIDED		
A. Day Care	Yes	No	At CFL	Elsewhere	No
B. Temporary Child Care	Yes	No	At CFL	Elsewhere	No
C. After School Care	Yes	No	At CFL	Elsewhere	No
D. Respite Care	Yes	No	At CFL	Elsewhere	No
E. Preschool/Headstart	Yes	No	At CFL	Elsewhere	No
F. Summer Youth Program	Yes	No	At CFL	Elsewhere	No
G. Recreation	Yes	No	At CFL	Elsewhere	No
H. Special Education	Yes	No	At CFL	Elsewhere	No
I. Special Ed. Evaluation	Yes	No	At CFL	Elsewhere	No
J. Project Youth	Yes	No	At CFL	Elsewhere	No
K. Employment Services	Yes	No	At CFL	Elsewhere	No
L. Job Referral	Yes	No	At CFL	Elsewhere	No
M. Tutoring	Yes	No	At CFL	Elsewhere	No

If a service was needed but not provided, please indicate what the service was and why it was not provided:

SERVICE	REASON NOT PROVIDED
1.__________	
2.__________	
3.__________	
4.__________	
5.__________	
6.__________	
7.__________	

APPENDIX B.4

TELEPHONE SURVEY OF A RANDOM SAMPLE OF PARENTS OF CHILDREN SERVED IN THE AFTER-SCHOOL PROGRAM

A structured telephone survey was completed with a random sample of parents of children currently in the after-school program (n = 139). The questionnaire was based upon information gathered from focus groups of parents of children who were served in the after-school program. The survey was conducted in Spanish, English, and Cantonese.

Questionnaire for Telephone Survey Parents of Children Currently in After-School Program

Introduction: Hello. My name is __________. I am calling as part of the research group that is conducting a study for the Center for Family Life. I believe you recently received a letter from _________ explaining that we would be calling. It will take about ten minutes for me to ask you the questions we hope you'll be willing to answer.

Is this a convenient time to talk? If no, when would it be convenient for me to call you again?

If yes, is it all right to start now? Everything you say will be confidential. We will not share anyone's individual comments with the people at the center.

1) **How many of your children have used the after-school program at P.S. 314/P.S. 1**

   ___ **How many years have you had at least one child attending the program?**

2) **Have any of your children gone to the summer camp program?___**

   If yes, for how many summers?___

3) **What are the three most important things the after-school program does for your child(ren)?** (Don't read code list, but check as appropriate.)

   __Keeps them safe/off the street
   __Provides recreation/fun
   __Helps with homework/schoolwork

__Teaches new skills, e.g., drama, dance, sports
__Teaches cooperation
__Teaches respect for one another, tolerance for different people
__Helps them to make friends
__Gives them self-esteem
__Provides role models for children
__Gives them something to aspire for as counselor-in-training (CIT)
__Gives them another adult to talk to re: problems

4) **What are the three most important things the after-school program does for you as a parent?** (Don't use code list, but check as appropriate.)

__Allows me to work/provides child care
__Makes me feel more secure about being away from home
__Helps me to learn how to raise children correctly
__Staff offer useful advice about how to handle different situations
__Get to meet other parents
__Gets me more involved in school/children's activities
__Gives my children another adult to talk with
__Other____________________

____

____

5) **Are there any things about the program that you would like to changed or improved?** (Again, don't read, but use possible codes.)

__Coverage for vacation times
__Hours of summer camp
__Other____________________

____

____

6) **Do you go to any of the programs the Center runs for parents?**

__ **If yes, which ones:** (Don't read; use possible codes.)

__Parent Council
__ESL Classes
__Parent Workshops
__Parenting Classes
__Other____________________

____

____

If no, why not?

____

____

7) Are you employed? __ If Yes, how many hours a week? __ What days and hours?_______________________________

8) We're just speaking hypothetically now, but just suppose the center's after-school program were not available. What would you do with your children after school?

   What do you estimate that would cost per week? ________________

9) Do you have any teenage children? __ If yes, do they participate in the teen center__ or CIT program? __

   If yes, what do you think are the two most important things about this/ these program(s)? (Again, don't read code list, but check as appropriate.)

   __Keeps them safe/off the streets
   __Teaches them new skills
   __Teaches them how to be responsible
   __Teaches them how to care for/work with children
   __Gives them an opportunity to socialize/make new friends
   __Gives them job skills
   __Keeps them busy
   __Gives my teenagers another adult to talk with
   __Other_____________________

   ____

   Do you see any disadvantages to their participating in this/these programs?

   __ If yes, what are they?

10) Is there anything I haven't asked you about that you'd like to tell me about the center's programs?

Thank you very much for taking the time to talk with me. Your answers are very important in helping us to understand the after-school program better.

Questionnaire for Telephone Survey of Parents of Children Formerly in After-School Program

Introduction: Hello. My name is __________. I am calling as part of the research group that is conducting a study for the Center for Family Life. I believe you recently received a letter from __________ explaining that we would be calling. It will take about ten minutes for me to ask you the questions we hope you'll be willing to answer.

Is this a convenient time for you to talk? If no, when would it be convenient for me to call you again? ____________

If yes, is it all right to start now? Everything you say will be confidential. We will not share anyone's individual comments with the people at the center.

1) **How many of your children have used the after-school program at P.S. 314/P.S. 1? __ How many years did you have at least one child attending the program? __**

2) **Have any of your children gone to the summer camp program? __ If yes, for how many summers? __**

3) **What are the three most important things the after-school program did for your child(ren)?** (Don't read code list, but check as appropriate.)

__Kept them safe/off the street
__Provided recreation/fun
__Helped with homework/schoolwork
__Taught new skills, e.g., drama, dance, sports
__Taught cooperation
__Taught respect for one another, tolerance of different people
__Helped them to make friends
__Gave them self-esteem
__Provided role models for children
__Gave them something to aspire for as counselor-in-training (CIT)
__Gave them another adult to talk to re: problems
__Other____________________

____

4) **What are the three most important things the after-school program did for you as a parent?** (Don't use code list, but check as appropriate.)

__Allowed me to work/provides child care
__Made me feel more secure about being away from home
__Helped me to learn how to raise children correctly
__Staff offered useful advice about how to handle different situations
__Got to meet other parents
__Got me more involved in school/children's activities
__Gave my children another adult to talk with
__Other____________________

5A) **When did your child(ren) stop attending the after-school program? (Month: ____ Year: _____)**

Why did you decide to stop using the after-school program for your children?

__Hours not convenient
__Children didn't like/didn't want to attend
__Parent stopped working/working schedule changed
__Wasn't satisfied with the program/quality of care provided
__Other____________________
____
____

5B) **Are there any things about the program that you would like to see changed or improved?** (Again, don't read, but use possible codes.)

__Coverage for vacation times
__Hours of summer camp
__Other____________________
____
____

6) **Have you gone to any of the programs the Center runs for parents __ If yes, which ones?** (Don't read; use possible codes.)

__Parent council
__ESL Classes
__Parent Workshops

__Parenting Classes
__Other____________________
____
____

If no, why not?

7) Are you employed? __ If yes, how many hours a week? __ What days and hours?_____________

8) We're just speaking hypothetically now, but just suppose the center's after-school program was not available. What would you have done with your children after school during the time that they attended the program?

What do you estimate that would cost per week?

9) Do you have any teenage children? __ If yes, do/did they participate in the teen center __ or CIT program?__

If yes, what do you think are the two most important things about this/these program(s)? (Again don't read code list, but check as appropriate.)

__Keeps them safe/off the streets
__Teaches them new skills
__Teaches them how to be responsible
__Gives them an opportunity to socialize/make new friends
__Gives them job skills
__Keeps them busy
__Gives my teenagers another adult to talk with
__Other____________________

Do you see any disadvantages to their participating in this/these program(s)? __ If yes, what are they?

10) Is there anything I haven't asked you about that you'd like to tell me about the center's programs?

Thank you very much for taking the time to talk with me. Your answers are very important in helping us to understand the after-school program better.

APPENDIX B.5

OUTLINE FOR FOCUS GROUP MEETINGS: PARENTS OF CHILDREN IN AFTER-SCHOOL PROGRAM AT P.S. 314

Introduction

1) Introduce selves and give brief explanation of Casey study and reason we wanted to meet with a few selected groups of parents, i.e., we want to gain a better understanding of what they view as the benefits and disadvantages of the program and its impact on their family life. Based on our discussion with them, we plan to identify the questions we should ask in a telephone survey of a larger sample of parents.

2) Explain reason for taping session, ask if anyone objects, and explain that tape will be turned off at any time that a member of the group requests. Assure them their individual responses will be held confidential and will not be shared with the staff of the center except in very general terms.

3) Ask members of the group to introduce themselves and give a little information about how many children they have involved in the program, how long their children have been attending, whether they had to stay on a waiting list first, etc.

4) Explain that we're going to ask some general discussion questions and may ask to go around the group sometimes, but we really want them to feel free to jump in and comment on anything that seems relevant to our discussion.

Discussion Questions

How do parents find out about the after-school center? How did you find out about it? After you applied, did you have to go on a waiting list? If yes, how long?

Why do you think some parents and children like to use the after-school center and others don't?

What have you liked about sending your children to the after-school center?

Probe: benefits for children
benefits for parents

What about the summer camp? Do your children attend this? Why do you think some parents have their children attend this and others don't? What are the benefits? Disadvantages?

Do any of you have older children? If yes, do they participate in the after-school program or evening center in any way? What do you see as the advantages for them of being involved in these activities? Are there any drawbacks to these activities from your perspective?

Have you volunteered to help in any way with the after-school or evening programs for youth? In what ways? How have you found this experience?

Which, if any, of the parent programs do you participate in? What do you like/not like about them? Why do you think some of the other parents don't participate?

What impact overall, if any, do you think the center's programs have had on your family life?

Do you think the center's programs have had any impact on your neighborhood?

What are the parts of the center's programs that you don't like or wish could be changed?

Probe: hours, days, actual activities, staff

Are there are any special questions you think we should include in the telephone survey to make sure we get everyone's honest opinion of the after-school program?

THANK PARTICIPANTS

APPENDIX B.6

FOCUS GROUP CFL P.S. 314 PROGRAM/ CFL P.S. 1 PROGRAM

The purpose of this meeting is to understand more about the CIT program. / I will be asking questions about your work and experience as a CIT. / These answers will help me describe the CIT program to others. / There are no right or wrong answers. / Everyone understands that no program is perfect. / It is all right to say positive and negative comments about the program./ It is important for you to be open and speak your mind./ Because I will be talking to other groups of CITs, I ask you not to discuss these questions with them until I finish doing all of the groups. / I will be finished talking to all of the groups by this Thursday. / This meeting will take about an hour. / Thank you for helping out!!

Note: If someone wants a comment to be kept confidential, let me know before you say it. If you want me to stop recording, please tell me. Because I am taping, please, no side conversations. I won't be able to understand the tape. Please respect the privacy of others' comments in the group if they ask.

Encourage Everyone to Talk.

QUESTIONS:

How did you learn about the CIT program?

How long have you been a CIT?

Would you please describe the process from when you first heard about the CIT program, to the time you joined up, up until the present time.

Describe your responsibilities as a CIT?

Do you feel a responsibility toward the CIT program. Why or why not?

Do you feel a loyalty to the CIT program, why or why not?

How do you find being a CIT? Tough, easy, in between? Explain.

This instrument developed by Don Allen, doctoral research assostamt.

What are some of the good things and bad things about being a CIT?

How would you describe the relationship between the adults in the program and the CITs?

Would your life be different if you were no longer a CIT? How?

You know people your age that aren't CITs? How is their daily life difference or the same?

Do you think there is a difference in how the girls experience being a CIT and how the boys experience being a CIT?

APPENDIX B.7

PREVENTIVE SERVICES PROGRAM GUIDE FOR INTERVIEWS WITH WORKERS

1. When you compare the center's preventive services program with other center programs, do you see *similarities and differences in the clients* served?

2. What would you identify as the *key characteristics of the center's preventive services program*?

3. Are there *types, or categories, of cases* served by the preventive services program?

   If no:

   a) How would you *describe* the program's cases?

   b) Typically, what case *outcomes* are hoped for?

   c) What *approaches* are used by workers?

   If yes:

   a) What *characterizes* the different types of cases?

   b) What are the *outcomes* hoped for with the different types of cases?

   c) What *approaches* are used with different types of cases?

4. Are there *families who don't "work out"* with the preventive services program? (Probes: what are their characteristics? what do they have in common?)

5. There are several specific aspects of the program's services I would like to ask about:

   a) What is the role of *home visits*?

   b) What kinds of *referrals* are made internally (within the center, such as psychiatrist, after-school program) and externally? What is the basis for referrals?

c) What is the staff's thinking about client *no-shows*? (some programs close cases with no-shows)

d) Do services vary for different *ethnic groups*? (If yes, how?)

How do workers decide what *language* services are provided in?

6. In a typical week, how many *hours do you work?* How is that time allocated (hours or percentages)?

7. What *worker characteristics* would you identify as important to effectiveness in serving clients in this program?

8. What *draws* you to this work?

9. What *pressures or stresses* do you find in this work?

10. What *supports* you in this work? (Probe for supervision.)

11. Are there things that I haven't asked about that are important to understanding the center's preventive services program?

APPENDIX B.8

CASE STUDY INTERVIEWS WITH PREVENTIVE SERVICES WORKERS

If you were describing the family to another preventive services worker, what would you tell them about what it's like for you to work with this family?

In your experience in preventive services, is your work with this family typical of the work you do with the center? If yes, in what ways? If not, what is different or unique?

Referral, Connection

As best you know:

When did family first hear about the center? How did family first get to the center or get involved in a center program? When first contact with any center program? Who in family had first contact with center program? Which services have family members been connected with over time? (Probe for after-school program, advocacy program, employment program, thrift shop, etc.—may be useful to do a time line that captures this information.)

Been elsewhere for services? Same here or different? How?

Now using services in center in addition to prevention services? Services beyond center?

Definition of Problem, Focus of Work

Primary reason working with center staff?

Other reason

Nature of Work with P.S. Staff

Nature of your contact with this family? (Might ask to describe a recent contact—beginning to end.)

Frequency of your contact with this family?

Who (in family, others) meets with you? Why?

Where usually meet?

Have you referred this family to other center programs? If yes, which ones, what hoping for; if not, why not, expect to in the future?

Worker-Client Relationship

Describe relationship—worker, family members—when first met, now.

Had there been a previous worker(s)? If yes, was there a transfer or transition? Describe: how has the change in workers affected your current relationship?

Variables that affect relationship (differences, similarities in language, ethnicity, age, culture, religion, etc.)

Have there been particular or unique characteristics about your relationship with this family?

Contract and Various Perceptions of Desired Outcomes

What want outcome(s) to be? Your perceptions of what each family member wants outcome(s) to be? Workers' perceptions of what other center staff/community professionals want outcome to be?

How arrived at contracted outcome(s)?

Describe relationships within family. Changed? In what ways?

Describe children's development and behaviors. Changed? In what ways?

Is the counseling with this family working? If yes, why?

Ever think it's not working? If yes, why? What done about that?

How will you know when the work is ended?

Service Process

Given your work to date with this family, what do you expect may be the progression of your work together over time? Are there particular issues or concerns you have that you expect you will be dealing with in the future?

Things come up in the process hadn't expected?

Anything like to tell the family members that you haven't felt free to? What? Why not free?

Looking back on work so far, how account for where are now?

Have there been times or situations in your work with this family that have been particularly difficult? If what describe. What was helpful *to the worker* in dealing with this?

How would you describe the center's preventive services program (i.e., what characterizes the program)?

Things I haven't asked that are important for me to know about?

APPENDIX B.9

CASE STUDY INTERVIEWS WITH FAMILY MEMBERS

If you had a friend or family member with a situation similar to yours, what would you tell them about the center?

Referral, Connection

When first *heard* about the center? How family first got to the center or got involved in a center program? When first contact with any center program? Who in family had first contact with center program? Which services have family members been connected with over time? Was family receiving services previously for same problem as currently, different problem? If same problem, what prompted current involvement? (Probe for after-school program, thrift shop, advocacy program, employment program, etc.—may be useful to do a time line that captures this information.)

Been elsewhere for services? Same here or different? How?

Now using services in center in addition to prevention services? Services beyond center?

Definition of Problem, Focus of Work

Primary reason working with center staff?

Other reasons?

Nature of Work with PS Staff

Nature of your family's contact with preventive services staff? (Might ask to describe a recent contact, beginning to end.)

Frequency of family's contact with preventive services staff?

Who (in family, others) meets with P.S. staff? Why?

Where usually meet?

What actually occurs in a meeting? (Ask to describe a meeting, perhaps most recent meeting.)

Worker-Client Relationship

Describe relationship—worker, family members—when first met, now, how characterize relationship?

Did the family work with this worker or another worker previously? (Probes depend upon history with center identified above.) If yes to either, how has this affected current relationship with worker?

Variables that affect relationship (differences, similarities in language, ethnicity, age, culture, religion, etc.)?

Contract and Various Perceptions of Desired Outcomes

What want outcome(s) to be? Your perception of what others in family want outcome(s) to be? Family members' perceptions of what worker/other center staff want outcome to be?

How arrived at contracted outcome(s)?

Describe relationships within family. Changed? In what ways?

Describe children's development and behaviors. Changed? In what ways?

Is the counseling with P.S. staff working? If yes, why?

Ever think it's not working? If yes, why? What done about that?

How will you know when the work is ended?

Service Process

Things come up in the process hadn't expected?

Anything like to tell worker (family members), haven't felt free to? What? Why not free?

Looking back on work so far, how account for where are now?

Have there been times in your work that have been particularly difficult? If what, describe. What was helpful to you in dealing with this?

Things I haven't asked that are important for me to know about?

APPENDIX C

INITIAL AND FINAL FAF SCORES

■

TABLE C1

Initial and Final FAF Factor Scores: Full Sample

	Time			
FAMILY ENVIRONMENT	INITIAL	FINAL	t	SIG.
F1 Home Environment	7.74	7.91	ns	ns
F2 Community Environment	7.31	7.45	ns	ns
F3 Financial Stress	7.50	7.27	ns	ns
F4 Social Support	5.09	5.07	ns	ns
CAREGIVER CENTERED				
CG 1 Parent/Child Interaction	49.87	49.81	ns	ns
CG2 Caregiver Responsibility	22.92	22.48	1.93	.055
CG3 Caregiver Emotional Control	6.77	6.74	ns	ns
CG4 Factors Undermining Parenting	10.99	11.23	ns	ns
CG5 Caregiver's Self-esteem	13.66	13.78	ns	ns
CG6 Historical Factors	7.52	7.71	ns	ns
CHILD CENTERED				
K1 Behavioral Difficulties	39.22	38.24	3.27	.001
K2 Developmental Difficulties	21.08	20.25	1.72	.088
K3 Emotional Disturbance	11.80	11.17	2.33	.021
K4 Relating Difficulties	5.64	5.28	1.93	.056
K5 Health Difficulties	4.14	4.33	ns	ns
K6 Learning Difficulties	10.47	9.62	3.60	.000
K7 Serious Emotional Disturbance	7.36	7.32	ns	ns
K8 Indicators of Maturity	8.05	7.84	ns	ns

NOTE: F1, F2, F4, CG1, CG2, CG3, CG5, K8: high scores are positive effects. F3, CG4, CG6, K1, K2, K3, K4, K5, K6, K7; high scores are negative effects.

TABLE C.2

Initial and Final FAF Factor Scores: Closed Cases

	Time			
FAMILY ENVIRONMENT	INITIAL	FINAL	t	SIG.
F1 Home Environment	7.68	7.83	ns	ns
F2 Community Environment	7.47	7.36	ns	ns
F3 Financial Stress	7.44	7.47	ns	ns
F4 Social Support	5.24	5.37	ns	ns
CAREGIVER CENTERED				
CG 1 Parent/Child Interaction	48.79	48.99	ns	ns
CG2 Caregiver Responsibility	22.89	22.24	2.42	.017
CG3 Caregiver Emotional Control	6.68	6.73	ns	ns
CG4 Factors Underming Parenting	10.93	11.22	ns	ns
CG5 Caregiver's Self-Esteem	13.76	13.90	ns	ns
CG6 Historical Factors	7.57	7.73	ns	ns
CHILD CENTERED				
K1 Behavioral Difficulties	39.89	38.61	1.95	.055
K2 Developmental Difficulties	22.41	20.38	4.91	.000
K3 Emotional Disturbance	12.51	11.89	ns	ns
K4 Relating Difficulties	6.69	5.91	4.01	.000
K5Healh Difficulties	4.49	4.04	2.90	.005
K6 Learning Difficulties	11.31	9.87	4.72	.000
K7 Serious Emotional Disturbance	7.69	6.99	3.29	.001
K8 Indicators of Maturity	7.83	7.75	ns	ns

TABLE C.3

Initial and Final FAF Factor Scores: Open Cases

	Time			
FAMILY ENVIRONMENT	INITIAL	FINAL	t	SIG.
F1 Home Environment	7.97	7.80	ns	ns
F2 Community Environment	7.45	7.25	ns	ns
F3 Financial Stress	7.57	7.05	2.57	.012
F4 Social Support	4.78	4.89	ns	ns
CAREGIVER CENTERED				
CG1 Parent/Child Interaction	50.21	49.84	ns	ns
CG2 Caregiver Responsibility	22.95	22.76	ns	ns
CG3 Caregiver Emotional Control	6.85	6.75	ns	ns
CG4 Factors Underming Parenting	11.06	11.25	ns	ns
CG5 Caregiver's Self-Esteem	13.25	13.67	ns	ns
CG6 Historical Factors	7.48	7.69	ns	ns
Time				
CHILD CENTERED				
K1 Behavioral Difficulties	39.67	39.18	2.64	.007
K2 Developmental Difficulties	21.03	20.23	1.66	.099
K3 Emotional Disturbance	11.82	11.16	2.44	.016
K4 Relating Difficulties	5.70	5.37	1.75	.082
K5 Health Difficulties	4.15	4.34	ns	ns
K6 Learning Difficulties	10.51	9.59	3.83	.000
K7 Serious Emotional Disturbance	7.37	7.33	ns	ns
K8 Indicators of Maturity	8.04	7.81	ns	ns

SOURCES CITED

■

ACS Reform. N.d. In *NYC Administration for Children's Services*. New York: Administration for Children's Services.

Addams. Jane. 1960 [1910]. *Twenty Years at Hull House*. New York: Signet.

Agris, C. and D. A. Schon. 1978. *Organizational Learning*. Reading, Mass.: Addison-Wesley.

Ainsworth, M. 1991. Attachments and other affectional bonds across the life cycle. In C. M. Parkes, J. Stevenson-Hinde, and P. Marris, eds., *Attachment Across the Life Cycle*, pp. 33–51. New York: Routledge.

Ainsworth, M. 1967. *Infancy in Uganda: Infant Care and the Growth of Attachment*. Baltimore: Johns Hopkins University Press.

Ainsworth, M., M. Blehar, E. Waters, and S. Wall. 1978. *Patterns of Attachment: A Psychological Study of the Strange Situation*. Hillsdale, N.J.: Erlbaum.

Allen, M. and J. Knitzer. 1983. Child welfare: Examining the policy framework. In B. G. McGowan and W. Meezan, eds., *Child Welfare: Current Dilemmas, Future Directions*, pp. 93–141. Itasca, Ill.: Peacock.

Allen, M., P. Brown, and B. Finlay. 1993. *Helping Children by Strengthening Families: A Look at Family Support Programs*. Washington, D.C.: Children's Defense Fund.

Alwon, F. J. and A. L. Reitz. 2000. Empty chairs. *Children's Voice* 9:35–37.

Annie E. Casey Foundation. 1993. Background information for the evaluation of the Center for Family Life in Sunset Park. Unpublished paper.

Annie E. Casey Foundation. 1996. *Getting Smart, Getting Real: Using Research and Evaluation Information to Improve Programs and Policies*. Report of the Annie E. Casey Foundation's September 1995 research and evaluation conference. Baltimore: Annie E. Casey Foundation.

Bartholet, E. 1999. *Nobody's Children: Abuse and Neglect, Foster Drift, and the Adoption Alternative*. Boston: Beacon.

Bernstein, B., D. Snider, and W. Meezan. 1975. *Foster Care Needs and Alternatives to Placement*. New York: New York State Board of Social Welfare.

Berry, M. 1992. An evaluation of family preservation services: Fitting agency services to family needs. *Social Work* 37:314–321.

Besharov, D. 1994. Looking beyond thirty, sixty, and ninety days. *Children and Youth Services Review* 16:445–452.

Bowlby, J. 1958. The nature of a child's tie to his mother. *International Journal of Psychoanalysis* 39:350–373.

Bowlby, J. 1969. *Attachment and Loss.* Vol. 1: *Attachment.* New York: Basic.

Bowlby, J. 1973. *Attachment and Loss.* Vol 2: *Separation: Anxiety and Anger.* New York: Basic.

Bowlby, J. 1988. *A Secure Base: Parent-Child Attachment and Healthy Human Development.* New York: Basic.

Bremner, R., ed. 1971. *Children and Youth in America: A Documentary History.* Vol. 2. Cambridge: Harvard University Press.

Bronfenbrenner, U. 1979. *The Ecology of Human Development.* Cambridge: Harvard University Press.

Burt, M. and R. Bayleat. 1977. *A Comprehensive Emergency Services System for Neglected and Abused Children.* New York: Vantage.

Campbell, D. 1987. Problems for the experimenting society in the interface between evaluation and service providers. In S. Kagan, D. Powell, B. Weissbourd, and E. Zigler, eds., *America's Family Support Programs: Perspectives and Prospects,* pp. 345–351. New Haven: Yale University Press.

Center for Family Life in Sunset Park. 1979. *Center for Family Life Annual Progress Report.* New York: Center for Family Life.

Center for Family Life in Sunset Park. 1980. *Center for Family Life Annual Progress Report.* New York: Center for Family Life.

Center for Family Life in Sunset Park. 1998. *Center for Family Life Annual Progress Report.* New York: Center for Family Life.

Center for Family Life in Sunset Park. 2000. *Center for Family Life Annual Progress Report.* New York: Center for Family Life.

Cheetham, J. 1992. Evaluating social work effectiveness. *Research on Social Work Practice* 2 (July): 265–287.

Child Welfare Fund. 1999. *Critique of the Special Child Welfare Advisory Panel's Report: Placement Issues in the New York City Child Welfare System.* New York: Center for the Study of Family Policy, Hunter College.

Citizens' Committee for Children of New York. 1998. *Keeping Track of New York City's Children.* New York: Citizens' Committee for Children of New York.

Citizens' Committee for Children of New York. 1999. *Keeping Track of New York City's Children.* New York: Citizens' Committee for Children of New York.

Citizens' Committee for Children of New York. 2000. *Keeping Track of New York City's Children.* New York: Citizens' Committee for Children of New York.

Citizens' Committee for Children of New York. 2002. *Keeping Track of New York City's Children.* New York: Citizens' Committee for Children of New York.

City of New York, Department of City Planning. 1993. *Socioeconomic Profiles: A Portrait of New York City's Community Districts from the 1980 and 1990 Censuses of Population and Housing.* City of New York, Department of City Planning.

City of New York, Department of City Planning. 1996. *Socioeconomic Profiles: A Portrait of New York City's Community Districts from the 1980 and 1990 Censuses of Population and Housing.* City of New York, Department of City Planning.

City of New York, Department of City Planning. 2002. Brooklyn Community District 7. http://www.ci.nyc.ny.us/html/dcp/html/lucds/bk7lu.html#data

Cobb, J. and D. Griffin. 1939. *Process Theology: An Introductory Exposition.* Philadelphia: Westminster.

Cole, E. and J. Duva. 1990. *Family Preservation: An Orientation for Administrators and Practitioners*. Washington, D.C.: Child Welfare League of America.
Comer, J. 1996. *Rallying the Whole Village: The Comer Process for Reforming Education*. New York: Teachers College Press.
Compton, B. 1981. The family-centered project revisited. Unpublished paper presented at the Council on Social Work Education Annual Program Meeting.
Cousins, E. 1971. Introduction: Process models in culture, philosophy, and theology. In E. Cousins, ed., *Process Theology*, pp. 1–17. New York: Newman.
Crawford, S. 1995. Personal communication.
Denzin, N. 1978. *The Research Act*. 2d ed. Englewood Cliffs, N.J.: Prentice Hall.
Dore, M. 1993. Family preservation and poor families: When "Homebuilding" is not enough. *Families in Society* 74:545–556.
Dore, M. and L. Alexander. 1996. Preserving families at risk of child abuse and neglect: The role of the helping alliance. *Child Abuse and Neglect* 20:349–361.
Drisko, J. 1997. Strengthening qualitative studies and reports: Standards to promote academic integrity. *Journal of Social Work Education* 33:185–197.
Dryfoos, J. 1990. *Adolescents at Risk: Prevalence and Prevention*. New York: Oxford University Press.
Dryfoos, J. 1994. *Full-Service Schools: A Revolution in Health and Social Services for Children, Youth and Families*. San Francisco: Jossey Bass.
Emlen, A., J. L'Ahti, and S. Downs. 1976. *Barriers to Permanency for Children in Foster Care*. Portland: Regional Planning Initiative, Portland State University.
Erikson, E. 1959. Identity and the life cycle. *Psychological Issues* 1:50–164.
Family to Family: Reconstructing Foster Care. 1998. Baltimore: Annie E. Casey Foundation.
Fanshel, D. and E. Shinn. 1972. *Dollars and Sense in Foster Care*. New York: Child Welfare League of America.
Fanshel, D. and E. Shinn. 1978. *Children in Foster Care: A Longitudinal Investigation*. New York: Columbia University Press.
Feldman, L. 1990. *Evaluating the Impact of Family Preservation Services in New Jersey*. Trenton: New Jersey Division of Youth and Family Services, Bureau of Research, Evaluation and Quality Assurance.
Foucault, M. 1980. *Power/Knowledge: Selected Interviews and Other Writings*. New York: Pantheon.
Fraser, M., K. Nelson, and J. Rivard. 1997. Effectiveness of family preservation services. *Social Work Research* 21:138–153.
Fraser, M., P. Pecora, and D. Haapala, eds. 1991. *Families in Crisis: The Impact of Intensive Family Preservation Services*. Hawthorne, N.Y.: Aldine de Gruyter.
Garbarino, J. 1987. Family support and the prevention of child maltreatment. In S. Kagan, D. Powell, B. Weissbourd, and E. Zigler, eds., *America's Family Support Programs: Perspectives and Prospects*, pp. 99–114. New Haven: Yale University Press.
Gabinet, L. 1983. Shared parenting: A new paradigm for the treatment of child abuse. *Child Abuse and Neglect* 7:403–411.
Geertz, C. 1973. *The Interpretation of Cultures: Selected Essays*. New York: Basic.
Geertz, C. 1983. *Local Knowledge: Further Essays in Interpretive Anthropology*. New York: Basic.

Germain, C. 1973. An ecological perspective in casework practice. *Social Casework* 54:323–330.
Germain, C. 1976. Time: An ecological variable in social work practice. *Social Casework* 57:419–426.
Germain, C. 1978a. General systems theory and ego psychology—ecological perspective. *Social Service Review* 52 (4): 535–550.
Germain, C. 1978b. Space: An ecological variable in social work practice. *Social Casework* 59:515–523.
Germain, C. and A. Gitterman. 1980. *The Life Model of Social Work Practice*. New York: Columbia University Press.
Glaser, B. 1978. *Theoretical Sensitivity: Advances in the Methodology of Grounded Theory*. Mill Valley, Cal.: Sociology.
Glaser, B. and A. Strauss. 1967. *The Discovery of Grounded Theory: Strategies for Qualitative Research*. New York: Aldine de Gruyter.
Glesne, C. 1999. *Becoming Qualitative Researchers*. 2d ed. New York: Longman.
Goldstein, J., A. Freud, and A. Solnit. 1973. *Beyond the Best Interests of the Child*. New York: Free.
Goldstein, J., A. Freud, and A. Solnit. 1979. *Before the Best Interests of the Child*. New York: Free.
Gordon, K. 1991. Improving practice through illuminative evaluation. *Social Service Review* 65:365–378.
Gruber, A. 1978. *Children in Foster Care: Destitute, Neglected, Betrayed*. New York: Human Sciences.
Halpern, R. 1988. Parent support and education for low-income families: Historical and current perspectives. *Children and Youth Services Review* 10:283–303.
Halpern, R. 1990. Poverty and early childhood parenting: Toward a framework for intervention. *American Journal of Orthopsychiatry* 60:6–18.
Halpern, R. 1991. Supportive services for families in poverty: Dilemmas of reform. *Social Service Review* 65:343–364.
Halpern, R. 1997. Good practice with multiply vulnerable young families: Challenges and principles. *Children and Youth Services Review* 19:253–275.
Halpern, R. 1999. *Fragile Families, Fragile Solutions*. New York: Columbia University Press.
Hamilton, G. 1951. *Theory and Practice of Social Casework*. 2d ed. New York: Columbia University Press.
Hare, B. 1987. HARE self-esteem scale (HSS). In K. Corcoran and J. Fischer, eds., *Measures for Clinical Practice*, pp. 393–395. New York: Free.
Hartman, A. 1970. To think about the unthinkable. *Social Casework* 51 (October): 467–474.
Hartman, A. 1994a. In search of subjugated knowledge. In A. Hartman *Reflection and Controversy: Essays on Social Work*, pp. 23–28. Washington, D.C.: NASW.
Hartman, A. 1994b. Many ways of knowing. In A. Hartman, *Reflection and Controversy: Essays on Social Work*, pp. 11–16. Washington, D.C.: NASW.
Hartman, H. 1958. *Ego Psychology and the Problem of Adaptation*. New York: International Universities.
Hess, P. 1995. Reflecting in and on practice. In P. Hess and E. Mullen, eds., *Practitioner-Researcher Partnerships*, pp. 56–82. Washington, D.C.: NASW.

Hess, P. and G. Folaron. 1993. *The Professional Review Action Group (PRAG) Model: A User's Guide*. Washington, D.C.: Child Welfare League of America.

Hess, P., B. McGowan, B. and C. Meyer. 1996. Practitioners' perspectives on family and child services. In A. Kahn and S. Kamerman, eds., *Children and Their Families in Big Cities*, pp. 121–137. New York: Columbia University School of Social Work Cross-National Studies Research Program.

Hess, P., B. McGowan, and M. Botsko. 1997. *Final Report of a Study of the Center for Family Life in Sunset Park: Greater Than the Sum of Its Parts*. Baltimore: Annie E. Casey Foundation.

Hess, P., B. McGowan, and M. Botsko. 2000. A preventive services program model for preserving and supporting families over time. *Child Welfare* 79 (3): 227–265.

Hess, P., G. Folaron, and A. Jefferson. 1992. Effectiveness of family reunification services: An innovative evaluative model. *Social Work* 37:304–311.

Hollis, F. 1964. *Casework: A Psychosocial Therapy*. New York: Random House.

Hyman, J. B. 1999. Spheres of influence: A strategic synthesis and framework for community youth development. Paper presented at Urban Affairs Association Annual Conference, Louisville, Kentucky.

Janchill, Sister M. P. 1969. Systems concepts in casework theory and practice. *Social Casework* 50:74–82.

Janchill, Sister M. P. 1981. *Guidelines to Decision-making in Child Welfare*. New York: Human Services Workshops.

Janchill, Sister M. P. 1997. Neighborhood Foster Family Care. Unpublished program description.

Janchill, Sister M. P. and Sister M. G. Tobia. 1995. Letter to the editor: The society that pretends to love children. *New York Times Magazine*, November 5, p. 16.

Jenkins, S. 1981. *The Ethnic Dilemma in Social Services*. New York: Free Press.

Johnson, Y. 1997. Sunset Park, a changing Brooklyn neighborhood: Can a historical study inform social work? Unpublished paper.

Jones, M., R. Neuman, and A. Shyne. 1976. *A Second Chance for Families: Evaluation of a Program to Reduce Foster Care*. New York: Child Welfare League of America.

Kagan, S. 1994. Defining and achieving quality in family support. In S. Kagan and B. Weissbourd, eds., *Putting Families First: America's Family Support Movement and the Challenge of Change*, pp. 375–400. San Francisco: Jossey-Bass.

Kagan, S., D. Powell, B. Weissbourd, and E. Zigler, eds. 1987. *America's Family Support Programs: Perspectives and Prospects*. New Haven: Yale University Press.

Kagan, S. and A. Shelley. 1987. The promise and problems of family support programs. In S. Kagan, D. Powell, B. Weissbourd, and E. Zigler, eds., *America's Family Support Programs: Perspectives and Prospects*, pp. 3–18. New Haven: Yale University Press.

Kagan, S. and B. Weissbourd, eds. 1994. *Putting Families First: America's Family Support Movement and the Challenge of Change*. San Francisco: Jossey-Bass.

Kamerman, S. B. 1996. The new politics of child and family policies. *Social Work* 41:453–465.

Kamerman, S. B., and A. J. Kahn. 1997. *Child Welfare in the Context of Welfare "Reform."* New York: Cross National Children's Program, Columbia University School of Social Work.

Kemp, S., J. K. Whittaker, and E. M. Tracy. 1997. *Person-Environment Practice: The Social Ecology of Interpersonal Helping*. Hawthorne, N.Y.: Aldine de Gruyter.

Kinney, J., B. Madsen, T. Fleming, and D. Haapala. 1977. Homebuilders: Keeping families together. *Journal of Clinical and Counseling Psychology* 43:667–673.

Kinney, J., D. Haapala, and C. Booth. 1991. *Keeping Families Together: The Homebuilders Model*. Hawthorne, N.Y.: Aldine de Gruyter.

Kixmiller, J. and H. Onserud. 1995. A community center model for current urban needs. In R. Kurland and R. Salmon, eds., *Group Work Practice in a Troubled Society*, pp. 203–216. New York: Haworth.

Knitzer, J., M. L. Allen, and B. G. McGowan. 1978. *Children Without Homes*. Washington, D.C.: Children's Defense Fund.

Kubisch, A. C., C. H. Weiss, L. B. Schorr, and J. P. Connell. 1995. Introduction. In J. P. Connell, A. C. Kubisch, L. Schorr, and C. H. Weiss, eds., *New Approaches to Evaluating Community Initiatives*, pp. 1–21. Aspen: Aspen Institute.

Kurland, R. and R. Salmon. 1998. *Teaching a Methods Course in Social Work with Groups*. Alexandria: Council on Social Work Education.

Lerner, S. 1990. *The Geography of Foster Care: Keeping the Children in the Neighborhood*. New York: Foundation for Child Development.

Lightburn, A. and S. Kemp. 1994. Family-support programs: Opportunities for community-based practice. *Families in Society* 75:16–26.

Lindblad-Goldberg, M., M. Dore, and L. Stern. 1998. *Creating Competence from Chaos: A Comprehensive Guide to Home-Based Services*. New York: Norton.

Lindsey, D. 1994. Family preservation and child protection: Striking a balance. *Children and Youth Services Review* 16:279–294.

Maas, H. and R. Engler. 1959. *Children in Need of Parents*. New York: Columbia University Press.

MacDonald, H. 1994. The ideology of family preservation. *The Public Interest* 115:945–60.

MacDonald, H. 1999. Foster care's underworld. *City Journal* 9:44–53.

McCroskey, J., R. Nishimoto, and K. Subramanian. 1991. Assessment in family support programs: Initial reliability and validity testing of the Family Assessment Form. *Child Welfare* 70:19–33.

McCroskey, J. and W. Meezan. 1997. *Family Preservation and Family Functioning*. Washington, D.C.: Child Welfare League of America.

McCroskey, J. and W. Meezan. 1998. Family-centered services: Approaches and effectiveness. *Future of Children* 8:54–71.

McGowan, B. G. 1988. Helping Puerto Rican families at risk: Responsive use of time, space, and relationship. In C. Jacobs and D. Bowles, eds., *Ethnicity and Race: Critical Concepts in Social Work*. Silver Springs: NASW.

McGowan, B. G. 1990. Family-based services and public policy: Context and implications. In J. Whittaker, J. Kinney, E. Tracy, and C. Booth, eds., *Reaching High-Risk Families: Intensive Family Preservation in Human Services*, pp. 65–87. Hawthorne, N.Y.: Aldine de Gruyter.

McGowan, B. G. 1994. *Asking New Questions: Introducing a Family Needs Assessment Into an Employment Program*. New York: Foundation for Child Development.

McGowan, B. G. with A. Kahn and S. Kamerman. 1990. *Social Services for Children, Youth and Families: The New York City Study*. New York: Columbia University School of Social Work.

McGowan, B. G. and E. M. Walsh. 2000. Policy challenges for child welfare in the new century. *Child Welfare* 79:11–27.

McGowan, B. G., J. Bertand, A. Kohn, and A. Lombard. 1987. *The Continuing Crisis; A Report on New York City's Response to Families Requiring Protective and Preventive Services*. New York: Neighborhood Family Services Coalition.

Maluccio, A., ed. 1981. *Promoting Competence in Clients*. New York: Free.

Maluccio, A. 1991. The optimism of policy choices in child welfare. *American Journal of Orthopsychiatry* 61:606–609.

Meezan, W. 1995. Personal communication.

Meezan, W. and McCroskey, J. 1996. Improving family functioning through family preservation services: Results of the Los Angeles experiment. *Family Preservation Journal* 1 (Winter): 9–29.

Metis Associates. 1999. *Sunset Park Neighborhood Survey Findings*. New York: Metis Associates.

Meyer, C. 1970. *Social Work Practice: A Response to the Urban Crisis*. New York: Free.

Meyer, C. 1976. *Social Work Practice*. 2d ed. New York: Free.

Meyer, C., ed. 1983. *Clinical Social Work in the Eco-Systems Perspective*. New York: Columbia University Press.

Miller, B. 1995. *Out-of-School Time: Effects on Learning in the Primary Grades*. Wellesley: School Age Child Care Project.

Murphy, P. 1993. Family preservation and its victims. *New York Times*, June 19, p. 21.

National Research Council Panel on High-Risk Youth. 1993. *Losing Generations: Adolescents in High-Risk Settings*. Washington, D.C.: National Academy.

Nelson, D. 1991. The policy implications of family preservation. In K. Wells and D. Biegel, eds., *Family Preservation Services: Research and Evaluation*, pp. 207–222. Newbury Park, Cal.: Sage.

Nelson, K. 1997. Family preservation—What is it? *Children and Youth Services Review* 19:101–118.

Nelson, K., M. Landsman, and W. Deutelbaum. 1990. Three models of family-centered placement prevention services. *Child Welfare* 69 (1): 3–21.

New York City Administration for Children's Services. 1999. *Request for Proposals for Child Welfare Services*. New York: New York Administration for Childrens Services.

Northouse, P. G. 2001. *Leadership: Theory and Practice*. 2d ed. Thousand Oaks, Cal.: Sage.

Nowicki, S. and B. Strickland. 1987. Nowick-Strickland locus of control scale (N-SLCS). In K. Corcoran and J. Fischer, eds., *Measures of Clinical Practice*, pp. 402–404. New York: Free.

The One and the Many. 1978. Brooklyn, New York: Center for Family Life in Sunset Park.

Orum, A., J. Feagin, and G. Sjoberg, eds. 1991. *A Case for the Case Study*. Chapel Hill: University of North Carolina Press.

Overton, A., and K. Tinker. 1957. *The Casework Notebook*. St. Paul: Greater St. Paul Community Chest and Councils.

Pecora, P., M. Fraser, K. Nelson, J. McCroskey, and W. Meezan. 1995. *Evaluating Family-Based Services*. Hawthorne, N.Y.: Aldine de Gruyter.

Persico, J. 1979. *Who Knows? Who Cares? Forgotten Children in Foster Care*. New York: National Commission on Children in Need of Foster Parents.

Peters, T. and N. Austin. 1985. *A Passion for Excellence: The Leadership Difference*. New York: Sarner.

Peters, T. J., and R. H. Waterman Jr. 1982. *In Search of Excellence: Lessons from America's Best-Run Companies*. New York: Harper and Row.

Pittenger, W. N. 1971. Process thought: A contemporary trend in theology. In E. Cousins, ed., *Process Theology*, pp. 23–35. New York: Newman.

Posner, J. and D. Vandell. 1994. Low-income children's after-school care: Are there beneficial effects of after-school programs? *Child Development* 65:440–456.

Powell, D. 1994. Evaluating family support programs: Are we making progress? In S. Kagan and B. Weissbourd, eds., *Putting Families First: America's Family Support Movement and the Challenge of Change*, pp. 441–469. San Francisco: Jossey-Bass.

Putnam, R. D. 2000. *Bowling Alone: The Collapse and Revival of American Community*. New York: Simon and Schuster.

Reynolds, B. D. 1980 [1934]. *Between Client and Community: A Study in Responsibility in Social Casework*. Silver Spring, Md.: NASW.

Roditti, M. G. 1995. Child day care: A key building block of family support and family preservation and programs. *Child Welfare* 74:1043–1068.

Rosenblatt, R. 1985. A Christmas story. *Time*, December 30, pp. 18–30.

Rosenblatt, R. 1995. The society that pretends to love children. *New York Times Magazine*, October 8, pp. 58–61, 90, 106–107.

Rosenfeld, J. M. and B. Tardieu. 2000. *Artisans of Democracy: How Ordinary People, Families in Extreme Poverty, and Social Institutions Become Allies to Overcome Social Exclusion*. Lanham: University Press.

Rossi, P. 1992. Assessing family preservation programs. *Children and Youth Services Review* 14:77–97.

Scopetta, N. 1996. *Protecting the Children of New York: A Plan of Action for the Administration for Children's Services*. December 19. New York City: Mayor's Office.

Schorr, L. B., with D. Schorr. 1988. *Within Our Reach*. New York: Doubleday.

Schorr, L. B. 1997. *Common Purpose: Strengthening Families and Neighborhoods to Rebuild America*. New York: Anchor/Doubleday.

Schorr, L. B. and A. L. Kubisch. 1996. New approach to evaluation: Helping Sister Mary Paul, Geoff Canada, and Otis Johnson while convincing Pat Moynihan, Newt Gingrich, and the American Public. In Annie E. Casey Foundation, *Getting Smart, Getting Real: Using Research and Evaluation Information to Improve Programs and Policies*, pp. A-15–A-29. Report of the Annie E. Casey Foundation's September 1995 research and evaluation conference. Baltimore: Annie E. Casey Foundation.

Schuerman, J. R. 1997. Best Interests and Family Preservation in America. Chapin Hall Center for Children at the University of Chicago discussion paper, October.

Schuerman, J. R., T. L. Rzepnicki, and J. Littell. 1994. *Putting Families First: An Experiment in Family Preservation*. Hawthorne, N.Y.: Aldine de Gruyter.

Senge, P. 1990. *The Fifth Discipline: The Art and Practice of the Learning Organization.* New York: Doubleday/Currency.

Shapiro, M. 1997. Parental guidance. *New York*, March 17, pp. 42–47.

Shapiro, M. 1999. *Solomon's Sword.* New York: Times.

Sheffer, E. 1992. *The Center for Family Life and the Sunset Park Community.* New York: Surdna Foundation, Foundation for Child Development.

Simon, B. L. 1994. *The Empowerment Tradition in American Social Work: A History.* New York: Columbia University Press.

Simon, B. 1995. A community of interests: An account of the connection between the Center for Family Life and the neighborhood of Sunset Park, Brooklyn, 1978–1995. Unpublished paper.

Smith, C. and B. Carlson. 1997. Stress, coping, and resilience in children and youth. *Social Service Review* 71:231–256.

Special Child Welfare Advisory Panel. 2000. *Advisory Report on Front Line and Supervisory Practice.* March 9. New York: Special Child Welfare Advisory Panel.

Spradley, J. 1980. *Participant Observation.* Fort Worth: Harcourt College.

Stake, R. 1994. Case study. In N. Denzin and Y. Lincoln, eds., *Handbook of Qualitative Research*, pp. 236–247. Thousand Oaks, Cal..: Sage.

Stake, R. 1995. *The Art of Case Study Research.* Thousand Oaks, Cal.: Sage.

Stake, R. 1998. Case studies. In N. Denzin and Y. Lincoln, eds., *Strategies of Qualitative Inquiry*, pp. 86–109. Thousand Oaks, Cal.: Sage.

Stein, T., E. Gambrill, and K. Wiltse. 1978. *Children in Foster Homes: Achieving Continuity of Care.* New York: Praeger.

Sunley, R. 1970. Family advocacy: From case to cause. *Social Casework* 51 (6): 347–357.

Taylor, S. and R. Bogdan. 1984. *Introduction to Qualitative Research Methods: The Search for Meanings.* 2d ed. New York: Wiley.

Temporary State Commission on Child Welfare. 1975. *The Children of the State: A Time for a Change.* Albany: Temporary State Commission on Child Welfare.

Tracy, E., N. Bean, S. Gwatkin, and B. Hill. 1992. Family preservation workers: Sources of job satisfaction and job stress. *Research on Social Work Practice* 2:465–487.

Tropp, E. 1976. A developmental theory. In R. Roberts and H. Northen, eds., *Theories of Social Work with Groups*, pp. 198–237. New York: Columbia University Press.

Turner, B. 1981. Some practical aspects of qualitative data analysis. *Quality and Quantity* 15:225–247.

U.S. Department of Education and U.S. Department of Justice. 1998. *Safe and Smart: Making the After-school Hours Work for Kids.* Washington, D.C.: U.S. Department of Education and U.S. Department of Justice.

Watching the numbers. 2000. *Child Welfare Watch* 6 (Winter): 15.

Weisberg, R. 1991. *Our Children at Risk.* New York: WNET.

Weisman, M. L. 1994. When parents are not in the best interest of the child. *Atlantic Monthly*, July, pp. 43–63.

Weiss, H. and K. Horsch. 1998. Learning from the Annie E. Casey Foundation's Evaluation Grants Program. *Evaluation Exchange* 4:2–4, 15.

Weiss, H. and F. Jacobs. 1988. *Evaluating Family Programs.* Hawthorne, N.Y.: Aldine de Gruyter.

Weissbourd, B. 1987. A brief history of family support programs. In S. Kagan, D. Powell, B. Weissbourd, and E. Zigler, eds. *America's Family Support Programs: Perspectives and Prospects*. pp. 38–56. New Haven: Yale University Press.

Weissbourd, B. 1994. The evolution of the family resource movement. In S. L. Kagan and B. Weissbourd, eds., *Putting Families First*, pp. 28–47. San Francisco: Jossey-Bass.

Weissbourd, B. and S. Kagan. 1989. Family support programs: Catalysts for change. *American Journal of Orthopsychiatry* 59:20–31.

Wells, K. and D. Biegel, eds. 1991. *Family Preservation Services: Research and Evaluation*. Newbury Park, Cal.: Sage.

Wells, K. and D. Whittington. 1993. Child and family functioning after intensive family preservation services. *Social Service Review* 67:55–83.

Wells, K. and E. Tracy. 1996. Reorienting intensive family preservation services in relation to public child welfare. *Child Welfare* 75:667–692.

Wells, K. and R. Freer. 1994. Reading between the lines: The case for qualitative research in intensive family preservation services. *Children and Youth Services Review* 16:399–415.

White, R. 1959. Motivation reconsidered: The concept of competence. *Psychological Review* 66:297–333.

White, R. 1963. *Ego and Reality in Psychoanalytic Theory*: New York: International Universities.

Whittaker, J. and E. Tracy, eds. 1990. *Reaching High-Risk Families*. Hawthorne, N.Y.: Aldine de Gruyter.

Winnick, L. 1990. *New People in Old Neighborhoods: The Role of New Immigrants in Rejuvenating New York's Communities*. New York: Russell Sage Foundation.

Wulczyn, F. 1995. Child welfare reform, managed care, and community reinvestment. In A. Kahn and S. Kamerman, eds., *Children and Their Families in Big Cities: Strategies for Service Reform*, pp. 199–229. New York: Cross-National Studies Research Program, Columbia University School of Social Work.

Wulczyn, F. 1996. Personal communication.

Wynn, J., R. Costello, R. Halpern, and H. Richmond. 1994. *Children, Families, and Communities: A New Approach to Social Services*. Chicago: Chapin Hall Center for Children at the University of Chicago.

Yin, R. 1994. *Case Study Research: Design and Method*. 2d ed. Thousand Oaks, Cal.: Sage.

Zhou, M. 2001. Chinese: Divergent destinies in immigrant New York. In N. Foner, ed., *New Immigrants in New York*, pp. 141–172. New York: Columbia University Press.

Zigler, E. and K. Black. 1989. America's family support movement: Strengths and limitations. *American Journal of Orthopsychiatry* 59:6–19.

INDEX

■

Page numbers in italics denote illustrations; tables are indicated by *t* after the page number.